Breaking the
PANZERS

The Bloody Battle for Rauray
Normandy, 1 July 1944

Kevin Baverstock

Foreword by Her Late Majesty
Queen Elizabeth The Queen Mother

SUTTON PUBLISHING

First published in 2002 by
Sutton Publishing Limited · Phoenix Mill
Thrupp · Stroud · Gloucestershire · GL5 2 BU

British Library Cataloguing in Publication Data
A catalogue record for this book is available from the British Library

ISBN 0 7509 2895 6

In these pages that you view
Our contact with the past
The vivid memories of the few,
Whose souls live on as cast.

Pte John Munro
Intelligence Section, 1st Tyneside Scottish

Typeset in 10/13pt Sabon.
Typesetting and origination by
Sutton Publishing Limited.
Printed and bound in England by
J.H. Haynes & Co. Ltd, Sparkford.

TABLE OF CONTENTS

The 49th Division Memorial near Fontenay-le-Pesnel.

The Fontenay-le-Pesnel War Cemetery.

LIST OF MAPS, DIAGRAMS AND PHOTOGRAPHS

CLARENCE HOUSE
SW1A 1BA

I am so pleased that this account of action
undertaken on 1st July 1944 in Normandy by The
Tyneside Scottish has been written by the son of
a former member of the Regiment.

It is a story of courage and fortitude which
resulted in the award of a Regimental Battle Honour,
and I am confident that all who read this history
will feel a sense of pride in the achievements of
a famous Territorial Battalion.

ELIZABETH R

Colonel-in-Chief
The Black Watch
(Royal Highland Regiment)

February 2002

FOREWORD

BY BRIGADIER G.C. BARNETT OBE,
COLONEL, THE BLACK WATCH

I am delighted to contribute this foreword to such a marvellous account of one day in the life of some 700 men serving in one of our battalions during the Second World War, a day which the Tyneside Scottish, at that time one of our territorial battalions, distinguished itself in the best traditions of the Black Watch. The Defence of Rauray on 1 July 1944 is one of our Regimental Battle Honours.

Over the last 260 years, since our first parade at Aberfeldy, many authors, including Bernard Fergusson, one of my predecessors, have written books about the Black Watch. This book is quite different. While the memoirs of Field Marshals and Generals are important, they seldom communicate the realities of fighting. There are so many unpublicised stories that should be told by former NCOs and Privates that deserve to be published. I listen to them after dinners and reunions and find them fascinating, moving and deeply humbling. Too often the natural modesty of those involved has meant that they have kept the details from all except close friends (often those who served with them) and family.

This book is one of the few written from the perspective of the fighting soldier doing his duty for his country. It is unconventional in that it focuses on the events of one long hard-fought day in the life of all ranks serving in the Tyneside Scottish in Normandy. It is also unusual in that it is written by a son of the Regiment writing with pride about events in which his father and his comrades were involved rather than himself.

While the centrepoint is the description of that day in Normandy, it does not ignore the backcloth of general history and training. With the not inconsiderable help from the Royal Artillery in support of the Battalion, over thirty tanks were destroyed that day, their hulks spread around the defensive position. How many other infantry battalions of any army have met with such success in a little more than twelve hours?

This Battalion of the Black Watch, the Tyneside Scottish, fought as one would expect from Black Watch soldiers throughout our history – with the courage, conviction and selflessness we have always come to rely upon. The Battalion held a pivotal position on the Allied front, helping to frustrate the desperate attempts by the Wehrmacht to break through between the 15th and 49th Divisions of the Allied centre in Normandy. The German assault by a formidable Panzer force was repulsed, and The Defence of Rauray on 1 July 1944 was recognised by Commanders at Division, Corps and Army level as making a significant contribution against overwhelming odds.

Mr Baverstock is to be congratulated on his hard work and long hours spent in research. Although he has no military experience himself, you will find that he has captured the spirit of his father's generation. The photographs, maps and diagrams do much to enhance the text. His cleverness in combining the brief accounts of those who were involved in the battle and making much use of the work of Major John Samson, and his skill in weaving them together with the recollections of many others, has resulted in a readable and important book. I have not come across another quite like it.

It is a privilege to commend this book to all those who are proud of our past and recognise the great contribution made by those who gave their lives at Rauray. We salute the Geordie Jocks. They did their duty nobly.

Garry Barnett

15 February 2002

PREFACE

This book records the part played by the 49th (West Riding) Infantry Division in a day-long defensive action at Rauray in Normandy on 1 July 1944. Among the British units which played a major role that day, particular mention is given to the 1st Tyneside Scottish (Black Watch). Renowned for their sacrifices in the First World War, little has been written about the men of the Tyneside Scottish in the Second World War, and, despite the fact that they gained a battle honour for their efforts at Rauray, their story has largely been forgotten.

In the mid-1980s, Major J.L.R. Samson FSA (Scot), a Tyneside Scot and author of a short history of the Battalion, began sending out questionnaires to as many veterans of the battle as he could obtain addresses for, asking them to write down anything they could remember about the day's action. In response he managed to collect over forty accounts ranging from one or two lines to vividly detailed recollections. Along with meticulous notes he had taken from the 1st Tyneside Scottish War Diary, the whole presented John Samson with enough material to write a book about Rauray. Sadly, aged sixty-two, he died suddenly of a heart attack at his Wiltshire home on 18 May 1988.

Major John L.R. Samson FSA (Scot)

After my father's death in 1981, a small collection of wartime keepsakes that he had gathered together in an old shoulder bag and placed at the back of a dark, cavernous wardrobe once more saw the light of day. His Army service record card showed that he had been a private in the Intelligence Section of the 1st Tyneside Scottish (Black Watch) from December 1940 to their break up in August 1944, after which he had served in the 1st Black Watch until his release in 1946. Fascinated by the contents of the bag, I carefully made an inventory of all the items and filed them in a new binder, with a view to making a more detailed study at a later date.

On the 50th anniversary of D-Day in 1994, I naturally became interested in the activities of the 1st Tyneside Scottish during the Battle of Normandy. Determined to find out all there was to know, I set out for the Public Record Office at Kew on that well-trodden path known to all military researchers, amateur and professional alike, which eventually ends at a small letter-coded desk in the Document Reading Room. With the War Diaries of the 1st Tyneside Scottish open in front of me, it soon became clear that this Battalion had taken part in a singularly bloody encounter with elite German SS troops near to the village of Rauray on 1 July 1944. Although my father rarely spoke about his wartime experiences, he had on one occasion described this day as the most momentous of his life in the Army. Having this in mind, the Rauray

The author's father – Private Leonard G. Baverstock, Intelligence Section, 1st Tyneside Scottish

battle became the focus of my research and I began a long quest of discovery. The Black Watch Regimental Museum in Perth most generously offered useful advice and addresses of people who might help, including Patrick Delaforce, the writer of several army divisional histories. He kindly informed me that Gordon Cowie had served with the 1st Tyneside Scottish at Rauray and suggested I contact him. When I finally met Gordon on Tyneside in September 1999, he explained that Major Samson's dossier had been left in his charge, and it soon became clear that with his help I should be able to extend my research to produce a definitive book about the Rauray battle. Unfortunately, Gordon's health deteriorated during our collaboration and he passed away towards the end of 2001. However, during our brief acquaintance he managed to provide a great deal of useful material and helped me make contact with several other Rauray veterans, including Brian Stewart, the 2nd i/c of the 1st Tyneside Scottish Anti-tank Platoon, who was extremely enthusiastic in offering his assistance – he had already corresponded with Major Samson during his quest for statements from Rauray survivors in the 1980s. Despite the fact that his career had kept him in Asia after the war, he had managed to keep in touch with the Black Watch over the years and was able to offer a wealth of expert knowledge and useful contacts. Throughout the last two years of my research, both Gordon and Brian were enormously supportive and I owe them a great deal.

The result is *Breaking the Panzers*, a memorial to the work of Major John Samson, without whose persistent efforts an authentic story of the action at Rauray on 1 July 1944 could not have been told.

Kevin Baverstock 2002

GLOSSARY

AFV	Armoured Fighting Vehicle	Corps	A formation of two or more divisions
AGRA	Army Group Royal Artillery	D-Day	The name given to the first day of Operation 'Overlord'
AP	Armour-piercing shell	D+6	Six days after D-Day
Bocage	Normandy fields bordered with high double-bank and ditch hedgerows	DG	Official abbreviation for Royal Dragoon Guards (also known as RDG)
'Bomb-happy'	A term used to describe a nervous state caused by constant exposure to heavy shelling or mortaring	Division	A formation of two or three infantry brigades with integrated artillery, engineer and administration support
Besa	Czech/British machine gun mounted in Sherman tanks	DLI	Durham Light Infantry
Bren	Light machine gun	ENSA	Entertainment National Service Association
Bren Carrier	See Universal Carrier		
Brew up	A term first used to describe making tea, which later also referred to a tank being explosively set on fire	'Epsom'	Code name for British military operation involving VIII Corps in extending the Normandy bridgehead south to the Odon and thence to the Orne River south of Caen
Brigade	A formation of three infantry battalions, tank or other regiments	HE	High-explosive shell
Bund	A raised embankment	Hitlerjugend	Hitler Youth. As a fighting force they formed the 12th SS-Panzer Division
BW	The Black Watch (Royal Highland Regiment)		
CANLOAN	A scheme whereby Canadian officers were loaned to the British Army	'Hohenstaufen'	Family name of medieval German kings used as an honorary title by the 9th-SS-Panzer Division
Carden Loyd	Pre-war carrier		
CO	Commanding Officer		
Crocodile	British Churchill tank with flame-throwing attachment	KG	Kampfgruppe (battlegroup). German ad hoc unit formed for

	a specific task or to bring together remnants of shattered formations into a battleworthy force. Usually took the name of the force commander
LMG	light machine gun
Loyd Carrier	A small open tracked carrier vehicle, most commonly used as a prime mover for anti-tank guns (sometimes inaccurately described as 'Carden Loyd' in memory of the pre-war carrier of that name)
Maquis	French resistance movement
'Martlet'	Code name for British military operation involving XXX Corps in securing the right flank of VIII Corps prior to and during Operation 'Epsom'
Mike target	An artillery codeword ordering all available Field Regiment guns to open fire
'Moaning Minnie'	Nickname given by British troops to the Nebelwerfer in reaction to the monotonous high-pitched sound of its delivery
NAAFI	Navy, Army and Air Force Institute
Nebelwerfer	German 6-barrelled rocket mortar
OB West	Oberbefelshaber West, or Commander-in-Chief of German forces in France, Holland and Belgium
'O' Group	Orders group of commanders of sub-units
OP	Observation Post (usually a forward artillery lookout)

'Overlord'	Code name given to the Allied operation to invade the Normandy beaches
Panther	German Panzerkampfwagen Mk V tank
Panzer	A German term; literally meaning armour, commonly used to describe a tank
Panzerfaust	'Armour fist'. German single-shot, one-man rocket launcher, capable of knocking out a tank at ranges of 80 yards or less
Panzerschreck	'Tank Terror'. German 2-man rocket launcher, effective at ranges of up to 150 yards
Polar Bears	The 49th Infantry Division
PIAT	Projector Infantry Anti-tank. British 1-man short-range, spring-loaded anti-tank weapon
POWs	Prisoners of war
RAP	Regimental Aid Post
RAC	Royal Armoured Corps
RDG	Royal Dragoon Guards
Ring contour 110	Contour line south of Rauray shown on War Office maps, used by the British Army as a landmark
Sabot	High-velocity tungsten anti-tank gun dart, favoured for its ability to penetrate tank armour
SHAEF	Supreme Headquarters, Allied Expeditionary Force
Sherman	American M4 tank, also used by the British Army
Spandau	Allied term used to describe the German

	MG42, a light machine gun with a distinctive high rate of fire
Sten	Light automatic sub-machine gun
Stonk	A concentration of shell or mortar fire on an objective
SS	Schutzstaffeln, the protective guards of the Nazi Party, not generally under Army control (see Waffen-SS)
StuG	Sturmgeschütz. A German self-propelled assault gun
TOS	Tam-o'-shanter. A Scottish broad flat cap or bonnet named after Tam o' Shanter of the poem by Robert Burns
TS	Tyneside Scottish
Uncle target	An artillery codeword ordering all guns available to a division to open fire.
Universal Carrier	A lightly armoured, open-topped tracked vehicle. Used in wide variety of roles including:

	reconnaissance, supply, carrying weapons and casualty evacuation (also known as Bren Carrier)
Verey (Very) light	Coloured rocket flare signal invented by Lt E.W. Very
Verey (Very) pistol	Firearm used to discharge a Verey light to provide a signal
Vickers	British heavy .303 machine gun, most often employed by specialist units in a support (indirect fire) role
Victor target	An artillery codeword ordering all available Corps guns to open fire. Could also include naval guns during Battle of Normandy
Waffen-SS	SS fighting in elite military formations. They were under Army control for operations, but had their own command and supply chains
WT	Wireless Telegraphy

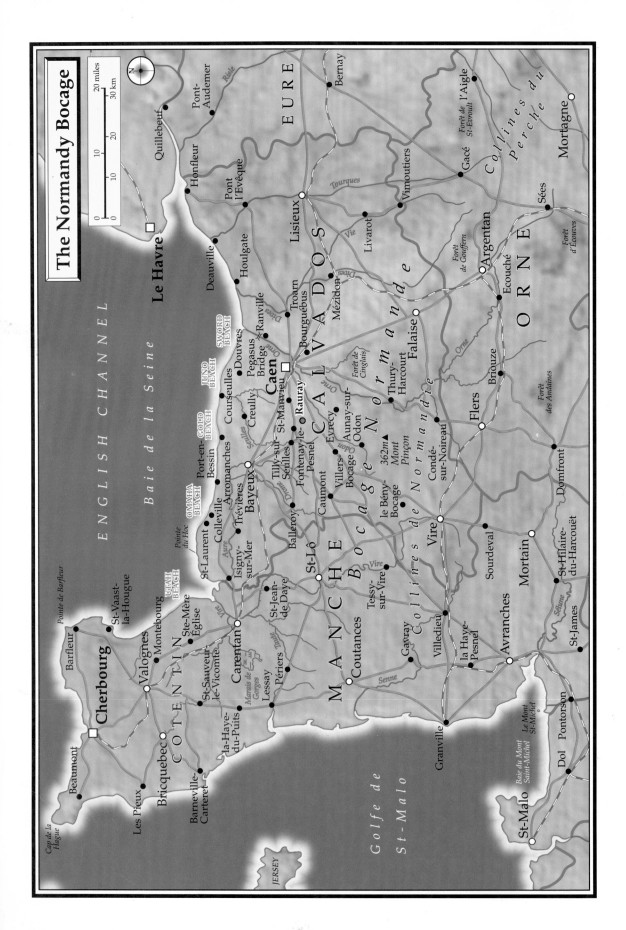

The Normandy Bocage

20 miles
30 km

ENGLISH CHANNEL

Baie de la Seine

Le Havre

Quillebeuf
Pont-Audemer
Honfleur
Pont l'Evêque
Deauville
Houlgate
Lisieux
EURE
Bernay
Forêt de l'Aigle
St-Erroult
Gacé
Collines du Perche
Mortagne
Sées
Vimoutiers
Livarot
Vie
Forêt de Gouffern
Argentan
ORNE
Forêt d'Ecouves

Troarn
Bourguébus
Mézidon
Dives
Ranville
Pegasus
Bridge
Douvres
SWORD BEACH
Courseulles
JUNO BEACH
Creully
GOLD BEACH
Port-en-Bessin
Arromanches
Bayeux
OMAHA BEACH
Pointe du Hoc
St-Laurent
Colleville
Trévières
Isigny-sur-Mer

Caen
CALVADOS
St-Manvieu
Rauray
Tilly-sur-Seulles
Fontenay-le-Pesnel
Evrecy
Aunay-sur-Odon
Villers-Bocage
Caumont
Falaise
Thury-Harcourt
Forêt de Cinglais
Orne
362m Mont Pinçon
le Bény-Bocage
Condé-sur-Noireau
Flers
Briouze
Forêt des Andaines
Ecouché

Balleroy
St-Lô
MANCHE
Bocage
Tessy-sur-Vire
Vire
Collines de Normandie
Vire
Villedieu
la Haye-Pesnel
Sourdeval
Mortain
St-Hilaire-du-Harcouët
Domfront

UTAH BEACH
Ste-Mère-Eglise
Montebourg
St-Vaast-la-Hougue
Pointe de Barfleur
Barfleur
Cherbourg
Valognes
COTENTIN
St-Sauveur-le-Vicomte
Carentan
Marais de Gorges
Lessay
Périers
Coutances
Gavray
Granville

Beaumont
Bricquebec
Barneville-Carteret
les Pieux
Cap de la Hague
la-Haye-du-Puits

Avranches
St-James
Sée
Pontorson
Dol
St-Malo
Le Mont St-Michel
Baie du Mont Saint-Michel
Golfe de St-Malo

JERSEY

St-Jean-de-Daye

Bocage de Normandie

Tourques
Drôme
Aure
Vira
Taute
Senne

INTRODUCTION

Whenever one considers fateful moments in the history of the British Army, the mind readily focuses on 1 July 1916, the first day of the Battle of the Somme. Among the many thousands for whom the battle was a story of supreme sacrifice was the first formation of men calling themselves Tyneside Scottish. By the evening of that calamitous day, 940 of them, including eighty officers, had been killed and 1600 wounded – nearly 80 per cent of the entire force of four Tyneside Scottish battalions.

Exactly twenty-eight years later, a new generation of Tyneside Scottish, now part of the Black Watch, also faced an enemy head-on, only this time in defence rather than attack. Arriving in Normandy one week after D-Day in 1944, the 1st Tyneside Scottish formed part of the 49th (West Riding) Division. From 26 June onwards, it fought hard to force a way through the bocage countryside south of Fontenay-le-Pesnel, battling against German Waffen SS units fanatically committed to defending the area west of Caen. By the time the Battalion eventually reached the high-ground south of the village of Rauray, the impact of over two weeks of bitter fighting had begun to tell; it was already badly under strength and had lost nine officers. Even for a battalion of battle-hardened regular soldiers, these losses would have been a grievous blow. Highly regarded senior personnel who had worked and trained with the Battalion for years were now gone and their replacements were strangers whose capability and trustworthiness had to be taken at face value.

During the early hours of 1 July, as the defenders of Rauray waited silently in their slit trenches, tanks were heard in the distance preparing for battle. Once again, as in 1916, the Tyneside Scottish were about to experience a sacrificial moment – dawn would herald a sharp counter-attack by infantry of Kampfgruppe Weidinger from the 2nd SS-Panzer Division 'Das Reich', and tanks of the 9th SS-Panzer Division 'Hohenstaufen', designed to punch a hole in the British front.

Today, some modern historians writing about this phase of the Battle of Normandy dismiss the German counter-attack of 1 July as being of little significance. They claim that the disruption caused by RAF bombing raids prior to the attack had reduced the threat of a major enemy assault, and that the few tanks that did make it to the front were quickly dispersed by artillery fire. Those who were at Rauray would disagree. The 1st Tyneside Scottish actually fought for over fourteen hours and eventually destroyed around a third of the total claims of more than thirty AFVs knocked out on its front. Nonetheless, what happened at Rauray has widely been forgotten and very few historians bother to mention it at all. True, Lord

Montgomery wrote about it in 1947 (see page 178), and Patrick Delaforce gives a full account of the battle in his excellent book about the 49th (West Riding) Division *The Polar Bears: Monty's Left Flank*, but such modern narratives are rare. Sadly, the 1st Tyneside Scottish are remembered more often than not as a territorial unit broken up in Normandy to create reinforcements. In order to delve deeper, one must seek sources contemporary to the battle.

One Battalion officer described the action at Rauray in the 1947 history of the 1st Tyneside Scottish, *Harder than Hammers*, as '*a defensive battle that will always be remembered by those who fought and survived, one of which all who served have full and just right to feel considerable pride, and one in which the Battalion acquitted itself according to the best Scottish traditions*'. It would appear that this sense of pride was fully felt in the immediate aftermath of the battle, as great care was taken to preserve detailed intelligence of the day's action in the 1st Tyneside Scottish War Diary (Public Record Office WO171/1382). In this document, an Intelligence Diary of 100 accurately timed signal reports lists details of radio messages sent from positions all over the battlefield, providing a minute-by-minute record of each and every major event which took place, from the moment when the first mortar bombs landed in Rauray, to the final reports confirming that all the Battalion's positions had been retaken. This chronological document allows us to closely follow the battle's progress, placing us in much the same position as those who received the information on the day (the author's version of the Intelligence Diary may be found on pages 150–3). In addition, Lt C.B. Mitchell, the Battalion's Intelligence Officer (later killed at Mézidon), wrote freely about the battle in a special report he compiled at the end of the fighting. His account, which forms an appendix to the standard war diary entry for 1 July 1944, is written in longhand and vividly conveys the thoughts of a man who knew he had witnessed an exceptional effort from his battalion.

Similarly, The Immediate Report No. 25 – Repulse by 49th Division – Rauray 1/7/44 (CAB106/963), written by Lt Col A.E. Warhurst, GSOI(L), 49th Division (one of the few Divisional Intelligence Reports from the Battle of Normandy still in existence in the Public Record Office), goes into great detail and offers a wealth of information about the parties engaged at Rauray and their losses and gains throughout the day. Warhurst was a major Second World War historian and therefore his account can be seen as a key reference. The report also includes a sketch-map of the battlefield. Following on from this report, The Immediate Report No. 26 – Narratives of a 6-pounder anti-tank gun – 31/7/44 (CAB106/963), provides official confirmation of some of the crucial anti-tank gun actions.

Book Three of The Official Histories of WW2 (CAB44/250) includes a map showing the locations of a number of German AFVs destroyed during the battle, compiled from an RAF reconnaissance photograph. This aerial photograph was originally part of the 70th Brigade War Diary No. 369 (WO171/653), but is unfortunately now missing from this document. However, a similar photograph showing numerous knocked-out AFVs on the 1st Tyneside Scottish front at Rauray can be found among the collection of Major-General E.H. Barker's documents, held by the Imperial War Museum. Copies of photographic reconnaissance runs (© Ministry of Defence) can also be obtained from the Air Photo Library at Keele University, providing a unique image of the battlefield, still fresh with the scars of shell and mortar bomb damage.

After the battle was over, Military Observers and War Correspondents visited Rauray to see for themselves the extent of the carnage left lying in the bocage fields surrounding the village. One Ministry of Information document written shortly afterwards, entitled 'Northern Troops in the Memorable Battle', includes important details of the action, some of which derive from conversations with 1st Tyneside Scottish soldiers who had taken part in the battle.

As far as the other units who were involved in the battle are concerned, several significant written accounts and records exist which provide useful additional information. Perhaps the most important among them are: 'None Had Lances', the story of the 24th Lancers by Leonard Willis, David Rissik's '10th and 11th Durham Light Infantry History'; and the War Diary of the 55th Anti-tank Regiment. Also of interest are: 'The Kensingtons', a document produced by the Regimental Old Comrades Association, which provides information about the machine gun companies of the 2nd Kensingtons, and Otto Weidinger's book *Comrades to the End – The 4th SS-Panzer-Grenadier Regt 'Der Führer' 1938-45*, which includes a short record of the day's actions from the German point of view.

MAJOR JOHN SAMSON'S DOSSIER

During the 1980s, Major J.L.R. Samson, FSA (Scot), a Tyneside Scottish anti-tank gunner who fought at Rauray, compiled a dossier of personal accounts by 1st Tyneside Scottish veterans. Unfortunately, his efforts were made difficult by the fact that, forty years after the end of the war, many senior officers who might have had something important to recall had either died or become impossible to track down. As far as the Battalion's Commanding Officer is concerned, it is believed that Lt Col R.W.M. De Winton was tragically shot by an unbalanced Italian woman while inspecting troops in Trieste on 10 February 1947. Despite these tribulations, Major Samson managed to obtain over forty accounts from a suitably wide cross-section of the Battalion, including HQ, Intelligence, Support (Anti-tank, Mortar and Carrier Platoons), as well as all four rifle companies. As a result of the passage of time, the memories of the veterans are understandably sometimes confused, but their individual descriptions of events correspond extremely well with each other, and overall, John Samson's dossier presents a remarkably authentic picture of a battalion caught in the grip of battle. As the basis for any study of the Rauray encounter it is a priceless record, and as a battalion account of a one-day battle drawing on the memories of all ranks, it is one whose quality many military historians might well regard as unique.

When asked for his thoughts about Major Samson's dossier, Capt (Retd) Brian Stewart CMG, the 2nd i/c of the 1st TS Anti-tank Platoon at Rauray, observed that Martin Middlebrook's book *The First Day on the*

Somme (Allan Lane, 1971), quotes a private from the 4th Tyneside Scottish as follows: 'On the far side of no man's land I found the wire well cut but there were only three of our Company to go past, the Lieutenant, a sergeant and me. The officer said "God! God! Where are the rest of the boys?"' By the end of 1 July 1916, thousands of men had been killed or wounded. Middlebrook's attempt to bring together the surviving voices from the Somme followed a visit to the war graves in Flanders in the 1960s; he managed to interview 546 survivors who still remembered, with awful clarity, their experiences in that tragic battle. John Samson was attempting something very similar with his dossier, allowing the combatants to tell the battle story themselves. One of the first known examples of this approach is Siborne's *History of Waterloo*, but his survey only covered surviving commissioned officers. Middlebrook, like Samson, sought material from all ranks. John Samson's dossier thus follows an established tradition, but with no exact precedent: Middlebrook looked at a whole army, Siborne at the officers of an army, while Samson deals with one battalion only.

COMPILATION NOTES

By referring to the accounts of Normandy veterans, regimental histories, war diary intelligence reports, official summaries and aerial photographs, *Breaking the Panzers* attempts to trace the sequence of events and construct a graphic description of the battle by using a series of diagrammatic maps.

The day's action is split into twelve stages, each stage having its own map and descriptive text. Most of the twelve stages cover a period of one hour. The specific times listed and highlighted in the text, e.g. 1 • 0005 hrs, refer to actual signal reports sent in by units on the battlefield and logged by the 1st Tyneside Scottish Intelligence Section in their diary. A reference number (1) has been added to help the reader connect each report with its graphic description and location on the map.

Accounts of Rauray veterans are shown in italics; the ranks and duties given were those held on 1 July 1944. In general, most accounts are sound and have been, for the most part, transcribed as they were written, but those which clearly contain errors due to lapses in memory (such as spellings of names, etc.) have been corrected or restyled for *Breaking the Panzers* in order to maintain clarity. In some cases, further explanations by the author have been added in plain type, between parentheses. Where possible, each separate event described in a veteran's account has been extracted as an excerpt and woven into its correct position within the time frame of the twelve battle stages. In order to tell the complete story of the Rauray battle one would of course require accounts from veterans of all the units that took part – both British and German. However, while every effort was made to locate as many veterans as possible, the only unit to be successfully represented in any number is the 1st Tyneside Scottish. As has already been mentioned, the reason for the large number of Tyneside Scottish accounts is almost entirely due to the efforts of Major John Samson. His 1984 dossier was compiled at a time when most of the veterans were in their early sixties. Fifteen years on, the author's chances of tracing further candidates who could complete a questionnaire were considerably reduced. Despite these difficulties, another fourteen accounts were added to the Samson dossier during 1999–2001, making a total of fifty-five. The resulting tapestry of narratives virtually represents one continuous Battalion account interspersed with intelligence reports and recollections of men from other units (see page 181 for a full list of the veterans who contributed to *Breaking the Panzers*).

The complete absence of photographic material directly relating to actions which took place on 1 July 1944 is hardly surprising, given the tremendous pressure of battle conditions. However, a series of photographs and film clips taken by the Army Film and Photographic Unit at Rauray can be found in the Imperial War Museum archives. They depict British 49th Division troops in action in the days immediately before and after the main Rauray battle, and several shots and film stills from the series are shown in this book. The two photographs shown on pages 72 and 76 from the collection of Major-General E.H. Barker held by the Imperial War Museum show the arena around ring contour 110. They were taken during a visit to Rauray sometime after the war and are probably as near as one could get to images of the 1 July 1944 battlefield.

Some modern-day photographs of the Rauray battlefield, taken in April 2002 by Ian Daglish, have also been included to highlight some of the locations mentioned in the text. These clearly show how the landscape has altered since 1944 and to what extent the bunds of the bocage hedgerows have been reduced in height.

BATTALION ORGANIZATION

BATTALION HQ

In addition to the normal command set up, HQ contained a small Regimental Aid Post, Regimental Police Section and an Intelligence Section with Intelligence Officer working with eight snipers.

HQ COMPANY

Signal Platoon: Two sections provided communications by line or wireless. Administrative Platoon: Divided into two Echelons – 'A' and 'B'. 'A' Echelon was the forward administrative area responsible for providing vehicles to carry ammunition. 'B' Echelon was situated back from the front, and provided vehicles for supply, clothing, food and stores. It was also used as a rest camp and troop reinforcement holding area.

SUPPORT COMPANY

Mortar Platoon: Three sections of two mortars each with a total of seven Universal carriers.

Carrier Platoon: Four sections with a total of thirteen open armoured tracked Universal carriers, provided mobile reserve firepower as well as supplies of ammunition and stores. Carriers also assisted with the evacuation of wounded from the battlefield.

Anti-tank Platoon: Three sections, each with two detachments of 6-pounder anti-tank guns. Each detachment had a Bren gun and 2-inch mortar. The Platoon had twelve Loyd carriers and one Universal carrier for Platoon HQ use (see page xxvi for full details of an anti-tank platoon).

Assault pioneer Platoon: Three sections dealt with the laying and lifting of mines, booby traps, minor demolitions, bridging, camouflage and the construction of command posts.

RIFLE COMPANIES

An infantry battalion had four rifle companies; 'A', 'B', 'C' and 'D'. Each company consisted of an HQ and three platoons. Platoons, numbered 7–18, were made up of three sections and were armed with a PIAT (projector infantry anti-tank weapon), 2-inch mortar and small arms including light machine guns, Sten guns, rifles and grenades. Sections usually had one NCO and from six to nine men.

PERSONNEL

At full strength 1st Tyneside Scottish consisted of: from thirty-six to forty-three commissioned officers, eight warrant-officers (including one regimental sergeant major), six quartermaster-sergeants, thirty-eight sergeants, seventy-three corporals, 685 privates and five pipers – just over 850 men in all, fewer than half of whom were in rifle companies.

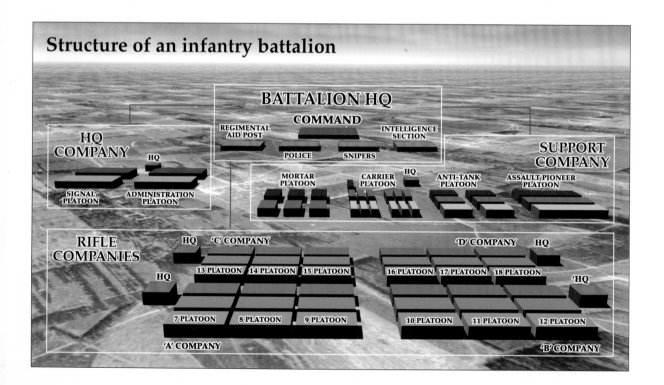

Structure of an infantry battalion

BATTALION HQ
COMMAND
REGIMENTAL AID POST
INTELLIGENCE SECTION
POLICE SNIPERS

HQ COMPANY
HQ
SIGNAL PLATOON ADMINISTRATION PLATOON

MORTAR PLATOON CARRIER PLATOON HQ ANTI-TANK PLATOON ASSAULT PIONEER PLATOON

SUPPORT COMPANY

RIFLE COMPANIES
HQ 'C' COMPANY
HQ
13 PLATOON 14 PLATOON 15 PLATOON
7 PLATOON 8 PLATOON 9 PLATOON
'A' COMPANY

'D' COMPANY HQ
16 PLATOON 17 PLATOON 18 PLATOON
'HQ
10 PLATOON 11 PLATOON 12 PLATOON
'B' COMPANY

A SOLDIER'S EQUIPMENT IN NORMANDY

Cpl G. Cowie, Section Commander, 18 Platoon, 'D' Company, 1st Tyneside Scottish:

Apart from entrenching tools, each company section was issued with spades and a couple of picks. We all carried one or the other, and they were either shoved down one's back under the small haversack or carried through the web belt at the front, with the metal spade protecting some of the body's vital parts. Both tools sometimes had their handles shortened to allow this. In addition to these ways of positioning entrenching tools, other methods of carrying equipment were newly devised, i.e. positions for bayonets, water bottles, respirator etc. New buckles were put on our small haversacks to allow us to carry more gear, including mess tins, emergency rations, spare shirt, socks, toilet gear and a few personal items. A gas cape was folded and placed on top of the haversack. Bren gun pouches also had new buckles in order to make it easier to fit magazines into them. We also had the new type steel helmet, while some in other divisions were to carry on wearing the old type.

As a section commander in Normandy, I also carried on my web belt wire-cutters, a machete and eight Sten gun magazines in two pouches. In addition, I was equipped with an Army pocket watch, compass and binoculars. It was quite a load. How we envied our carrier and truck drivers. Section bundles were carried on our QM truck. These bundles contained one groundsheet and one blanket each. Later, the greatcoat was included. If we had been in a position for two or three days, these bundles came up to us, as did containers of tea, stew and rice. Meanwhile we just survived, probably eating our emergency rations (without orders).

Shown here is an example of the actual kit list handed out to 1st Tyneside Scottish rank and file soldiers in 1944.

Soldier's kit list (TOS – Scottish battalions favoured a tam-o'-shanter).

Men's Kit and Where it is to be Carried.

Haversack (modified with straps moved)

Mess Tins
Gas Cape
Holdall
P.T. Shoes
Socks
Housewife
Cap Comforter
Shirt
Soap & Cleaning Kit
2x 24 Hr Rations one in each half of the mess tin.
1 Tommy Cooker
12 Fuel Tablets
1 Water Sterilizing outfit

Pack (modified with straps moved)

Great Coat
Boots
2 Prs Socks
Denims
Pants
P.T. Vest
P.T. Pants
Towel
Shirt
TOS
Blanket

THE INTELLIGENCE SECTION

As part of its training in the UK, the 1st Tyneside Scottish Intelligence Section attended a special course in 1943 at the 49th Division Battle School, under GSO1 (I) Western Command, Presteigne. In January 1944, the CO gave orders to the Intelligence Section as part of a set of new training instructions, stating that personnel were to be trained in careful observation in the field, and be made aware that all enemy movement on the Battalion's front must be reported immediately, no matter how unimportant it may appear at first sight. They should also study the latest War Office weekly intelligence summaries in order to gain an insight into what would be expected of them on the battlefield.

Later on, after the Battalion had landed in Normandy, the 49th Division headquarters supplied a list of Standing Orders which included the following instructions for Intelligence Sections:

Members of the 1st Tyneside Scottish Intelligence Section and Signal Platoon.

INTELLIGENCE

Sitreps (situation reports) will be sent in twice daily by formation and divisional troop units showing the situation as at 1200 hrs, to reach Divisional HQ by 1400 hrs, and as at 2400 hrs to reach Divisional HQ by 0200 hrs. They will be franked IMMEDIATE and will contain the following information:

a) situation and estimated strength of enemy forces

b) all identifications

c) summary of enemy air activity since last report

d) general position of own troops

e) location of HQs

f) general summary of state of own troops and casualties

Events of importance will be reported immediately to the next higher formation, also to flank formations and other units affected.

Formations and units actively engaged with the enemy will ensure that the next higher formation is fully informed of all events, and of their own intentions.

The time at which events take place will invariably be stated in the text of the message as apart from the time of operation.

All incidents of air attack or shelling must be reported at once using the following letter-code:

A – time from

B – time to

C – map reference of observer

D – area being shelled or bombed

E – number and nature of guns or aircraft

F – number and nature of shells or bombs

G – damage done

H – bearing of flash or sound (for shelling only)

The message will be preceded by the code word BOMREP or SHELREP for bombing or shelling reports respectively.

These instructions give an excellent idea of some of the duties required of Intelligence Section members, and show how necessary it was for them to remain alert and in control during heavy bouts of enemy shelling and mortaring, when their basic instinct would have been to bury themselves in the nearest slit trench.

> ### Pte J. Munro, Intelligence Section, Battalion HQ, 1st TS:
> *One of the prime responsibilities of the Intelligence Section was to lay white guide tape in No Man's Land prior to an attack. Taped grids were laid out using compass bearings which ensured that the companies lined up and advanced together at the same time in the dark. The white tape was unrolled from a drum – two men to a team. One of the greatest fears was meeting an enemy patrol. If a Verey light went up, one stood still, no movement could be made.*

Pte John Munro.

The photographs on this and the facing page were taken by Pte John Munro using a camera he had found in a German backpack captured during the attack on Brettevillette on 28 June. Sadly, we will never know what was taken before that date as the German half of the film did not develop properly. However, John's shots now offer us a fascinating glimpse of life behind the lines in Normandy.

Far left: *Pte Leonard Baverstock.*

Left: *Pipe Major Tom Imrie (seated on harrow).*

> ### Pte J. Munro, Intelligence Section, Battalion HQ, 1st TS:
> *The camera was a cheap Agfa and the photographs were taken with the balance of the film left unexposed in it. I was told later by Lt C. Mitchell, my Intelligence Officer, that I had better hand such items to him in future. It is so long ago now that I cannot recall the exact locations of the photographs, but they all must have been taken in July, after the Rauray battle. The shattered farmhouse (above right) was the Regimental Aid Post.*

THE ANTI-TANK PLATOON

As the events described in this book will show, anti-tank guns played such a major role in front line defence during the Rauray battle, that a detailed section about these weapons has been included as a tribute to the training and achievements of the Tyneside Scottish gunners.

The anti-tank platoon first became an integral part of the infantry battalion during the desert campaign of 1942, when German tank superiority forced the British Army to create a strong defensive organization.

Lt B.T.W. Stewart, 2nd i/c, Anti-tank Platoon, 'S' Company, 1st TS:
The Anti-tank Platoon of the 1st Tyneside Scottish had been part of my life from its inception in late 1942 when it was presented with 6 2-pounder guns, handed down from the Royal Artillery who had been given 6-pounders. I had recently joined the Battalion as a newly commissioned 2nd/Lt Black Watch, having been posted to 'A' Company as a platoon commander. On subsequently being selected to join Support Company, I had the task of commencing the training of the Anti-tank Platoon before it became a Captain's command, when I then became the 2nd i/c. From then onwards, apart from Battle School as a student, and as an instructor after being wounded at Rauray, I spent my whole military career in the 1st Tyneside Scottish as an Anti-tank man.

TRAINING

The Anti-tank Platoon had a full year of constant practice: gun drills, exercises, sand table firing order practice, miniature and full scale range practices – as highly trained, I think, as any unbloodied Anti-tank platoon in the British Infantry. The best trained would clearly be a claim which I could not substantiate, but I remember putting a huge amount of time into training and it seemed to pay off! We sought every possible opportunity to fire live rounds, to practice the gun commanders and their crews so that command, judging of speed and distance, laying and gun drills became second nature. When we could not get a slot on a full calibre range, we designed do it yourself subcalibre .303 ranges, on the beaches of Wales, and the moors of England and Scotland, where we used Bren guns mounted on the barrels of the 6-pounders, and fired at towed targets. A great deal of time was also spent on DIY miniature ranges, where a .22 Rifle attached to the barrel of a 6-pounder added some interest to drill. Manhandling of our guns was practised repeatedly and brought to a fine art. I recall with great pleasure taking a section down to a gunnery range, somewhere in England, where I discovered from the Range Commandant that the record for manhandling 6-pounders around the obstacle course was held by the Scots Guards. I passed the word on to the Jocks who proceeded to knock a minute or so off the course record by ignoring the drill book methods of swinging the gun trail left and right, and running the gun straight over every obstacle.

Members of the 1st TS Anti-tank Platoon who gave key accounts of its actions at Rauray

Lieutenant Brian Stewart

Sergeant Sam Swaddle

Sergeant David Watson

Private Bill Cook

On another occasion I recollect that one of our gun towing carriers, which had been waterproofed, faltered in the middle of a water obstacle in a divisional competition. The men responded effectively and immediately to my exhortations to jump out, unhook the gun, and manhandle carrier and gun to dry land. The carrier recovered and rumbled away triumphantly with gun once more in tow, thus saving the face of the 1st Tyneside Scottish, albeit in an unorthodox manner, in the competition.

EQUIPMENT

By the time we set off for Normandy, the original 2-pounder anti-tank guns (peashooters against the latest German tanks) were a distant memory. The Royal Artillery had gone on to 17-pounders around the time I became 2nd i/c, and as in 1942 when we received their 2-pounders – we got their 6-pounders. The 2-pounder was a remarkable little contraption, hauled about in something called a 'Portee' – a vehicle like a small furniture van – into which it first had to be winched, the wheels eventually being removed before the gun could be fired. This made for exotic gun drill practice, with much bawling and sprinting about. The 6-pounder looked like, and was, a serious gun. It fired solid rounds, and exploding shells which were obviously useful for demolishing walls but not for killing tanks. The gun had a split trailer which was opened as soon as the gun was unlimbered from its towing Loyd carrier, so that the two legs of the trailer roughly formed a 45 degree stabilizer, the base plates digging into the ground as the gun was fired. The wheels were not removed, so the gun was ready for movement at all times, either by carrier or manhandling. The gun 'layer' and 'loader' were protected by a shield which stopped shrapnel splinters.

The 6-pounder was a high velocity gun and a very sharp crack accompanied its firing – I fear we all paid dearly in later years for the enthusiastic and frequent practice which formed the basis for the Platoon's success at Rauray. My hearing has never been the same since. Just before action in Normandy, the familiar 6-pounder ammunition was replaced (or augmented) by Sabot – a tungsten 'dart' encased in a plastic sleeve which disintegrated as the round was fired, leaving the dart to travel twice as fast as the old 6-pounder solid round and with infinitely greater penetration. The dart, if a hit was achieved, made quite a small hole in the tank's armour, but then whizzed around inside causing great damage to crew and equipment. Not having been trained in the use of Sabot, we only knew of these rounds in theory and we were probably less effective than we had been with the familiar 6-pounder round. The extra velocity changed the trajectory as well as making it less necessary to 'lay off' (allow for the speed of the target). On the other hand, there can be little doubt that when we achieved a hit it was more likely to penetrate (an account of Sabot ammunition in action appears on pages 127–8).

IN ACTION

The perfect sequence of action was: 1 – Unlimber the gun from the Loyd carrier and unload box of ammunition (once the gun was in position, the carrier could then widen its role carrying food, ammunition and wounded for the local rifle company). 2 – Face gun barrel to enemy and open trailer legs. 3 – Load. The breech-block was opened by hand, a round pushed in and block closed by loader who then raised his hand to show that the gun was ready to fire. 4 – Aim. The layer (aimer) would be looking through his telescope and adjusting his aim as the loader was doing his part. 5 – Fire. On the command of the Gun Detachment Commander, the gun would fire at the designated target. The layer had to use his judgement, possibly helped by the Commander, about the speed of the enemy tank and the Commander's orders about range. The Commander would be giving his target information to the layer as soon as the gun was in position. The loading would be automatic. Thus: 'Enemy tank, 400 (yards range) – Fire!'. If the first round hit and disabled the enemy tank, fresh orders would be given to identify and fire at the next target: 'Enemy tank, 2 o'clock, speed 20, range 500. If the first round travelled over or under the tank, the Commander would order: 'up 200!' or 'down 200!', and the aimer would adjust his telescope accordingly. Getting a hit fast was important before fire was returned by the enemy. As I previously mentioned, we practised this sort of drill endlessly, on parade grounds and in the countryside, so that it became instinctive. Of course, in battle, the confusion of moving targets, some using smoke to conceal their whereabouts, made accurate estimates of range and speed, which required laying off ahead of the tank (unless the speed was very low), difficult. In short, however good the drill, and I think we were as good as any, judgement and luck played a major part.

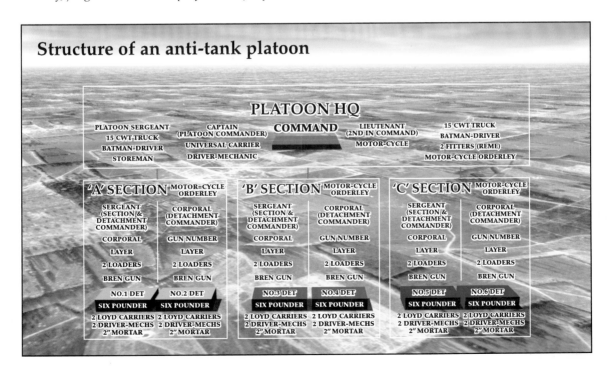

Structure of an anti-tank platoon

PLATOON HQ

COMMAND

PLATOON SERGEANT	CAPTAIN	LIEUTENANT	15 CWT TRUCK
15 CWT TRUCK	(PLATOON COMMANDER)	(2ND IN COMMAND)	BATMAN-DRIVER
BATMAN-DRIVER	UNIVERSAL CARRIER	MOTOR-CYCLE	2 FITTERS (REME)
STOREMAN	DRIVER-MECHANIC		MOTOR-CYCLE ORDERLY

'A' SECTION MOTOR-CYCLE ORDERLY

SERGEANT (SECTION & DETACHMENT COMMANDER)	CORPORAL (DETACHMENT COMMANDER)
CORPORAL	GUN NUMBER
LAYER	LAYER
2 LOADERS	2 LOADERS
BREN GUN	BREN GUN
NO.1 DET	NO.2 DET
SIX POUNDER	SIX POUNDER
2 LOYD CARRIERS	2 LOYD CARRIERS
2 DRIVER-MECHS	2 DRIVER-MECHS
2" MORTAR	2" MORTAR

'B' SECTION MOTOR-CYCLE ORDERLY

SERGEANT (SECTION & DETACHMENT COMMANDER)	CORPORAL (DETACHMENT COMMANDER)
CORPORAL	GUN NUMBER
LAYER	LAYER
2 LOADERS	2 LOADERS
BREN GUN	BREN GUN
NO.3 DET	NO.4 DET
SIX POUNDER	SIX POUNDER
2 LOYD CARRIERS	2 LOYD CARRIERS
2 DRIVER-MECHS	2 DRIVER-MECHS
2" MORTAR	2" MORTAR

'C' SECTION MOTOR-CYCLE ORDERLY

SERGEANT (SECTION & DETACHMENT COMMANDER)	CORPORAL (DETACHMENT COMMANDER)
CORPORAL	GUN NUMBER
LAYER	LAYER
2 LOADERS	2 LOADERS
BREN GUN	BREN GUN
NO.5 DET	NO.6 DET
SIX POUNDER	SIX POUNDER
2 LOYD CARRIERS	2 LOYD CARRIERS
2 DRIVER-MECHS	2 DRIVER-MECHS
2" MORTAR	2" MORTAR

A 'layer' adjusting the telescope on a 6-pounder anti-tank gun.

A 'loader' inserting a round.

A BRIEF HISTORY OF THE
1st TYNESIDE SCOTTISH
BEFORE ACTION IN NORMANDY

'HARDER THAN HAMMERS'

FOREWORD BY
LT COL (RETD) AMBROSE WALTON TD
PRESIDENT OF THE BLACK WATCH ASSOCIATION
(NEWCASTLE BRANCH)

As the only surviving member of the group of officers who were selected in 1939 to serve in the Battalion which eventually became the 1st Bn, Tyneside Scottish, The Black Watch (RHR), I have been asked to write a foreword to this brief history.

Prior to the outbreak of the Second World War, I was a serving officer in the 9th Bn The Durham Light Infantry (Territorial Army), stationed in Gateshead. In September 1939, the War Office ordered the 9th Bn to form a second line unit to be designated the 12th Bn Durham Light Infantry

Lt Col H.L. Swinburne, CO of the 1st Tyneside Scottish in 1939.

Col J.R. Hall, Hon Colonel of the Tyneside Scottish Committee.

(TA). The 2nd i/c of the 9th Bn, Major H.L. Swinburne, was to command the new unit and was elevated to the rank of Lieutenant Colonel. Lt Col Swinburne then selected four officers from the 9th Bn, of whom I was one. The 12th Bn was then based in Victoria Road Schools, where recruiting took place.

The raising of the 12th Bn then came to the notice of Col (Retd) J.R. Hall, who had held the rank of Honorary Colonel of the Tyneside Scottish Committee from the eve of the First World War war. In that capacity, J.R. Hall contacted Lt Col Swinburne and asked if he would be prepared to take on the regimental title of 'Tyneside Scottish' for his battalion. Lt Col Swinburne said he would only be agreeable provided the unit became part of a recognized Highland Regiment and not merely associated. Approach was then made to the Highland Division, resulting in an enthusiastic offer by the Black Watch (RHR). The matter was then put to the War Office who consented to the title – 1st Battalion Tyneside Scottish, The Black Watch (RHR).

In April 1957, I was included by the Chairman of the Black Watch Regimental Honours Committee as the member representing the Tyneside Scottish, and in September 1957 the Battle Honours awarded by the War Office to the Regiment were confirmed as including 'Defence of Rauray'.

Lt Col (Retd) Ambrose Walton, 2000

'GEORDIE AND JOCK'

Some would ask – 'Just who were the Tyneside Scottish? Were they simply a group of Newcastle men seeking Scottish ties, or were they a true mix of Tynesiders and Taysiders?'

In order to answer that question one must go back to the beginning of the First World War. In September 1914, an attempt was made to form a special battalion of Northumberland Fusiliers with Scottish blood to be known as the Tyneside Scottish, but such was the popularity of the idea among Tynesiders that within weeks over 4,000 men had volunteered for service with the unit, and by the middle of November 1914 it had rapidly expanded to a full brigade of four Tyneside Scottish battalions (20th–23rd Northumberland Fusiliers). As whole communities were enrolling in groups, it soon became clear that Northumberland folk would inevitably form a majority and plans to restrict membership to those with Scottish ancestry were abandoned.

Although keen to get to the front, the men of the Tyneside Scottish Brigade did not reach France until January 1916. Then began the breaking-in period, during which the men were gradually fed into the front line. At last, all four battalions were ready to face the enemy, but the cheerful optimism they had shown in volunteering was about to be cruelly shattered. When the time did finally come for them to be piped into battle, they went to their deaths like mayflies, many of them being among the thousands lost on the first day of the Battle of the Somme. Just before 0730 hrs on 1 July 1916, two gigantic mines were detonated below the German lines around the village of La Boiselle. A few minutes later, at the sharp blast of officers' whistles, the whole of the 34th Division, including all four Tyneside Scottish

Officers of the 1st Tyneside Scottish, the Black Watch (Royal Highland Regiment) – Totnes 1940. Left to right, back row: 2/Lts A. MacLagan, W.H.F. Armstrong, R. Dempster, R.W. Scott, H.R. Alexander, M.R. Tatham, K.P. Calderwood, F.T. Bell, T.D. Ross, A.P. Whitehead, H.B. Boyne, C.D. Elrick, Middle row: 2/Lts W.B. O'Hanlon, A.S. Lawrie, A.K.A. Ogg, R.M. McLeod, E.F. Carter, B.G. Kennedy, D.E. Salisbury, G.C. Paton, D.M. Leitch, J.S. Highmore, R.S.M. Stordy, H.G. Chudleigh, H.E. Parker, Sitting: lt H.S. Forrester, Lt A.L. Campbell, Capt W.K. Angus, Capt A. Walton, Major K.K. Walmsley, Lt Col C.W. McGregor, Capt J.K. Dunn, Capt R.N. Craig, Lt Qrmr J. Findlay, 2/Lt W.G. Brennan.

battalions, left their trenches and began what was to be for most of them the short walk to oblivion. However, despite its horrendous losses on the battlefields of the Somme, the Tyneside Scottish Brigade fought on till the last days of the war and it is thought that a complete list of decorations awarded to its men in the First World War would amount to about 400.

No attempt was made to re-form the original Brigade at the outbreak of the Second World War but a duplicate territorial battalion of the 9th Durham Light Infantry, initially known as the 12th, adopted the Tyneside Scottish title and sought affiliation to a Highland regiment (as Ambrose Walton has already explained in his foreword to this brief history). On being successfully adopted by a Scottish regiment, the Battalion took the name – 1st Battalion, Tyneside Scottish, The Black Watch (Royal Highland Regiment), and began wearing the Black Watch Tartan and Red Hackle. Although garrisoned in Perth, Scotland, the new unit remained in close contact with the Durhams, becoming part of the 70th Infantry Brigade alongside the 10th and 11th DLI.

There was no repeat of the enthusiasm of 1914, the ethos behind the original Tyneside Scottish 'Pals' Brigade having died along with so many of its men, but despite this, the Battalion's morale soared after the evacuation of Dunkirk as its Scottish ties began to be defined in Black Watch manpower as well as in name. As the intensive training progressed, the old Tyneside Scottish spirit was rejuvenated and enhanced. In 1944, the Battalion would truly go off to war as 'Geordie and Jock'.

While it would be practically impossible to clearly state the proportion of Tynesiders to Scots amongst those who set out for Normandy, a very rough estimate based on an address list of those men who served with the Tyneside Scottish during the Second World War would suggest that, among officers (the majority having originated from the Black Watch): 25 per cent were Tynesiders, 25 per cent Scots and 50 per cent others. Among other ranks: 45 per cent were Tynesiders, 35 per cent Scots and 20 per cent others.

Lt B.T.W. Stewart, 2nd i/c, Anti-tank Platoon, 'S' Company, 1st TS:
The Officers' Mess roughly conformed to the picture outlined by the above figures. The older officers were for the most part Geordies, originally from the Durham Light Infantry, the younger ones were all Scots who had been commissioned into The Black Watch before being posted to the 1st Tyneside Scottish. Amongst the senior officers there was a mixture of Black Watch regulars and Tyneside Scottish territorials. The CO, Lt Col Oxley, was a Tynesider (Territorial), Major McGregor had been a Black Watch Sergeant in Palestine before the war and Quartermaster Findlay was an ex-Black Watch RSM. I was not conscious of any gulf between Geordie and Jock, either in the officers Mess or outside it – old and new seemed to be well integrated.

FRANCE 1940

Despite the fact that its training was incomplete, the 1st Tyneside Scottish was sent to France in April 1940 as part of the British Expeditionary Force, to help build new airfields. A month later, the German Army invaded Belgium and the Battalion's role immediately became a more active one. On 17 May, having been unable to defend its position on the Canal du Nord against the rapid German *Blitzkrieg*, the Battalion fell back on the village of Ficheux. Three days later, after a final stand at the village crossroads, the strength of the attack proved too much for the defenders and they were overrun by advancing enemy tanks. However, it took Rommel's German Panzers five hours of desperate fighting to overcome this inexperienced territorial unit, whose brave efforts won vital time for the BEF trapped on the beaches at Dunkirk. Determined to do their duty to the last despite the hopelessness of their position, these brave men resolutely fixed bayonets when their ammunition finally ran out. German officers commenting on this day's action were astonished that their adversaries had come from the inexperienced 23rd Division, and expressed great admiration at the fighting performance of such an ill-equipped unit. Some of the weaponry issued to the Battalion had turned out to be for drill purposes only and thus incapable of firing a single shot. In all, the Battalion lost over 100 in the fighting, and only around 140 survivors made their way back across the Channel.

> **Major A. L. Campbell, 1st Tyneside Scottish 1940–43:**
> *The Battalion was reinforced with both officers and other ranks, as only a few of the former and less than 200 of the latter had managed to return from Dunkirk. The new arrivals soon settled down and the Battalion took good shape under the command of Lt Col C. Oxley, who was very ably assisted by the company commanders: Ken Dunn, Ken Calderwood, Bob Stordy, Bill Brennan and Ambrose Walton. Of particular merit at this time was the Adjutant, 'Cabby' McGregor, who really licked the Battalion into shape using his previous experience as a peacetime Company Sergeant Major with The Black Watch. He seemed to know exactly what was required to be done to re-form the Battalion. He was a very good disciplinarian, but also very helpful, so was greatly respected by the other officers and other ranks alike.*

During a stay in Modbury, and later in Kingsbridge, Devon, the Battalion found itself greatly scattered as it had been detailed to defend 17 miles of Devon coastline against the expected German invasion. Despite this display of vigilance, the Battalion's arms consisted mainly of rifles and bayonets, a situation hardly providing the equivalent of the coastal defences set up by the enemy across the Channel that the Allied invasion forces were to confront four years later.

> *We had a few Brens and also a few First World War Maxim machine guns – probably acquired from The Imperial War Museum! These fired a few rounds, then had a stoppage which required about ten minutes to rectify. We also had an anti-aircraft platoon to cope with the regular visits from German aircraft – the platoon's armaments consisted of six rifles, and they had six bicycles to keep them mobile. I was Intelligence Officer at the time, and as our transport was civilian vehicles still in their original paint, I had a*

splendid Ariel 500 motorcycle still in shining chrome!. The CO asked me to go all round the Battalion area and pinpoint all the defensive positions. Owing to the herring-bone type of road system, I travelled 250 miles to complete the job. Fortunately for the Battalion's 'thin red line' situation, the Germans did not attack. But looking back at that hopeless position we were in at the time, the morale in the Battalion was very high indeed, and I am quite sure that if the Germans had come, the defensive principle of 'to the last round and to the last man' would have applied without question by everyone in the Battalion. We became very defensive minded, and apart from preparing and manning our positions, very little training was done other than at section level. There was a great concern about fifth-column activity, and as IO, my main task seemed to be to dispel suspected cases; i.e. light signals to offshore submarines would turn out to be the evening sun reflecting on an opening and closing window moved by the wind, or a new kind of bomb or grenade washed ashore would turn out to be a ball-shaped metal container for German gas masks.

The Battalion was moved to Totnes around October 1940 to be re-equipped and made ready for action:

Our Quartermaster, Jimmy Findlay, did a marvellous job and in a very short time we were all ready, and after family farewells, our journey began and ended with our arrival in Iceland.

ICELAND

Having been successfully recharged in the UK with replacements from the Black Watch, the 1st Tyneside Scottish joined 'The Polar Bears' (49th Division) in Iceland. The main role of the Battalion as an Iceland (C) Force reserve unit was to counter-attack enemy penetration in the Reykjavik area (the C in brackets in the Force's name was introduced to avoid the chance of mail being sent to Ireland by mistake, typing errors being a common occurrence). A German attack on Iceland by sea or air was regarded at the time as a distinct possibility, the island being of great strategic value as Atlantic shipping routes were vital to the survival of Britain's war effort. Fear of the use of gas during a full-scale attack by the enemy was coupled with the belief that fifth columnists would provide assistance at such times. The War Office would herald the beginning of such an attack with a codeword. The Battalion was therefore told to stand by for 'JULIUS'. However, no such attack materialized, and the only enemy action experienced was an attack made by a German bomber on a platoon at Selfoss. Flying at a height of 100–200 ft, the enemy aircraft strafed the party, killing one man and wounding another in the arm.

Despite the lack of any serious combat action, the Battalion was rarely unoccupied. Seven-day Company route-marches were organized to keep the troops exercised and to engage them in various training schemes monitored by military observers. The result was a rapid building of fitness and a hardened edge which would prove invaluable later on in the war. Other exercises took the Battalion to Kleifarvatn, a valley 15 miles south

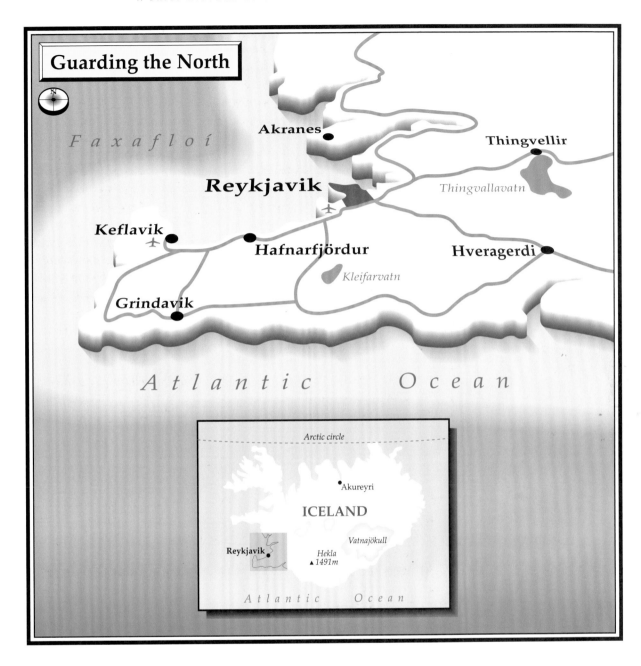

Guarding the North

Faxaflói

Akranes

Thingvellir

Reykjavik

Thingvallavatn

Keflavik

Hafnarfjördur

Hveragerdi

Kleifarvatn

Grindavik

Atlantic Ocean

Arctic circle

•Akureyri

ICELAND

Vatnajökull

Reykjavik•

Hekla
▲ *1491m*

Atlantic Ocean

of Reykjavik, where a set-piece attack was carried out with full artillery support, and to the mountain and snow warfare school at Akureyri, in the north of the island. At Akureyri, a Winter Warfare Course was run by a group of Army and Navy officers who were well experienced in Arctic conditions, along with a number of Norwegian Army representatives. The Norwegians gave skiing lessons and explained and demonstrated how their ski units operated in Norway.

Major A.L. Campbell, 1st Tyneside Scottish 1940–3:
The course was very interesting and good value as it showed us how to dress, live and exist in extremely cold conditions, as low as 30° below zero. We were shown how to build an igloo and spend

days and nights living on a glacier. The Norwegians also showed us how difficult it is to shoot a man skiing fast downhill. They used a life-sized target of a man on skis, which was released for twenty-four of us to fire on at will with five rounds each. When we examined the target afterwards, there were no hits.

The Battalion's camp was an untidy scattering of Nissen huts at Baldurshagi, near Reykjarvik, on the banks of a fast-flowing river, rich with superb trout and salmon.

Capt Brennan became very popular at the Baldurshagi camp because, a very keen and able fly-fisherman, he kept us supplied with delicious sea trout.

The 49th Division had its own newspaper, *The Midnight Sun*, and sports were encouraged – the Battalion football team won the final of a Force football competition, each winning team member being presented with a pencil! Events such as this were important for morale as long periods of guard duty (winter nights in Iceland lasted around eighteen hours) could be depressingly dull. Wind chill, in temperatures already way below freezing, meant the men had to be constantly aware of the danger of frostbite. My father wrote home about howling gales, during which he had to stand with his back against a wall to avoid being blown off his feet. However, despite the arctic weather conditions and the fact that Army welfare and entertainment was poor in Iceland, the men buckled down and made the best of it. Indeed, some found the island most agreeable, including an officer with the nickname 'Chocolate'.

The 1st Tyneside Scottish Pipe Band, Iceland 1941.

The mention of 'Chocolate Kennedy' reminds me of how that officer got his name. He boasted that if you booked for a night at the Borg Hotel and lowered a line with a bar of chocolate tied to the end, you would soon get a 'bite', and when you pulled in, you would find a young Icelandic lady hanging on to it! Another story about him (sworn to be true), was that after an all-night party in Reykjavik he arrived back at the Baldurshagi camp by taxi, got out and walked past the guardroom sentry exchanging salutes – then the sentry noticed that Kennedy was dressed in full dress uniform, but instead of a kilt, only a shirt tail was covered by the sporran. At 11.00 am another taxi arrived, and this time a young Icelandic lady leant out and handed a kilt over to the sentry saying 'for Mr Kennedy please!'. Much later, when back in the UK, he astounded everyone in the Battalion by applying for a course with a Commando or SAS unit the morning after a well-lubricated dinner. A couple of weeks later, to his dismay, he was actually accepted. He left the Battalion to attend the course and was never heard of again.

On 12 June 1941, a ceremonial parade took place in Reykjavik in celebration of the birthday of HM King George VI. The Battalion had become a regular feature of these occasions – their kilts, pipes and drums being hugely popular with the locals.

Lt B.T.W. Stewart, 2nd i/c, Anti-tank Platoon, 'S' Company, 1st TS:

The good people of Iceland were rivetted by the sight of kilted warriors marching through their streets to the stirring strains of pipes and drums. They were even more rivetted when an occasional slip on a patch of ice revealed all!

Later, the possibility of involvement by the United States of America in the war was suggested when US Marines landed in Reykjavik. They had been sent over to make preparations for future commitments. Then on 16 August, Winston Churchill visited Iceland on his way home from his historic meeting with President Roosevelt off the coast of Newfoundland, and the Battalion once again took part in a ceremonial march-past in Reykjavik.

Major A.L. Campbell, 1st Tyneside Scottish 1940–43:

The Battalion was ordered to prepare a Guard of Honour for a VIP who was shortly to visit the capital. Lt Col Oxley detailed me to measure our men for the job. I was able to hand-pick the men and QM Jimmy Findlay did us proud by issuing new uniforms to all. We were lucky to have the equivalent of a small barrack-square outside Ken Dunn's Company HQ, and I had a day or two to smarten up foot and arms drill. All the men really enjoyed the situation, and when the 'big day' did arrive, we were told that the VIP was none other than our Prime Minister, Winston Churchill. The drill and arms salute was carried out perfectly by the whole Guard of Honour, and the Prime Minister thanked and praised us all for our turn-out. I must not forget our pipe band! – they were a splendid sight to see, and a stirring sound to hear and march to. Scotland would have been proud of them, and so too, any Black Watch Battalion.

In November, the Battalion moved its base to Hafnarfjördur, a fishing town 10 miles along the coast from Reykjavik, where it remained until its relief by the US Army the following month.

TRAINING IN THE UK

A tired but happy group of Tyneside Scots finally arrived in Llanelli, South Wales, on Christmas morning 1941, having travelled all night from Gourock in Scotland where they had disembarked after the long sea voyage from Iceland. Llanelli, or 'Slash' as it was called (presumably because of the Welsh double 'l'), became the Battalion's second home, and

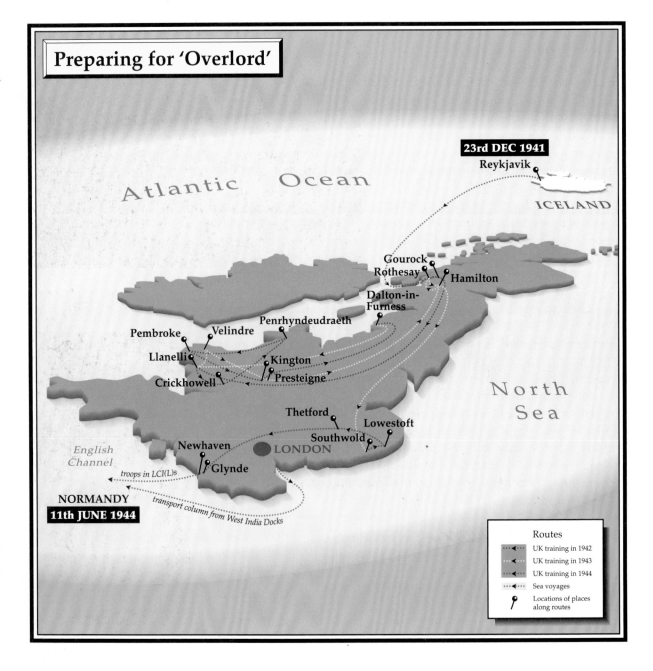

Preparing for 'Overlord'

23rd DEC 1941
Reykjavik

Atlantic Ocean

ICELAND

Gourock
Rothesay
Hamilton
Dalton-in-Furness

Penrhyndeudraeth

Pembroke
Velindre
Llanelli
Kington
Crickhowell
Presteigne

North Sea

Thetford
Lowestoft
Southwold

English Channel
Newhaven
Glynde
LONDON

troops in LCI(L)s

NORMANDY
11th JUNE 1944
transport column from West India Docks

Routes

◄····	UK training in 1942
◄	UK training in 1943
◄····	UK training in 1944
◄····	Sea voyages
⚲	Locations of places along routes

announcements of forthcoming marriages between Tyneside Scots and Llanelli girls rapidly became commonplace.

Cpl G. Cowie, Section Commander, 18 Platoon, 'D' Company, 1st TS:

Previously in a Home Defence Unit, I volunteered for service with the 1st Tyneside Scottish in 1942, who at that time were stationed at Llanelli in South Wales. My impression was that I was with real soldiers for the first time. Although an easy-going body, they seemed a pretty tough crowd. There were a number of Dunkirk veterans amongst them, some sporting Military Medals and one officer wore a Military Cross. All had been toughened by eighteen months service in Iceland, but the Battalion was nowhere near up to standard at this stage.

However, the joy of being home again was tempered with knowledge that the Battalion was about to take up a role involving a long and extremely rigorous period of training. Still part of the 49th (West Riding) Division, it took part in a series of exercises in Wales and Scotland designed to turn it into a mountain troop unit. Mountain training began in earnest during the spring of 1942 at Penrhyndeudraeth in Snowdonia, the object being to attack and advance over high ground in mountainous country using horses and mules as pack transport. As spring turned to summer, the Battalion moved south again. First to Pembroke, then to Kington in Herefordshire to continue its mountain training in the Brecon Beacons. At Pembroke, a football match was arranged with a local team and the Battalion's footballing 'Geordies and Jocks' once again showed their enthusiasm for the game. They were a crack team, comfortably winning all their 'friendlies' and 49th Division Competition matches. Among the Tyneside Scots was Sgt J.D. Wright, who had recently won an England International cap in a match against Norway.

Lt Col C.W. Oxley, CO of the 1st Tyneside Scottish 1940–43.

Pte P. Birkett, Intelligence Section, Battalion HQ, 1st TS:

The Pembroke match kicked off and the Battalion soon began scoring goals. At 6 – 0, 'Dougie' Wright quietly suggested that some of the lads should swap shirts to even things up a bit.

After the war, Wright went on to make eighty-two appearances for Newcastle United FC and 233 for Lincoln City FC, an incredible

Sgt J.D. Wright.

achievement given that he had been seriously wounded in one leg while fighting in France with the Battalion in 1940.

The end of the year was spent at a camp in Dalton-in-Furness, from where the Battalion moved back, with much satisfaction, to Llanelli. However, the move was made with many of the Jocks carrying sore heads, as the hour of departure came at the crack of dawn on New Year's morning 1943. In February, the 1st Tyneside Scottish reached peak fitness in route marching, on one occasion covering a distance of 50 miles over the hilly roads of South Wales while under the temporary command of Major W.L. McGregor. He marched along with the companies, covering the distance in exactly 23 hours and 12 minutes, including a three-hour halt for a meal and a rest. This phenomenal effort was part of the preparation for 'Exercise Spartan', the biggest military manoeuvres ever held in the UK at that time.

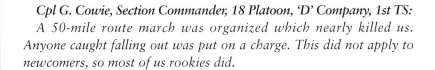

Cpl G. Cowie, Section Commander, 18 Platoon, 'D' Company, 1st TS:
A 50-mile route march was organized which nearly killed us. Anyone caught falling out was put on a charge. This did not apply to newcomers, so most of us rookies did.

Lt Col A.J.H. Cassels, CO of the 1st Tyneside Scottish 1943–44 (seen here in his later Major-General's uniform).

After a brief spell at Hamilton Park, Lanarkshire, the Battalion was shunted back to South Wales again, this time to the small village of Velindre just north of Carmarthen. Special train facilities were arranged so that the troops could visit Llanelli on their days off. At Velindre, the CO, Lt Col C.W. Oxley, left the Battalion and was succeeded by Lt Col A.J.H. Cassels, a Seaforth Highlander.

Cassels was a very highly respected soldier, and many would say, including the author's father, that he was largely responsible for bringing the 1st Tyneside Scottish up to a level of combat fitness. *Harder than Hammers* glowingly mentions:

The TS soon recognised that in 'Jim' Cassels, who had been General Ritchie's chief staff officer in the 52nd Division, they had a CO in a thousand. In six brief months he brought the Battalion up to absolute concert pitch, and in the process got to know personally almost every man under his command. As soon as his six months 'in command of troops' had expired he was whisked away again, to serve under General Ritchie as Brigadier (General Staff) of 12th Corps. But in that brief period he left a mark on the TS which was never to be erased. No commanding officer has ever been paid a more genuine tribute than the way in which the troops turned out en masse – quite spontaneously – to bid him farewell when he left Battalion HQ at Southwold for the last time.

Cassels took over command of the 152nd Brigade, 51st (Highland) Division, at the end of June 1944, the Division itself in May 1945, and later commanded the 1st Commonwealth Division during the Korean War. He was CGS from 1965–68 and finished his career as a Field Marshal.

Around the time that Lt Col Cassels joined the Battalion, command of the 49th Division passed to Major-General E.H. (Bubbles) Barker, who took firm control of the Polar Bears, changing the motif of their divisional sign and tunic patch from a passive bear, as worn in Iceland, to an aggressive one with its head lifted in an expression of defiance (the Polar Bear patch was also worn by the US First Marine Brigade while they served in Iceland). Keen to improve physical fitness, Barker greatly encouraged field training at the Division's Battle School.

Lt B.T.W. Stewart, 2nd i/c, Anti-tank Platoon, 'S' Company, 1st TS:
The 49th Division Battle School at Presteigne Manor in Radnorshire, under GSO1 (I) Western Command, was established soon after I joined the Battalion in late 1942. Lt K.D. Buchanan and I, who were the newest joined subalterns, were chosen to be the Battalion's guinea-pig students. The school seemed, to put it mildly, an unattractive prospect for the older officers, but for Lt Buchanan and me, fresh from university and OCTU, it was pretty easy stuff. The emphasis on physical fitness and endless obstacle courses was something we were well used to, and I think we both found it a very natural transition from all we had already been doing at OCTU. There was one big difference however; at the Battle School, every exercise was conducted with live ammunition to remind the students what it sounded like to be at the receiving end of rifle and machine gun fire. The programme started at 'sparrows' every morning and was not pleasant if there had been a party the night before, but generally the physical side held few terrors as far as I was concerned. We encouraged the students to clamber over hedges, under barbed-wire, through tunnels, down cliffs and across chasms – many of the techniques being very familiar to me as one who at Oxford had climbed into College to avoid fines.

Soon after graduation from the school, I went to Netheravon to study the theory and practice of anti-tank gunnery and learn about the two-pounder, but I had hardly taken over my new job as the Anti-tank Platoon Commander than I was whisked off to Presteigne again, this time as an instructor. Since at the end of my spell at Battle School I returned to the Anti-tank Platoon, I never had the opportunity to put the theories I had learnt at Netheravon into practice. Inevitably, the determination to make the exercises as realistic as possible, firing live ammunition on fixed lines and demanding that students learnt to deal with dangerous obstacles, led to the occasional tragedy. In my relatively short time as an instructor, three of my students died. The first was a particularly sad case of a Major who was presumably afraid to admit to a fear of heights. When climbing down a rock face gripping a rope, he suddenly fell to his death. The second case was an inexpert student firing a 2-inch mortar smoke bomb during an attack on my section. The projectile struck my student on the head, killing him instantly. The third victim was killed during a night exercise by a round from a Verey pistol, which at point blank range is of course lethal.

During my first few months as a new subaltern, I commanded a platoon in Major McGregor's Company. This redoubtable officer had been in The Black Watch before the war and had brought to his position a great deal of military experience. He was, perhaps understandably, less than impressed by the abilities of some of those around him and he could be a very hard task master. At an early stage he said to me, 'Laddie, your noo a verra guid shot, you'll gae doon to the range every day until you reach sniper standard'. I did not object, he was quite right and practice made perfect.

Cpl J.W.H. Tipler, Section Commander, 18 Platoon, 'D' Company, 1st TS:

The only memory I have of a one-day sniping course is of Major McGregor's final warning on the need for honesty in claims: 'It's no good you claiming that you shot at and killed a General when in fact you shot at and killed a cook!'

In October 1943, the Battalion spent four weeks in Rothesay, Isle of Bute, climbing in and out of landing craft as part of its training for the invasion of the Continent. For the next few weeks, the Firth of Clyde took the place of the English Channel and the men got a real sense of what it would be like to make an amphibious landing and attack coastal defences. Live ammunition and explosives were used in a full-scale programme of practice assaults. The whole Battalion, in groups of seventy, embarked in landing-craft and proceeded to jump into the sea. Before the exercise, the following orders were given out:

a) parties will be organized so that, as far as possible, swimmers and non-swimmers jump in together
b) weapons and bayonets will not be carried
c) steel helmets will be worn and tied down to the wearer to avoid being lost when the men jump into the water

Cpl G. Cowie, Section Commander, 18 Platoon, 'D' Company, 1st TS:

This was good. We approached the beaches firing live ammunition, then wading ashore we blew the wire with our 'Bangalore torpedoes' and dug-in, spending the night in the slits still soaking wet. To give us confidence, we were taken out in landing-

craft, and several yards from the promenade we were ordered to jump into the sea wearing our 'Mae Wests'. The 'Mae Wests' were half inflated and one had to further inflate them if and when one surfaced. I lost my steel helmet and began drifting out to sea on my back like several others who were non-swimmers. I was eventually picked up by a boat manned by Royal Marines, on duty for that purpose.

At the end of November, the Battalion was ordered to Southwold where most of the unit were installed in a girls' school. Here, the CO jokingly complained that when he pressed the bell in his bedroom marked 'Ring for Mistress', nothing happened.

In January 1944 the Battalion moved to Lowestoft, where it took part in Exercise 'Elk II' – attacking an enemy strongpoint defended by a deep minefield. This exercise, watched by General Eisenhower and the Chief of Imperial General Staff (CIGS) Alanbrooke, included secret armoured invasion weapons. It was at Lowestoft that the Battalion came under the command of Lt Col R.W.M. de Winton, a Gordon Highlander who had taken part in the 51st Highland Division's desert and Sicily campaigns. At the end of the month, a further switch of location took the Battalion to Thetford, where it received its final training, on one occasion being visited by HM King George VI (see photograph above).

HM King George VI inspecting the 1st Tyneside Scottish at Thetford Station, 27 April 1944 (Capt J.R. Alexander, the Battalion Adjutant, walks behind the King).

Cpl G. Cowie, Section Commander, 18 Platoon, 'D' Company, 1st TS:
The hard work really started at Thetford. Training became far more realistic, with Brigade and Divisional exercises, nearly always using live ammunition. Everyone learnt to use the new PIAT anti-tank weapon. It was not liked. One could be pushed back a few feet after firing and probably hit in the eye by a metal cap from the bomb. Theoretically, one could disable an enemy tank at a distance of about 100 yards and knock one out at 30 yards. It was a suicide job. Each platoon appointed a couple of PIAT men in the same way as their 2-inch mortar teams. As regards digging slit trenches, this was never taught, one had to find out the hard way later when it was usually the case of 'dig or die'.

During the early hours of 7 June, D + 1, the main body of the Battalion left Thetford by train bound for Sussex (the transport party had already departed for West India Docks in London), and by 1000 hrs had reached Glynde Camp where it was to be marshalled before leaving for France. The following day an advance party headed for Normandy to prepare for the Battalion's arrival. There was no training as such in the days leading up to embarkation, but the camp was still a hive of activity with plenty of briefings. News bulletins about the progress of the fighting across the Channel were broadcast over the camp Tannoy system. Each man was given the equivalent of £1 in French paper money (printed in England) and the best the Army could provide in the way of 'comforts' – cinema shows, ENSA and NAAFI all helping to give them a spirited send-off. However, behind the cheerful revelry of these last few days on native soil there lay an urgency for departure. A number of men held deep memories of the sacrifices the Battalion had made in France in 1940, and the need to return and reverse the result of Dunkirk was strong. There was now a confidence in the Battalion built up by months of training in all weathers, which suggested that this time things might be different.

ARRIVAL IN NORMANDY

O n 30 May, during a talk given by the CO, a message of encouragement was passed on to all ranks from General Montgomery, Commander of the 21st Army Group and mastermind of Operation 'Overlord'. Despite the fact that an Allied invasion was imminent and on everyone's mind, the 1st Tyneside Scottish, along with the rest of the 49th (West Riding) Division, was not destined to be part of the famous D-Day operations of 6 June, but would join the action as part of a follow-up force a week later.

Lt B.T.W. Stewart, 2nd i/c, Anti-tank Platoon, 'S' Company, 1st TS:
The Duke of Wellington, fanatically interested as all the best military commanders have been in having good intelligence, often spoke of wanting to know what was on the other side of the hill. He would have been pleased with the combined efforts of the British Intelligence and Security Services before D-Day – the Allies were extremely well informed. The Duke would also have been astonished at the new technology for intelligence collection, radio intercept, radar and aerial photography. Our radio intercepts were sometimes deciphered, translated and delivered to our commanders before the German addressee had read them.

At our level, we had to make do with our Commander's hearty address at Thetford, when wrecking the beautiful symmetry of the serried ranks of our Brigade, Monty ordered us to cluster round his jeep and assured us that we would soon be hitting the Germans for six. But neither he nor anyone realized how successful our Intelligence and Security Service had been in totally bamboozling the enemy about our strength. The Germans believed that we had a spare Army Group with 23 Divisions up our sleeve in south-east England called FUSAG (First US Army Group), commanded by General Patton and poised to attack the Pas de Calais, and that our main thrust would be in that area. It was a brilliant hoax. The FUSAG was a phantom; there were no fighting troops, AFVs or guns, only communicators and radios. It was only after the war was over, when German generals had given their stories to Allied interrogators, that the full picture emerged of the factors which contributed to the German failure to mass their forces against our bridgehead on D-Day, before we had time to consolidate. The picture that slowly emerged was as follows:

a) The Germans, from Hitler downwards, having been convinced by our deception operation, were afraid to move troops from the Pas de Calais.

b) Having assumed that the Allies would wait for a good weather forecast, the enemy did not expect the invasion to take place as early as 6 June, so most of the senior officers were away from their HQs.

c) Allied bombing and shelling, and sabotage by their agents assisted by the Maquis, had been highly successful in destroying railway and road bridges, thus severely affecting the movement of reinforcements. Sabotage had also played a useful part in the destruction of communications.

d) Rommel and von Rundstedt were at loggerheads over the type of counter-attack that should be launched. Rommel wanted an immediate counter-attack, piecemeal. Von Runstedt wanted a measured response with massed armour.

e) Although the Atlantic Wall defences, which Rommel had been strengthening all year, had by no means been destroyed by our bombardments and bombing, nevertheless, the troops manning the 'Wall' had been stunned and demoralized by the weight of such strikes.

f) Our pre-invasion hammering of the German radar and radio jamming stations had eliminated all their electronic defences.

g) The Germans had 300 miles of European coast to defend, and the ten Panzer Divisions available were thinly spread behind this coastal perimeter.

h) The German assessment that our main attack would come across the Pas de Calais was based not only on our deception plan, but also on their conviction that we would choose to attack there in an attempt to cut off their forces in Normandy by a rapid armoured thrust.

Cpl G. Cowie, Section Commander, 18 Platoon, 'D' Company, 1st TS:
We all now felt that we could not have been better trained for the job in hand. Morale was sky high. Of course, most of us did not have a clue what to really expect, we knew it would not be a walkover but we could never have possibly imagined how bad it would actually be (as the Battalion began to suffer casualties in Normandy its numbers altered dramatically and replacements came from anywhere and everywhere. By the end of the Normandy Campaign, the 'Geordie and Jock' effect was to vanish, along with over half the Battalion).

11 JUNE

At 1045 hrs on 11 June, the marching troops were driven from Glynde Camp to Newhaven Harbour.

Cpl G. Cowie, Section Commander, 18 Platoon, 'D' Company, 1st TS:
All the chaps had a surplus of English coins, ranging from old pennies to half-crowns. These were thrown to the lads of Newhaven, dozens of whom ran after the slowly moving trucks. They had a field day. We paraded in a large shed alongside the quay – and waited! – eventually embarking during the early evening.

The Battalion embarked onto landing-craft together with the 10th Durham Light Infantry – one of its fellow battalions of the 70th Brigade. These craft, known officially as LCI(L)s – Landing-craft Infantry (Large) – were full of rations including ingenious cans of self-heating soup. Anti-seasickness pills were handed out and everyone eagerly awaited the hour of departure.

We had got used to these craft during our training at Rothesay. Some stretcher cases were being landed nearby, I think they were naval personnel. I shouted across to a Durham I knew in a craft moving alongside. I never saw him again.

At 2300 hrs, a convoy of six LCI(L)s left Newhaven harbour and moved out, unescorted, into a choppy sea.

I was on deck during the night, and could just about see two long lines of craft heading towards France. I saw no escort. The meals were good, morale was still high and the naval chaps were very cheerful, even though they had been at it since D-Day. The sky above

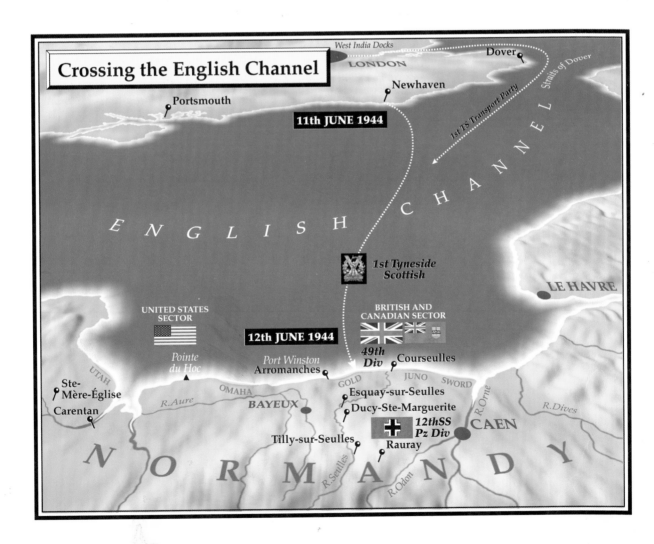

them was murky to begin with, but eventually it cleared and from then on the crossing was made in starlight. A number of flares were seen at one point which gave a moment's alarm, but otherwise the journey was uneventful (see map on page 19).

12 JUNE (D + 6)

At about midday on 12 June, D + 6, the main body of the 1st Tyneside Scottish arrived off the coast of Normandy at a point somewhere between la Rivière and le Hamel, the advance party having already been ashore twelve hours. Craft of all descriptions could be seen in huge numbers: warships, steamers, ferries, launches, ships unloading supplies, boats towing sections of Mulberry harbour into position – the traffic was endless.

I will never again see such a sight, there were ships everywhere. Before we disembarked, a Messerschmitt 110 flew over, rather slow. Everything opened up on it and it soon disappeared. Many of the craft were flying a type of barrage balloon.

About 1500 hrs, the men started to disembark, laden with equipment. Most made it without getting their feet wet, but some had to plunge into the sea up to their necks and wade ashore; their 'swimming in full kit' training off the Scottish coast finally being put to the test.

Lt B.T.W. Stewart, 2nd i/c, Anti-tank Platoon, 'S' Company, 1st TS:
We anchored well off the beach, and the platoon's carriers, waterproofed and fitted with vertical exhaust pipes, disappeared under the waves so completely that only the heads of the occupants were visible. But to my relief, they all rumbled safely up the beach.

Cpl G. Cowie, Section Commander, 18 Platoon, 'D' Company, 1st TS:
We were transferred into a smaller landing craft which carried a platoon. The craft I was in had its ramp jammed, not properly closed. Sea water was coming in, and the coxwain explained that it had been damaged a few days earlier. We were therefore sitting or standing in about a foot of water. The craft landed about 50 yards from the beach and we waded ashore. Water was up to my thighs. We deposited our 'Mae Wests' on a gigantic pile on our left. On the right, I noticed a large pile of para collapsable folding bikes. 'B' Company, the so-called 'Cycle Company', who had been issued with these, were depositing their folding bikes too. This particular beach area was in King sector of GOLD beach, near to the hamlet of le Hamel. The 50th (Northumbrian) Division had gone ashore here on D-Day. There was much debris about and we could hear gunfire coming from an area a few miles inland.

First-class administration once again took control. All the exits from the beaches were clearly marked. Windsocks showed the way for vehicles – black and white for tracked and dark blue for wheeled. Personnel exits were marked as such, and led to assembly areas where staff collected

```
PERSONNEL LANDING CARD

WHERE TO GO WHEN YOU LAND

1. On landing go immediately via the nearest personnel exit
   to:-

   49 DIV SUB SECTOR OF THE

        ASSEMBLY AREA    SHELLEY

   and report to 49 Div SECTOR CONTROL.


2. You will then receive orders whether to remain in the
   Assembly Area or move to your concentration area "C".
```

landing cards and gave the marching troops the route forward to their concentration areas. The landing cards (see example above) gave basic instructions about where to go in case anybody got lost as the result of being put down in the wrong area. This prevented stranded men from drifting around and getting in the way.

Lt B.T.W. Stewart, 2nd i/c, Anti-tank Platoon, 'S' Company, 1st TS:
I knew Normandy had been the richest region of France in peacetime; a picture postcard scene of lush pastures, rich arable fields, verdant hedgerows, dense woods, vast dairy herds, picturesque orchards, mellow châteaux, half-timbered farmhouses and famous seaside resorts. However, I was as yet unaware of the dire consequences for an attacking force of all these beautiful hedgerows and their attendant sunken roads. Our first view of the Normandy coast had not of course been at all like the tourist dream. Every building had been smashed, and the beaches, sand dunes and fields beyond them were littered with burnt-out tanks and vehicles and all the debris of war. At the back of the beaches were the concrete walls, anti-tank barriers and barbed wire of the German coastal defences which had been breached on D-Day. Trees, if still standing, were torn and battered, and the only animals to be seen were French cattle or German horses lying dead – putrefying and stinking in the hot summer sun.

The 1st Tyneside Scottish had approximately seven miles to march to the 70th Brigade concentration area at Esquay-sur-Seulles (see map opposite). The advance party had already marked out the battalion's designated area, and on arrival the men dug-in and waited. For the next 48 hours or so there was little to do as the process of bringing equipment and supplies up from the beach to the concentration area proved to be somewhat slow.

Cpl G. Cowie, Section Commander, 18 Platoon, 'D' Company, 1st TS:
We marched south for about six miles or so. Unlike in training, we had been told that all weapons had to be loaded. At our first halt, two shots were fired immediately behind me. Someone looked sheepish and I bawled him out! All safety catches should have been on, the culprit's was not. I found that his Bren gun was on automatic – his finger must have brushed the trigger when he had put his weapon down, firing a quick burst of two rounds. Also the gun must have been cocked. He had got it all wrong. We had to learn to be more careful. The Sten gun could be even more dangerous when the cocking handle was not in the safety slot. The weapon, whether cocked or not, fired a round if thumped by the butt.

Lt B.T.W. Stewart, 2nd i/c, Anti-tank Platoon, 'S' Company, 1st TS:
Our instructions on landing were to follow Divisional (Polar Bear) signs, Brigade signs and then look for the Battalion. In my case, we failed to find the Brigade signs and proceeded towards Caen, until halted by Canadians who informed us that if we went any further round the corner we would meet the Germans. I did a smart about turn on my motor-cycle and turned the column round. As we moved inland, the scenery continued to be battle scarred, the detritus of battle on every side. Occasionally we found areas which had somehow escaped the ravages of war, and in one farmhouse I had a memorable supper of rabbit stew, camembert cheese and vintage calvados (apple brandy). But I was not tempted to think that this was just another exercise, with a Norman girl standing in for a friendly British farm wifie, as even in reserve the sounds of war were loud in our ears; with 15-inch naval shells whooshing overhead like express trains amid the crash, bark and crump of artillery, the dull thud of mortars, the rattling of machine guns and the noisy passage of our droning air armadas and screaming fighters.

15 JUNE

At 0900 hrs on 15 June, the battalion discovered that it was not to be used in its original role as advance guard, and so a move was made further inland to the village of Ducy-Ste-Marguerite, where HQ was set up in an old mill. Here the Battalion was fully briefed about the situation on its front and given details about its new role. For the immediate future, the Battalion would be held in reserve along with the rest of the 70th Brigade. The weather was quite warm and the men spent much of their time exploring the area.

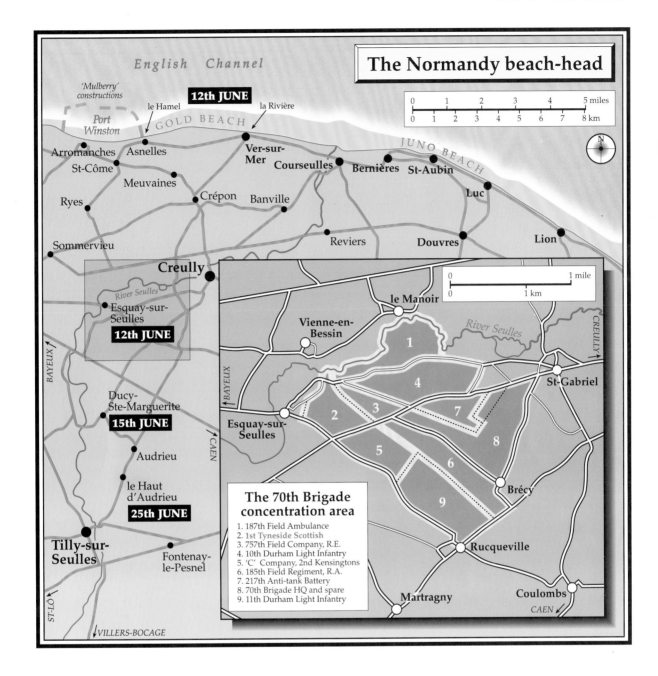

The Normandy beach-head

English Channel

'Mulberry' constructions

12th JUNE

le Hamel · la Rivière

GOLD BEACH

Port Winston

JUNO BEACH

Arromanches · Asnelles
St-Côme
Meuvaines
Ryes
Sommervieu
Crépon · Banville
Ver-sur-Mer · Courseulles · Bernières · St-Aubin
Luc
Reviers · Douvres · Lion

Creully

River Seulles

12th JUNE
Esquay-sur-Seulles

BAYEUX

Ducy-Ste-Marguerite

15th JUNE

CAEN

Audrieu

le Haut d'Audrieu

25th JUNE

Tilly-sur-Seulles

Fontenay-le-Pesnel

ST-LÔ

VILLERS-BOCAGE

le Manoir
Vienne-en-Bessin
River Seulles
CREULLY
St-Gabriel

1
4
2 · 3 · 7
8
5
6
9
Brécy

Esquay-sur-Seulles

BAYEUX

Rucqueville

Martragny
Coulombs
CAEN

The 70th Brigade concentration area

1. 187th Field Ambulance
2. 1st Tyneside Scottish
3. 757th Field Company, R.E.
4. 10th Durham Light Infantry
5. 'C' Company, 2nd Kensingtons
6. 185th Field Regiment, R.A.
7. 217th Anti-tank Battery
8. 70th Brigade HQ and spare
9. 11th Durham Light Infantry

Pte J. Munro, Intelligence Section, Battalion HQ, 1st TS:

We sometimes played chess, wrote letters and occasionally took a trip on a motorcycle, only the drawback was that the dust tended to attract Jerry artillery.

Cpl G. Cowie, Section Commander, 18 Platoon, 'D' Company, 1st TS:

Our new Platoon Commander was Captain R. J. Gelston from Montreal, Canada. We had several of these CANLOAN officers. They came mainly from The Black Watch of Canada. All had volunteered to serve with the British Army for the invasion and had been welcomed as there was a general shortage of subalterns even *then (up until Capt Gelston's arrival I had been acting Platoon Commander). They were great chaps. They wore the same regimental and formation badges as us, but above the 49th Divisional (Polar Bear) sign they displayed the CANADA flash. In addition, they wore the ribbon of the Canadian Volunteer Medal, which had a small maple leaf affixed to the centre. The Canadians nicknamed the medal – 'McKenzie King's Breeches' or '60 days away from mother' (McKenzie King was the Canadian Prime Minister). Soon all the 49th Division had seen action apart from the 70th Brigade. Eventually, we were told that the 10th DLI were in action, suffering casualties at St-Pierre. Tension increased, we knew we would be next.*

BATTLE TACTICS IN NORMANDY

In order to understand why the Normandy landscape is often regarded as having been one of the bloodiest and most hard-fought battlefields of the Second World War, one must look carefully at its land structure. A particular characteristic of the Norman countryside, and one which strongly determined the nature of fighting during the campaign, was the pattern of agricultural enclosures known locally as bocage. This patchwork of fields – bordered by high, earth-banked hedgerows, and criss-crossed with tracks and narrow sunken lanes – presented the attacking Allied forces with considerable problems. Perfectly suited to defence, the bocage engendered a type of warfare very different from any they had previously experienced. In contrast, the Germans had a well-tried set of battle tactics and employed all the tricks needed to defend such terrain.

GERMAN TACTICS

The Germans had the heaviest and best-armed tanks in Normandy, and they frequently used these as well dug-in gun platforms covering lines of advance. German infantry were equally well armed. A *Gruppe* (squad) could comprise up to ten men supporting an MG42 machine gun team – the heart of its firepower. This gun was also known as the 'Spandau' by the Allies, as its metal was often stamped with this name. Personally directed by the *Gruppenführer* (squad leader), the *Gruppe* consisted of one – *Richtschütze*, an MG *Schütze* who fired the gun; two – *Zwo*, an MG *schütze* who assisted and changed its barrels; three – *Munitionschütze* and four to nine – *Gewherschützen*. As all *Gruppe* members were trained to use it, an MG42 could be kept in action as long as someone remained alive to fire it. By 1944, the Germans had developed the art of suppressive fire: a quick burst delivering a high-speed stream of bullets with the characteristic ripping sound – 'brr-brr-bpt!' Carefully positioned Spandaus could create deadly fields of rapid fire across empty pastures, and camouflaged snipers, hidden high up in the trees, helped to further pin down attackers. Mortar pits were placed at strategic points where attacking infantry, ranged well beforehand, could be suddenly halted and put into a state of utter chaos and confusion. The Germans also had the Panzerfaust – a hand-held rocket launcher, and Panzerschreck ('tank terror') – a superior bazooka-type weapon.

When the Germans themselves attacked a defensive position, small parties would try to infiltrate along the field edges, some carrying belts of ammunition for machine guns (huge amounts were needed to feed the Spandau's voracious appetite), keeping well hidden in the ditches between the high-banked hedgerows. The Germans were experts at this form of fighting, and because they had the basic building block of the gruppe, they could generate specially organized formations. These ad hoc battlegroups, known as Kampfgruppen (the term was usually coupled with the name of a prominent commander, such as Kampfgruppe Weidinger) could be drawn together at short notice to make swift counter-attacks. In the Caen area, such Kampfgruppen involved men from SS-Panzer Divisions – the elite troops of the German Army, who had earned strong reputations for military prowess and were galvanized with supreme confidence and morale, sometimes fanatical, always totally committed. If German-held ground was lost, an opponent's moment of victory, sometimes hard-won after many hours of heavy fighting, was often cut short by an immediate counter-attack. This classic tactic frequently sapped the attacker's strength as he strove to advance through the Normandy bocage.

ALLIED TACTICS

Although we can generalize to a certain extent here in terms of Allied tactics, the scope of any book covering the Rauray battle would not readily extend far beyond the British/Canadian sector, and therefore this section does not purport to give specific details of American tactics in Normandy.

Among the Allied forces in attack, British tanks and infantry found cooperation difficult in Normandy. It took time for a rapport to develop between them and good relationships could suddenly be lost with a switch of armoured brigades. Contact could easily be lost when the tanks came up against high-banked hedgerows. This became a problem, as experience quickly proved that it was essential for tanks and infantry to attack together. If the tanks attacked alone in the bocage without the close cooperation of infantry, they risked heavy casualties from hidden dug-in enemy tanks, anti-tank guns and Panzerfausts. The most successful types of attack were those where infantry located the enemy's hidden armour by infiltration along hedgerows and then directed the tank's fire onto its target. However, during Operation 'Martlet', tanks and infantry regularly set off together across open fields in large groups.

Lt B.T.W. Stewart, 2nd i/c, Anti-tank Platoon, 'S' Company, 1st TS:
I am uncertain that we made use of the tactics the Battle School taught. The emphasis there was on section and platoon tactics in an attack situation, using fire and movement to carry out flanking attacks in a rapid and unhesitating drill, but what little I observed in Normandy, and what I have learnt in conversation with regular soldiers, suggest that the theory was seldom put into practice in the field. Companies pushed forward en masse rather than manoeuvring by sections and platoons.

This large-scale form of attack could be successful in the bocage if pressed home in a determined fashion, but it usually needed to be preceded by a creeping barrage of artillery fire laid down in front of the troops as they advanced (as at the start of the 1st Tyneside Scottish attack on Brettevillette on 28 June, described on page 40). Failure to support infantry groups with a sufficient artillery barrage often led to company attacks becoming bogged down in exposed positions where the enemy, camouflaged by the bocage, could snipe, rocket and pound them, unseen, with heavyweight tank fire. At times, dug-in German heavy tanks could only be destroyed at point-blank range by man-handling anti-tank guns into close positions. The British and American infantry had, respectively, the PIAT and bazooka as individual hand-held anti-tank weapons, but their operators had to be suicidally close to their target before they could realistically hope to make a successful kill. The British equivalent of the German MG42 machine gun was the Bren, although its inferior rate of fire made it considerably less dominant and specialist MG battalions using Vickers machine guns were attached to divisions to compensate. The Bren was usually fired in bursts, ideally five rounds, at a target. Bren gunners and riflemen tended to take turns alternating fire and movement. In terms of ripping power, the American .50 calibre machine gun was outstanding. Tactically, the Americans generally used their M1 rifles as a fire base, with BAR rifles in support.

On the whole, the Allies increasingly preferred to rely on artillery and air strikes as a means of dislodging the enemy's defences. However, the dominant use of artillery rather than infantry by the British Army was understandable given that it could ill afford to lose men. The steep rise in casualties in the weeks that followed D-Day meant that its soldiers were seriously dwindling in number. Only rarely did Montgomery advance his troops beyond the umbrella of the artillery. The seemingly unlimited supply of Allied equipment and firepower did of course have a devastating effect on the German's will to defend Normandy, but the speed of the breakout through the bocage was frequently reduced to a desperate slog. Artillery shoots required dangerously exposed forward observation officers, backed up by infantry, to monitor the progress and concentration of shelling if they were to be fully successful, and the launching of carefully coordinated air strikes often had to be postponed due to unsuitable weather conditions over air bases in the UK. Not only that, carpet bombing of German AFV formations usually only succeeded in disrupting their ability to counter-attack in force rather than wiping them out altogether. In the end, Allied firepower proved overwhelming, but not before both the efficiency of the German Panzer Divisions and the natural defences of the Normandy terrain had caused weeks of intense and bitter fighting, creating scenes more commonly associated with the First World War.

In describing the hourly events of the Rauray battle, subsequent pages in this book will illustrate the advantages and disadvantages of bocage fighting and the battle tactics used by the opposing forces – a kind of microcosm of the Eastern Front of the Battle of Normandy. We will see German Waffen-SS troops attempt a classic dawn attack, using small parties of Panzer-Grenadiers supported by AFVs, and the British secure the advantage of being in defence by retaining enough of their forces in key frontal positions in order to guide defensive artillery fire onto enemy targets.

NORMANDY TIMELINE

DATE	THE BATTLE OF NORMANDY	OPERATION 'MARTLET'	OPERATION 'EPSOM'
6th June 1944	D-Day. Start of Operation 'Overlord'.	–	–
12th June	Carentan captured by First US Army.	–	–
13th June	7th Armd Div halted at Villers-Bocage.	–	–
13th June	German V-1 flying bombs strike London.	–	–
16th June	Hitler responds to Allies in Normandy.	–	–
19–22nd June	The Great Storm hits the English Channel.	–	–
25th June	–	Start of Operation 'Martlet'. 49th Div attack Fontenay.	–
26th June	The fortress of Cherbourg surrenders.	1st Tyneside Scottish attack la Grande Ferme.	Start of Operation 'Epsom'. 15th Div attack Cheux.
27th June	The port of Cherbourg surrenders.	11th DLI clear the enemy from Rauray.	15th Div take Tormauville. 11th Armd Div reach Hill 112.
28th June	–	1st Tyneside Scottish attack Brettevillette.	2nd Argylls reach the bridge at Gavrus.
29th June	–	10th DLI defend Rauray spur.	VIII Corps absorb counter-attacks by I & II SS-Pz Korps.
30th June	–	70th Brigade prepare to defend Rauray.	VIII Corps pulls in the perimeter of its defences.
1st July	Last major German counter-attack on British front.	**Defence of Rauray.**	VIII Corps defends the 'Epsom' salient.
7th–8th July	Operation 'Charnwood' captures northern Caen.	–	–
15th July	Operation 'Greenline' west of Caen.	–	–
18th–20th July	Operation 'Goodwood' captures the rest of Caen.	–	–
19th July	First US Army captures St-Lô.	–	–
20th July	Attempt to assassinate Hitler.	–	–
25th July	Operation 'Spring' by II Canadian Corps.	–	–
25th–28th July	Operation 'Cobra' by VII US Corps.	–	–
30th July–6th Aug	Operation 'Bluecoat' by Second British Army.	–	–
6th–8th Aug	Operation 'Lüttich', the Mortain counter-attack.	–	–
8th–11th Aug	Operation 'Totalize' by First Canadian Army.	–	–
15th August	Operation 'Dragoon', the landings in the S. of France.	–	–
14th–17th Aug	Operation 'Tractable' Capture of Falaise.	–	–
20th–22nd Aug	Closure and emptying of Falaise pocket.	–	–
23rd-24th Aug	Disbandment of the 70th Infantry Brigade.	–	–
25th August	Liberation of Paris ends Battle of Normandy.	–	–

BUILD-UP TO THE RAURAY BATTLE

Three weeks after D-Day, the Allies were desperately trying to force a breakout from Normandy. Storms in the English Channel had dealt heavy blows on the two Mulberry harbours causing delays in the arrival of crucial supplies of vehicles and ammunition. This allowed the German *Generalfeldmarschall* Rommel extra time to reinforce his army in the Caen sector, a major blow for Montgomery as he had always regarded the taking of Caen as a pivotal move in the breakout from the Normandy beaches. Frustrated by these bad weather conditions, he decided on a full-scale operation for the newly arrived British VIII Corps. Code-named 'Epsom' and scheduled to begin on 26 June, this major offensive would involve the 15th (Scottish) and 43rd (Wessex) Divisions in a drive from the railway line just south of Bretteville-l'Orgueilleuse to the River Odon, where a crossing would be made. The 11th Armoured Division would then pass through the leading units and take up a commanding position on the high-ground known as Hill 112. If successful, VIII Corps would then advance across the River Orne and grasp the area south of Caen. This would compel the enemy to reinforce its defences in the British sector, giving the US Army room to break out in the west.

In order to protect the right flank of VIII Corps during 'Epsom', XXX Corps would attempt to secure the high-ground to the south of the village of Rauray in an operation code-named 'Martlet'. On 25 June, starting a day earlier than 'Epsom', 'Martlet' would involve the 49th (West Riding) Division in a three-stage advance, the objectives being: 'Barracuda' – the road between Juvigny-sur-Seulles and Fontenay-le-Pesnel, 'Walrus' – Tessel Wood and the farm at St Nicholas, and 'Albacore' – Rauray and the spur of high-ground (see map on page 31). The first 'Barracuda' attack would involve three infantry battalions – the 4th Lincolns to the west near St-Pierre, the Hallamshires in the centre and the 11th Royal Scots Fusiliers to the east near le Parc de Boislande. The 1st Tyneside Scottish would occupy a position a mile back from the front in reserve. An artillery barrage would be fired by nine field and four medium regiments. In addition, two companies of 4.2-inch mortars would provide support on the flanks along with two machine gun companies from the 2nd Kensingtons.

From the point where the three battalions were to form up for the attack, the land gently fell away down a slope, through rich cornfields and on to bocage country beyond. Shortly after 0400 hrs, on the right flank of the 'Barracuda' attack, the 4th Lincolns, with tanks of the 24th Lancers in

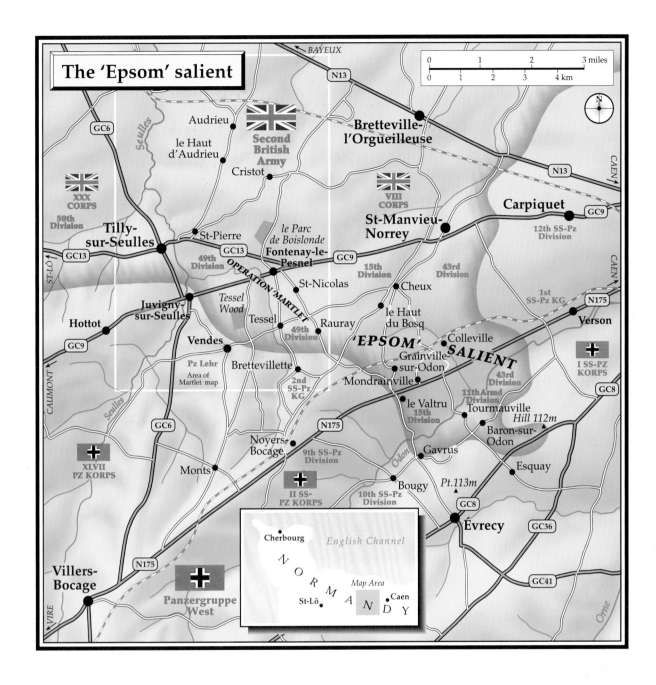

The 'Epsom' salient

support, crossed the taped start line, which was eerily lit by lights, and edged their way forward down the slope and into a thick enveloping mist which lay in the valley below. Within an hour, their crackling radio signals had weakened and died, isolating them, and there was much confused shouting in the mist, the enemy adding smoke and mortar bombs to the fog of battle as the desperate Lincolns tried in vain to recognize their own groups. Eventually, the attackers reached 'Barracuda' and dug in, having overcome several close encounters with the enemy, including a group of half-track vehicles which the Lincolns destroyed with grenades, and a German officer who was silenced while attempting to rally his Panzer-Grenadiers by blowing on a bugle.

Meanwhile, the Hallamshires in the centre had experienced similar problems with the thick mist. Their painfully slow advance could only be carried out by way of careful compass work, with bearings taken every few yards. On finally reaching the Fontenay road (GC 9), the Hallams were subjected to intense tank and machine-gun fire as they were met by a determined effort to drive them back. 'Barracuda' was being defended by tanks from the 8th Company of II/SS-Pz Regt 12, and infantry from the 10th and 11th Companies of III/SS-PzGR 26, 12th SS-Panzer Division – 'Hitlerjugend', under the command of *SS-Sturmbannführer* (Major) Erich Olboeter. Steeped in the fanatical discipline of Nazi doctrine, the teenagers of the Hitler Youth were formidable adversaries despite their young age and inexperience. The tenacity with which they held on to every inch of ground often led to martyrdom, and their overall losses during the Battle of Normandy were enormous – most of the 12th SS-Panzer Division being completely wiped out. An example of this self-sacrifice is shown in an extract taken from a XXX Corps Intelligence Report (WO 171/337) which narrates a wireless broadcast given by *SS-Standartenführer* (Colonel) Kurt Meyer of the 12th SS-Pz Div on 1 July 1944: 'Yesterday, I saw one young fellow, imbued with the spirit of self-sacrifice, leap on to an enemy tank and get blown up with it. But in doing so, he liberated his comrades by making a way out of the position in which they were imprisoned.' After a short encounter, during which two German tanks were knocked out by 6-pounder anti-tank guns, parties of Hallamshires set out east and west along the road between le Pont de Juvigny and Fontenay-le-Pesnel (GC 9), amid heavy shelling and mortaring, in order to link with the units on either side of them.

On the left flank of the attack, the 11th Royal Scots Fusiliers had set out at 'H-Hour' with the north side of Fontenay-le-Pesnel as their 'Barracuda' objective. As the Scots sank down into the smog, they immediately sustained heavy casualties. Visibility was virtually nil and men clung on to each other to avoid being lost, forming a ghostly chain. Recognition of one's fellow attacker could only be achieved by staring into his face. When the sun eventually came up, their losses began to increase as snipers and machine-guns opened up in front of them, and on reaching Fontenay, house-to-house fighting brought bitter confrontations. Despite many gallant attempts to penetrate the village and force the enemy out, its gardens and orchards provided the defenders with excellent cover and the Fusiliers were unable to pass beyond the road running westwards from the village to Tilly-sur-Seulles. Flanking fire was also coming in from Spandaus concealed in the Parc de Boislonde to the north-east – the thickly wooded area that had been the venue for a truly horrific battle between the Polar Bears and the Hitlerjugend on 17 and 18 June.

About 2030 hrs, the 7th Duke of Wellington's Regiment passed through what was left of the 11th RSF and managed to clear most of the western part of Fontenay, while the 12th SS-Panzer Division, supported by reinforcements from the 21st Panzer Division (sent from Caen) and Panzer Lehr Division (who were holding Vendes), held on ferociously to the rest of the village and the wood beyond.

While the 11th RSF had been locked in mortal combat all afternoon in Fontenay-le-Pesnel, the 'Walrus' phase of the 'Martlet' operation had

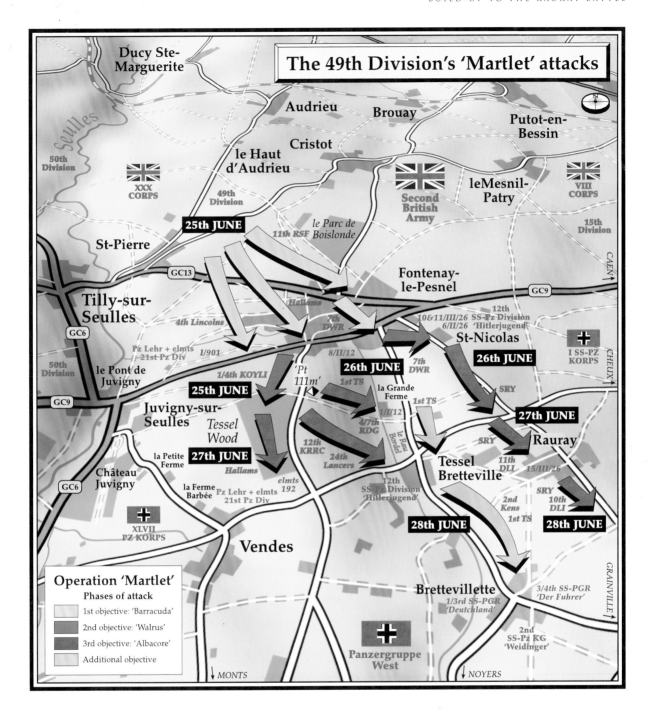

The 49th Division's 'Martlet' attacks

Duccy Ste-Marguerite

Audrieu Brouay Putot-en-Bessin

50th Division

Seulles

Cristot

le Haut d'Audrieu

leMesnil-Patry

XXX CORPS

49th Division

St-Pierre

le Parc de Boislonde

11th RSF

Fontenay-le-Pesnel

Second British Army

VIII CORPS

15th Division

CAEN

25th JUNE

GC13

Hallams

7th DWR

10&11/III/26 SS-Pz Division
6/II/26 'Hitlerjugend'

St-Nicolas

Tilly-sur-Seulles

4th Lincolns

8/II/12

I SS-PZ KORPS

CHEUX

26th JUNE

GC6

Pz Lehr + elmts
21st Pz Div I/901

1/4th KOYLI

'Pt
111m'

1st TS

26th JUNE

7th DWR

la Grande
Ferme

SRY

27th JUNE

50th Division

le Pont de Juvigny

GC9

Juvigny-sur-Seulles

Tessel Wood

25th JUNE

1/II/12

4/7th
RDG

1st TS

le Rau
Bordel

SRY

Rauray

11th
DLI 15/III/26

Château Juvigny

la Petite Ferme

27th JUNE

12th
KRRC

24th
Lancers

Tessel Bretteville

2nd
Kens
1st TS

SRY
10th
DLI

28th JUNE

GC6

Hallams

la Ferme
Barbée

Pz Lehr + elmts
21st Pz Div

elmts
192

12th
SS-Pz Division
'Hitlerjugend'

28th JUNE

GRAINVILLE

XLVII
PZ KORPS

Vendes

Brettevillette

3/4th SS-PGR
'Der Fuhrer'

1/3rd SS-PGR
'Deutchland'

Operation 'Martlet'
Phases of attack

1st objective: 'Barracuda'

2nd objective: 'Walrus'

3rd objective: 'Albacore'

Additional objective

Panzergruppe
West

2nd
SS-Pz KG
'Weidinger'

↓ MONTS

↓ NOYERS

begun on the western front. The plan was for the 1/4th (the first reserve of the fourth Battalion) King's Own Yorkshire Light Infantry to advance south, through the 4th Lincolns on the Fontenay road, to Tessel Wood. At 1200 hrs, the 1st Tyneside Scottish were moved to le Haut d'Audrieu to establish a firm base in support of the 'Martlet' attacks. Around the same time, the 1/4th KOYLI, supported by tanks of the 24th Lancers, began their attack, the start line once again being on the edge of cornfields. This time the land sloped upwards, but the Yorkshiremen made the first hundred yards or so in four minutes under the cover of a very heavy

See 'Epsom' salient map on page 29 for a guide to distances.

Nebelwerfer fully loaded with rockets.

artillery barrage. However, as the infantry toiled their way through the corn the enemy began bombarding them with Nebelwerfer mortars.

The Nebelwerfer was extremely effective as a launcher for rocket-powered mortar bombs, mainly because the screaming noise it made when fired was extremely alarming. It was operated by means of an electric switch attached to a junction box in the barrel assembly. The six barrels were fired separately in a fixed order, all six being discharged in ten seconds. A forty-foot flame meant the launch crew had to take cover while firing. The troops who were unlucky enough to be on the receiving end of these mortar bombs nicknamed them 'Moaning Minnies'.

Eventually, the 1/4 KOYLI covered the deadly mile or so up to the edge of the wood and its mortar platoon dug in. The enemy, once again Hitlerjugend troops of the 12th SS-Panzer Division, counter-attacked but were beaten off, losing two tanks to the 24th Lancers.

By the evening of this eventful day, the 49th Division had achieved a great deal against resolute opposition, but was still short of its main objective – the village of Rauray and the spur of high-ground which overlooked the area VIII Corps would attempt to burst through during 'Epsom'. The weather had been hot and sunny, but it was now beginning to cloud over – an ominous sign for what was to follow the next day. At 2030 hrs, Lt Col R.W.M. de Winton, the CO of the 1st Tyneside Scottish, was present at a divisional conference where plans were made for the Battalion to attack towards Rauray at dawn.

On 26 June, to the west of the main 'Epsom' assault, the 1st Tyneside Scottish put in its first 'Martlet' attack, supported by the 4/7th Royal Dragoon Guards – part of the 8th Armoured Brigade. For the majority of the young men in the Battalion, this was to be their initiation into the real horrors of war, and they were to witness several disturbing sights even before they had reached the start line.

> *Pte P. Lawton, rifleman, 18 Platoon, 'D' Company, 1st TS:*
> *Most of us were 18 to 20 year olds with no combat experience, just our military training to fall back on. We debussed at Fontenay-le-Pesnel, and as we moved round the end of a row of terraced cottages, I was struck by a feeling of apprehension which was not helped by the smell of burning cordite combined with that of putrefying flesh. This early in our front line experience, we were not to know that this was far more likely to emanate from dead cattle rather than human remains. Reaching our start line, we had some time to wait before moving forward into our first action. It was a bit of a shock when an ME 109 flew quite low over our heads. It was the first time we had seen an enemy aircraft since our arrival in Normandy. It came and went very, very quickly and I don't recall whether anyone was able to get off a shot in its direction. Eventually, we moved forward in open order across a field and took up positions along a hedgerow and ditch to await our next move. The field in front of us was littered with debris, dead cattle and a knocked-out Sherman. Shells and mortar bombs were bursting round about. I think we found the air-burst shells particularly disturbing, I know that I was worried in case a piece of shrapnel drove part of my helmet into my skull. I am sure that many other soldiers must have been troubled by such irrational thoughts in these traumatic times.*

> *Cpl J.W.H. Tipler, Section Commander, 18 Platoon, 'D' Company, 1st TS:*
> *We went through a field where the pioneers had laid out 20 or so soldiers who had been killed in the area in recent days. There were several dead cows, their bodies bloated and legs sticking up in the air.*

The steady accumulation of dead flesh – animal and human – meant that the air quality over the Calvados region became so bad that reconnaissance aircraft were sometimes forced to fly at higher altitudes to evade the overpowering fumes that rose from the rotting carcases. Decaying dairy produce was also a problem. In July, the 11th DLI reserve positions were smitten by the stinking aroma of a nearby abandoned Camembert cheese factory, making them almost glad to go forward into battle.

> *Pte J. Munro, Intelligence Section, Battalion HQ, 1st TS:*
> *One of the worst experiences was the terrible stench that hung over Normandy – hundreds of cows, dead and blown-up to twice their normal size, lying with legs outstretched, until after a while they*

burst. Human bodies too, lay decaying where they fell, covered by 2 to 3 inches of soil until the War Graves Commission could collect and bury them. Ahead of our landing point, a unit had run into machine gun fire and lay scattered in the fields. Another type of smell, similarly penetrating, was that of the German equivalent of DDT. It was very noticeable in all their billets and trenches. I imagine they had the same problem with our smell.

At the start line of the Tyneside Scottish attack, infantry and tanks faced east-south-east towards their first objective – la Grande Ferme – with Tessel Wood on their right. Once past the wood, their open right flank would be protected by armoured cars of the 12th King's Royal Rifle Corps Motor Battalion, who would later attack Tessel Bretteville along with the 24th Lancers. At 0650 hrs, the rising drone of the bagpipes signalled that the moment had come for the Tyneside Scottish to go into battle. 'A' Company (1st TS) and 'C' Squadron (4/7th RDG) formed the van, followed by 'B', 'C', 'D' and HQ Companies (1st TS). A tactical group from HQ Company took up a position behind 'A' Company. Things were somewhat confused owing to the fact that the tanks and infantry were not properly aligned, a scene later described by Major J.D.P. Stirling, the 4/7th RDG historian, as 'a badly organized partridge shoot'.

A major disadvantage would be the absence of a substantial artillery barrage, the majority of the 49th Division's firepower having been transferred over onto the 'Epsom' front to support the main attack by VIII Corps. The effects of this were soon felt; restricted by the lack of artillery support, the leading troops immediately came under heavy fire from enemy tanks and machine guns, and within the first hour 'A' Company had an officer killed (Lt P.A. McDowell) and two others wounded (Capt A.P. Whitehead and Major W.L. McGregor, the Company Commander and one of the main driving forces behind the Battalion). It would be impossible to say just how much the loss of such an influential figure as Major McGregor may have contributed to any future shortcomings 'A' Company experienced after this, in particular at Rauray on 1 July, but it is not hard to imagine the space left by his departure.

Lt B.T.W. Stewart, 2nd i/c, Anti-tank Platoon, 'S' Company, 1st TS:
My final glimpse of Major Mac was of a bloody figure being carried back on a stretcher having been badly wounded by a mortar bomb. I was lying behind a bank, awaiting orders to move forward behind 'A' Company, but the Germans were too well dug-in for our armour.

The prospects of the Battalion reaching its first objective, let alone Rauray, began to look bleak and the men of 'A' Company could only stare at one another as they tried to keep their heads below the relentless fire from the hidden Spandaus. The exact position of the enemy was difficult to locate as the 'close' nature of the landscape allowed his forces to remain concealed among the trees and leafy hedgerows. In fact, the Germans were so well camouflaged that it was a tough job to spot them even with binoculars. This was typical Norman bocage: fields surrounded by high

Major W.L. McGregor.

double-hedges with earth banks which rendered them practically impassable for the tanks. As the Shermans drove hard at these barriers in an attempt to surmount the crest, their momentum launched them skywards, leaving their hulls dangerously exposed to the enemy. Casualties began to mount as the men desperately fought to clear a way forward through this hellish obstacle course, and it soon became apparent that the attack faced two major problems.

To begin with, the enemy was using Nebelwerfer rocket mortars to great effect. Enemy snipers and Spandau guns were pinning the Tyneside Scottish infantry down, coaxing them to take cover against a particular bocage bank which had been carefully ranged by the Nebelwerfer teams. Once the troops had been forced into the trap – over came the screaming rocket-mortars, which exploded high in the trees, blasting their canopy and the surrounding hedges into thousands of deadly splinters. I remember my father once describing these tree splinters as devastating – some tiny, others like great spear shafts. He recalled some of the splinter-peppered men after the Nebelwerfer attack near Tessel Wood as being pitiful to behold, and believed the tearing effect of jagged wood to be as bad, as, if not worse than, shrapnel. The wounds they inflicted were extremely difficult to treat as fragments that had penetrated deep could rapidly spread infection. In addition to the tree splinters, intermittent shelling rained metal down on the men, causing further injury.

Pte J. Munro, Intelligence Section, Battalion HQ, 1st TS:
Tessel Wood was on a riverside escarpment. There was heavy use of 'air-burst' from Jerry which extended back beyond Tactical HQ – our first experience of this. They exploded overhead and showered the ground in shrapnel. In effect, one was a smaller target standing up!

The other problem lay several hundred yards ahead on the far side of le Bordel Rau, a stream running across the Battalion's front. It was here that four well-dug-in tanks of I/SS-Pz Regt 12, 12th SS-Panzer Division 'Hitlerjugend' were effectively holding up the whole attack. The Germans also had the 7th Company of II/SS-PzGR 26 around la Grande Ferme (a large farmstead whose long buildings lay adjacent to the stream), with elements of PzGR 192, 21st Panzer Division in the Tessel Wood area.

Lt B.T.W. Stewart, 2nd i/c, Anti-tank Platoon, 'S' Company, 1st TS:
The anti-tank Platoon was invited, by 'A' Company, to knock down an orchard wall behind which a German tank was hiding and sniping. We did so most efficiently; manhandling a 6-pounder into position, knocking down the offending wall and manhandling the gun back out of the rifle company's position. They were not grateful – they were stonked!

At about midday, 'B' Company passed through a battered 'A' Company and managed to get a platoon across le Bordel Rau to where their youthful adversaries lay firmly dug in. However, they were soon pinned down by Spandau fire and became isolated. The 4/7th RDG tried to follow them but lost six tanks in trying to reach la Grande Ferme, the surviving occupants having to crawl away from their burning Shermans beneath the ripping fire of the hostile Spandaus.

> ### Cpl J.W.H. Tipler, Section Commander, 18 Platoon, 'D' Company, 1st TS:
> *A squadron of Shermans joined us at Tessel Wood and during one 'stonk' I saw one of them suddenly blazing from the open cupola – presumably a bomb had dropped right in there. One man got out of the driver's compartment and another came out of the turret. Both dropped to the ground and their mates went to help them.*

The four 'Hitlerjugend' tanks had defended their ground vigorously and in hull-down position they had been untouchable. At 1600 hrs, it was decided to bring the day's action to a close, and the 1st Tyneside Scottish was withdrawn three miles back to le Haut d'Audrieu, although a small party from 'A' Company remained behind and pushed on to la Grande Ferme. Casualties had been quite high – around fifty, most of which were taken by 'A' Company, whose surviving members left the battlefield lamenting their lost comrades in traditional Scottish fashion.

> ### Pte J. Munro, Intelligence Section, Battalion HQ, 1st TS:
> *'A' Company marched in section order, single file down the hill, to a lone piper.*

On the right of the 1st Tyneside Scottish, the 12th KRRC had attacked south towards Tessel-Bretteville, while the 24th Lancers skirted the eastern edge of Tessel Wood. The four tanks at la Grande Ferme which had given so much trouble to the Tyneside Scots and their supporting Dragoon Guards fired on the armoured cars of the 12th KRRC as they advanced, as did others positioned near Tessel-Bretteville. At the crossroads between Vendes and Tessel-Bretteville, the leading Sherman of an advancing troop of 'A' Squadron, 24th Lancers, fought a deadly duel with two Panthers. It managed to set one ablaze, but was simultaneously hit as it engaged the other, its ammunition exploding before all the crew could evacuate the tank's flaming body. The squadron's further progress was badly restricted by poor visibility in the sunken bocage lanes, but it finally succeeded in reaching the stream just north of its objective. The 12th KRRC also managed to reach the stream after several skirmishes, then carried on to the church on the western edge of Tessel-Bretteville. By now both units had lost a fair amount of armour in trying to force a way forward, and therefore had to abandon their efforts and return to Tessel Wood under the cover of smoke. Col M. Aird of the 24th Lancers described these events as 'a bloody day'.

On the Division's left, the 7th Duke of Wellington's Regiment, supported by tanks of the Sherwood Rangers Yeomanry, had begun their 'Walrus' assault from the outskirts of Fontenay-le-Pesnel. At 0930 hrs, Dukes 'C' and 'D' Companies attempted to advance south across the open ground leading to their objective – St-Nicholas – a farm less than half a mile away, occupied by the 6th Company, II/SS-PzGR 26, 12th SS-Panzer Division. However, the farm was so strongly defended by 'Hitlerjugend' snipers and

A lone piper leads the way.

carefully concealed tanks that the two companies of Dukes were forced to withdraw. A second attempt was made at 1550 hrs by 'A' and 'B' Companies, and this time, following a pulverizing 20-minute artillery barrage (*Gruppenführer* Kurt Meyer, the 'Hitlerjugend' Commander, described this barrage as an enormous steam roller which crushed all life as it rolled across the earth), the Dukes finally managed to take St-Nicholas and advance several hundred yards beyond it. From here, the SRY tanks found good ground and reached the crossroads north of Rauray, where they were joined at 2100 hrs by the 11th Durham Light Infantry, who dug in. It was important that Rauray was secured as soon as possible, therefore later on that evening an 11th DLI recce patrol made its way to the edge of Rauray, hoping to prepare the way for a night attack. Although RAF fighter bombers had rocketed the village earlier in the day, smashing its buildings and orchards into ruins, the Durhams unhappily found Rauray full of enemy troops, its surrounding woods echoing to the sound of tank movements. A lot of fighting would still need to be done before the 49th Division could claim 'Albacore' and bring about a successful conclusion to the 'Martlet' operation, which was now way beyond schedule.

Earlier in the day, to the east of the 49th Division, VIII Corps had begun its 'Epsom' advance two and a half hours after the 1st Tyneside Scottish had received its baptism of shell, mortar and Spandau fire at Tessel Wood. The going had been hard. Loss of air support due to bad weather meant that the main 'Epsom' attacks lacked the sting they needed to paralyse the enemy's defences. Lt Gen Miles Dempsey, the Commander of the Second British Army, described this as a great handicap in view of the heavy and detailed air plan which had been prepared to support the VIII Corps operations. The 15th Division had initially made steady progress from its start-line north of St-Manvieu-Norrey. 'Flail' tanks (Shermans with special rotating attachments, which flailed the ground ahead with lengths of chain in an attempt to clear it of mines) had led the Scottish troops as far as the village of Cheux, two miles due east of St-Nicholas. However, it was here that the enemy had fought back. Large elements of the 12th SS-Panzer Division 'Hitlerjugend', had defended the countryside around Cheux with great ferocity. Although they had sustained a huge number of casualties, they had held the German line and stopped the 11th Armoured Division's advance to the River Odon. Throughout the afternoon, the enemy had split its forces into small groups which had nipped away at the flanks of the VIII Corps advance and prevented a major salient being established. As had been feared, heavy shelling had come from the Rauray spur, still in enemy hands. However, one positive result of the day's efforts was that the German leadership became so alarmed by the situation north of the River Odon, that it felt it had no alternative but to rush the bulk of its SS-Panzer Divisions to the area before the British could achieve a breakthrough. Accordingly, Rommel reluctantly ordered the 1st, 9th, and 10th SS-Panzer Divisions to head for the Odon Valley immediately. In addition to these forces, elements from the 2nd SS-Panzer Division 'Das Reich' were to be sent from its base at St-Lô, 25 miles away.

The following day, 27 June, General Montgomery wrote to CIGS Alanbrooke describing the launch of 'Epsom'. He pointed out that

27 JUNE

although the RAF had been grounded due to rain and low cloud, he had decided to order the operation to go ahead as he could not give Rommel any more time to get organized. At 0700 hrs, the 1st Tyneside Scottish moved to Fontenay-le-Pesnel, where they lay in reserve while a fighting patrol from the 11th Durham Light Infantry tried for most of the morning to infiltrate Rauray, supported by tanks of the Sherwood Rangers Yeomanry. The village was being defended by the Hitlerjugend III/SS-PzGR 26, with Panzers and 88 mm guns giving flanking fire, and the SRY lost several tanks trying to wrest it from them. In the end, the SRY had to withdraw, leaving the Durham patrol to fight on alone. A forward platoon did eventually claw its way into the centre of the village, but its leader, Lt K. Hoggard, was badly wounded in the process. The rest of the 11th DLI suffered too, being struck with wicked accuracy by mortars directed from an observer's tree platform, complete with telephone, cleverly hidden in the undergrowth. Late in the morning, it was decided that something drastic had to be done, and even though it could not expect any further tank support, the 11th DLI put in a full-scale infantry attack. The Durhams fixed bayonets and slowly advanced in line abreast: 'B' Company on the right, with 'D' on the left. A platoon of 'C' Company waited in the rear to pass through the first assault parties once they had reached the village. A preliminary artillery barrage was laid on, but it appeared not to have much effect.

Cpl R.C. Baxter, 18 Platoon, 'D' Company, 11th Durham Light Infantry:

The attack on Rauray was timed for 1100 hrs. 'D' Company moved across a very flat field and were soon under fire from Spandaus. There was no cover at all and we could see the enemy quite clearly. After an attempt to advance further with help from our platoon mortars, a number of us were hit including myself.

Spandaus and hidden snipers picked off the attackers as they advanced, and both leading companies incurred heavy losses, 'B' Company losing several officers and NCOs. Around midday, a short cease-fire was agreed by both sides to allow the recovery of wounded and killed, but by 1400 hrs the attack had resumed and by 1600 hrs the 11th DLI had managed to clear Rauray of its teenage defenders and claim their part of 'Albacore'. Numerous among those Hitlerjugend found around the village were young snipers, some of whom were found tied by ropes to trees and perfectly camouflaged with foliage.

Earlier in the afternoon at 1430 hrs, Lt Gen Dempsey had met the Commander of XXX Corps, Lt Gen B.C. Bucknall, at St-Croix and told him that his task was to secure the British line, keeping the 8th Armoured Brigade in the Rauray area, and to gain and keep touch with the right flank of VIII Corps between Brettevillette and Grainville. On the other side of Tessel-Bretteville, the Hallamshires attempted to reach Vendes from Tessel Wood, and at 2100 hrs, the 1st Tyneside Scottish moved to an assembly point south of Fontenay-le-Pesnel in preparation for an attack on Brettevillette scheduled for the following morning. On the 'Epsom' front, little progress was made until the 2nd Argyll and Sutherland Highlanders

Opposite: A Hitlerjugend sniper captured by the Durham Light Infantry near Rauray, 28 June 1944.

managed, against all the odds, to take the bridge over the River Odon at Tourmauville. Then between 1900 and 2200 hrs, the 15th Division fought hard to establish a position beyond the bridgehead. Opposition was very strong, but some elements of the 11th Armoured Division did finally succeed in reaching their objective – Hill 112 – their tanks finally reaching the lower slopes near Baron as darkness fell. It was hoped that their next move would be to advance due east to the River Orne, but the Germans were not only determined to bar their way but were prepared to fight to keep control of the advantagious viewpoint that Hill 112 provided over the area around Caen.

28 JUNE

At 0700 hrs on 28 June, the 1st Tyneside Scottish formed up for their next attack, supported by machine guns of the 2nd Kensingtons. A heavy artillery barrage was laid ten minutes beforehand, very close to the start-line, so the men had to keep their heads well down as they prepared themselves for action. The attack began well, the troops advancing slowly through thick bocage, making sure that they kept just behind the rolling artillery barrage laid by an AGRA and four Field Regiments which hammered the country ahead of them. Some opposition was felt on the left, but on the whole the Battalion met little resistance and after about forty minutes the forward companies reached Tessel-Bretteville, code-named 'Jock'.

Cpl S. Hebdige, 9 Platoon, 'C' Company, 2nd Kensingtons:
The Germans had cut the road to Brettevillette, so our platoon officer, Lt J.T. Griffiths, decided to make a recce with myself and Sgt Bone to see if we could find another route to marry up with the Tyneside Scottish. We came across a Tyneside Scot in a slit trench at the bottom of a hedgerow, who told us that his HQ was on the other side of an open field. Lt Griffiths gave us the order in which we were to cross the field: he would go first, followed by Sgt Bone, then I would bring up the rear. As we were about to cross, a Spandau opened up and the Tyneside Scot in the slit trench shouted to us to get down, but we were already down with the bullets whipping through the hedge like a swarm of wasps. All three of us made it to the other side of the field and Lt Griffiths went off to talk to some Tyneside Scottish officers, later coming back with the information that the road was now open again and that we would return the way we had come and in the same order. I being the last to go again, felt that if they did not get the first two they would most certainly get me. So head down, I ran as fast as I could and caught my foot in a mole hill, twisting my knee so badly I could not put any weight on it. The Officer and Sergeant came back to me, thinking I had been hit, and when I told them what had happened, they told me to crawl towards the Tyneside Scottish as they were nearer. This I started to do, but had not got very far before a 'Moaning Minnie' opened up and I heard mortar bombs dropping in the field. I then found myself up and running, and it was not until I reached the Infantry that my knee gave way and I fell to the ground.

While 'C' and 'D' Companies, 1st TS, consolidated, 'A' and 'B' pushed on at midday heading for the next objective – 'Jones', the village of

Durhams stop to pose beside a knocked out SS-Pz Regt 12 Panther near Rauray, 27 June 1944.

Brettevillette. Once again, an artillery barrage assisted the attack, although this time it was less intense. The infantry gradually moved forward but soon began to run into Spandau fire. This became very strong, and the enemy added to the weight of their defence by shelling and mortaring the Battalion's rear. As the main resistance was being focused on 'A' Company's front, 'C' Company was brought up to give support and reinforce this side of the attack. Behind them, 'D' Company protected the Battalion's rear. Despite the heavy opposition, the Battalion doggedly kept moving forward and at 1430 hrs all four companies reported that they were on the objective and that hard fighting was going on in Brettevillette.

Pte P. Lawton, rifleman, 18 Platoon, 'D' Company, 1st TS:

On this occasion, I was No. 1 on the PIAT, a weapon weighing some 39 lbs which I carried in addition to my rifle, ammunition and grenades etc, the PIAT bombs being carried by the No. 2. We started to advance along a hedgerow, and the first thing we saw as was the mutilated and dying Pte Ross, who had been hit by shrapnel just a few moments earlier. Although still alive, it was patently obvious that he was not going to last more than a few minutes. On reaching the road leading into the village, I was instructed to set-up the PIAT to ensure that no nasty surprises in the form of enemy armour were able to come up in the rear of 18 Platoon. We had come under intermittent shellfire during the attack, and now, as we lay half expecting an enemy tank to appear round the bend, we could hear rifle and machine gun fire coming from the village behind us.

At 1500 hrs, reports from troops inside the village who were barely hanging on suggested a full-scale counter-attack by enemy infantry and tanks was in progress and that the situation was becoming serious.

This attempt to drive the 1st Tyneside Scottish back from Brettevillette was being made by Kampfgruppe Weidinger, a battlegroup composed of elite SS troops from the 2nd SS-Panzer Division 'Das Reich' under the command of SS Major Otto Weidinger. It was represented on 'A' Company's front by I/SS-PzGR 3 'Deutchland', and on 'B' Company's front by I/SS-PzGR 4 'Der Führer'. In his book about the 'Der Führer' Regiment – *Comrades to the End* – Otto Weidinger confirms that several penetrations were achieved against both these units, but were eliminated by immediate counter-attacks.

KG Weidinger had arrived in the Monts area the day before. 'Das Reich' had originally hoped to burst onto the scene and push the British back towards the coast, but had been constantly harassed by the RAF and the Maquis all the way to the front. The firepower of artillery and naval guns had also been crucial in preventing the Germans from building up enough forces in the area for a full-scale counter-attack, which meant they could only block gaps with depleted forces. However, the Panzer-Grenadiers of KG Weidinger were extremely tough opponents who had been battle-hardened on the Eastern Front. Having relieved Olboeter's battered Hitlerjugend who had been defending the area west of Rauray, they were firmly determined to hold on to Brettevillette, and for the next few hours the fighting was savage and at times totally confused as the 1st Tyneside Scottish tried in vain to consolidate. KG Weidinger had no tanks of its own, but it had tanks from I/Pz Regt 3 in support, the 2nd Panzer Division having provided one Panther company for the defence of Brettevillette. At one point, a tank broke through and destroyed two 2nd Kensingtons carriers, killing three machine gunners.

Lt J.T. Griffiths, Platoon Commander, 9 Platoon, 'C' Company, 2nd Kensingtons:

I was ordered to take the platoon forward to support an attack by the Tyneside Scottish on the village of Brettevillette. The route was difficult and by the time we got to the village the infantry had moved through it and were coming under attack from German infantry and tanks. Some of the wounded were returning out of the area. By standing on the engine compartment of my carrier, I was able to see beyond the edge of the village where enemy reinforcements were arriving. I manually signalled one of the sections to fire its two guns over the village at the enemy and this successfully disrupted them until a German tank emerged from the village, fired twice and destroyed and set on fire two of my carriers, killing three of the section (Cpl F.S. Bushnell, L/Cpl J.P. Wallace and Pte R.F.W. Perry) and wounding another, the section sergeant (Sgt Bone). Both gun teams had gallantly fired at the tank, but .303 bullets are no match for armour plate. Luckily for me in my exposed position, the tank withdrew without firing at the carrier I was standing on.

Cpl S. Hebdige, 9 Platoon, 'C' Company, 2nd Kensingtons:

The Tynesiders started out on the attack on the village and we moved forward with them to give them support. The platoon (9th) consisted of the Officer's carrier, then four machine gun carriers; Nos. 1, 2, 3 and 4. I was in the leading carrier (No. 1) with No. 2 on my right, then No. 3 behind me, and No. 4 behind No. 2. For some reason, Lt Griffiths stopped Nos. 1 and 2 carriers, and 3 and 4 passed through us to take up the lead. At this point, a German tank appeared to our right with infantry around it. Lt Griffiths gave the two leading carriers the order to fire. At the same time, the tank opened fire and knocked out No. 3 carrier, killing the gun crew and wounding Sgt Bone. A sheet of flame then shot across the lane and knocked out No. 4 carrier, with no loss of life. We regrouped and went to the end of the avenue where there was a hedge facing the village. Nos. 1 and 2 carriers were ordered to take their guns off their mountings and mount them in the hedge. The Tyneside Scottish then used us as a rallying point, and time and again they went forward into the village, only to be driven out again. Their CSM (CSM O. 'Paddy' Shanks) kept going in with them, telling them how well they were doing and letting them know how proud he was of them. We could not fire into the village ourselves as we would have been killing our own troops.

Lt J.T. Griffiths, Platoon Commander, 9 Platoon, 'C' Company, 2nd Kensingtons:

I was able to get the survivors back to join the other section and formed a defensive position where the retreating Tyneside Scottish would be able to consolidate and form a defence. I was relieved to see my company commander, Major Stanley Pinks, arrive in his jeep and help organise the defence. In fact, no serious attacks developed and the village was later bypassed and we withdrew. This was my first encounter with real warfare and it left me with a feeling of helplessness in dealing with casualties for we had only field dressings to help stem wounds which were not much use in the more serious cases. I also learned with some horror how much blood a human body contains. We had a paramedic with us who was better equipped but not always on the spot. Stanley saved me the worst horror. He ordered me away from the scene and arranged the recovery and burial of my dead comrades.

Pte T.H. Clark, Batman driver, 9 Platoon, Company HQ, 'C' Company, 2nd Kensingtons:

I drove a 15 cwt containing Capt Stanyer, 2nd i/c 'C' Company, two squaddies, supplies and tools that might be needed, to where the action had taken place in close proximity to a farm. On arrival we saw our three dead, plus other British dead and Germans – approximately ten in total. It was an eerie sensation, our three lads *were badly burned but the remainder were in crouching or standing positions behind the cover of vehicles etc., with little apparent injury. We dug a shallow rectangular grave in a rather exposed position in a nearby field. Suddenly, a German plane appeared from nowhere, but it passed over our position wiggling its wings – obviously he had seen that we were burying British and German dead.*

All the 1st Tyneside Scottish reserves had now been thrown into the attack, and two Company COs had been wounded – 'D' Company Commander, Major H.B. Boyne and 'B' Company Commander, Major J.K. Dunn. Eventually, the Battalion's forward position became so perilous that Lt Col de Winton decided to pull his troops back to Tessel-Bretteville.

Cpl J.W.H. Tipler, Section Commander, 18 Platoon, 'D' Company, 1st TS:

We had just reached the edge of the village when the Company runner came to me and told me that instructions from Company HQ were to withdraw as our own artillery was about to shell the village. I pulled my men back, and some time later in the general melee, joined two men, not of my section, tending to someone on the ground. It was Major Harry Boyne, our much-respected Company Commander, badly wounded in both legs. We did what we could, and a few minutes later a stretcher-bearing jeep arrived. We lifted Harry on to one of them, and I remember although his face was ashen, he managed a smile and said, "Good old 'D' Company!" We lifted the stretcher on to the jeep and it was driven away.

Pte P. Lawton, rifleman, 18 Platoon, 'D' Company, 1st TS:

After a while, we saw that some of our troops were starting to pull out of the village, and eventually we were informed that the whole Company was being withdrawn under the command of CSM 'Paddy' Shanks, the Company Commander, Major Boyne, having been badly wounded. We were told to remain in position until all the Company was out of the village, and then to withdraw as fast as we could. Pte Roper and I withdrew back along the hedgerow where we had advanced earlier in the day. About halfway down the field, there was a Bren carrier of the Kensingtons carrying a Vickers heavy machine gun, and as we approached, the officer in charge called me over and pointed out an enemy tank, with troops riding on the outside, driving along the road which only a few minutes earlier we had been guarding. He asked if I could do anything to stop the tank, but it was well out of PIAT range and I told him that we could only be effective if the tank turned and came towards us. On turning to look for my No. 2, I found that he had continued on his way and I was unable to attract his attention. Without the bombs he was carrying, the PIAT was no use whatsoever, so I had to carry on and rejoin the rest of the platoon. With hindsight, I realise that had the tank turned towards us he would probably have blasted the carrier to kingdom come without ever coming within the 100 yards range of the PIAT.

By 1800 hrs the Tyneside Scottish had re-grouped – 'D' Company holding a forward position with machine guns and two anti-tank guns, well dug-in about 400 yards short of Brettevillette, 'B' and 'C' Companies in front of Tessel-Bretteville and 'A' Company behind the village in reserve. By 2100 hrs, the situation was firm. Casualties in this operation had been double the number sustained during the attack on la Grande Ferme near Tessel Wood two days before, including two officers killed, but this time the Battalion had gained ground and had inflicted heavy casualties in return. Otto Weidinger confirms these German casualties, stating that heavy fighting continued all day while the British appeared to be steadily growing in strength. Artillery barrages landed on Noyers

and the 'Der Führer' command post, followed by severe naval gun shelling in the evening, with little response from the German guns. The Seventh German Army had also lost its Commander, *General-oberst* Friedrich Dollmann, who had died of a heart attack during the morning. *SS-Oberstgruppenführer* Paul Hausser immediately took over command.

At points along the road running through Rauray, the enemy had abandoned some of its heavier tanks. One Mk VI 'Tiger', probably of SS-Pz-Abteilung 101, which had been knocked-out sometime prior to the capture of the village by the DLI on 27 June, lay with its gun barrel jutting out into the road, and the Royal Engineers were called upon to deal with this obstruction.

German PzKmpfw Mk VI 'Tiger', probably of SS-Pz-Abteilung 101, that had been either knocked-out or abandoned in Rauray village prior to the action on 27 June.

Sapper W. Hudson, 757 Field Company, Royal Engineers:

At some point, while sitting in a halftrack, I was ordered by an officer to blow off the Tiger's gun barrel, as only a bren carrier could pass underneath.

First, the officer had a go himself, placing a ring of HE (plastic high-explosive) around the barrel. He came back to the halftrack while the explosion took place, and I told him that I did not think that it would blow it off – and it didn't. The charge was doubled, and I told him that I still didn't think it would blow it off – and it didn't. I was then ordered to blow it off myself, or I would be put on a charge for insubordination. So I took a handful of explosive and placed it down the barrel, with a detonator and a length of cortex attached. I followed this with soil packed in until it was over half full. This time, the barrel dropped off as the explosive took the weakest line of resistance – which was outwards. Previously, by placing the explosive around the barrel, as the officer had done, it had been fighting against the explosive on the opposite side.

Sapper Bill Hudson.

An abandoned Panzerkampfwagen Mk VI 'Tiger' on the edge of Rauray, 28 June 1944.

According to Craig Mitchell, the 1st Tyneside Scottish IO, it had been a very sticky day. It had been a sticky day for the VIIIth Corps as well. During the morning, the enemy had fought back along the whole length of the salient being formed by the 'Epsom' advance, the right flank being particularly vulnerable around the villages of Grainville-sur-Odon and Mondrainville. However, by midday the 11th Armoured Division, who had been pouring tanks across the River Odon, did reach the crest of Hill 112, but came under heavy fire from enemy guns positioned on the reverse slopes of the feature and from Point 113 to the west of Esquay. Although these counter-attacks went on throughout the afternoon, by the evening the villages of le Valtru and Grainville-sur-Odon had been cleared and the 2nd Argyll and Sutherland Highlanders had gone on and made their way up the Odon Valley as far as the bridge north of Gavrus. By nightfall, the VIIIth Corps positions north of the River Odon were secure, although a big German counter-attack remained a major threat. If the enemy were to counter-attack the VIII Corps salient, they would most likely strike out north-east from Noyers-Bocage, along the roads north and south of Grainville-sur-Odon. The northerly line of attack would take the enemy through Queudeville, just south of Brettevillette, giving further explanation to the reason why KG Weidinger was making such a supreme effort to hold on to these villages. In addition to defending the area from further attack by the 49th Division, KG Weidinger would also have to shield it from the enemy during German counter-attacks. East of Brettevillette, the 10th DLI and 4/7th RDG had advanced through the 11th DLI in Rauray and had spent the day in a very exposed position, contesting the high-ground south of the village near the inter-Corps boundary. During the afternoon, Lt Gen Dempsey had given instructions that XXX Corps should make very sure of this area and keep a strong force of armour there.

At first light on 29 June, it was clear that the guns of KG Weidinger, now firmly dug in, were forming an extremely aggressive defence, with heavy Spandau-fire breaking out along their front. The 1st Tyneside Scottish soon found it impossible to venture out beyond its forward positions and any movement immediately attracted devastating mortar fire. During the afternoon, forty replacements arrived in order to bring 'A' Company up to strength. Meanwhile, 'D' Company was being troubled by an enemy tank which every so often appeared at the end of the lane at Brettevillette and shot at its position. Eventually 'D' Company was ordered to withdraw in order to avoid the barrage being prepared for the start of an attack by the 11th DLI on Brettevillette. As soon as it began to move back, the enemy seized on the opportunity to open fire caused by its movement, and the ensuing Nebelwerfer attack inflicted a considerable number of casualties. Similar attacks were being felt by the 10th DLI to the south of Rauray where they spent hour after hour being shelled and rocketed by Nebelwerfers. Major J.D.P. Stirling, in his history of the 4/7th Royal Dragoon Guards, wrote this about the high-ground south of Brettevillette and Rauray: The place was stiff with dug-in tanks and anti-tank guns and we lost several tanks reconnoitring the feature. For days and days nothing that anyone could do could shift them. The tanks tried, the infantry tried and the gunners had a go with everything they had. It was still suicide to poke your nose out onto that forward slope.

The Germans were threatening to cut through the salient formed when VIII Corps had attacked the Odon Valley by piercing it at what appeared to be a weak point between the 15th and 49th Divisions, and at a midday meeting with his Corps Commanders, Lt Gen Dempsey once again stressed the importance of the inter-Corps boundary area between Rauray and le Haut de Bosq. At 1800 hrs, the 11th DLI attack was cancelled as it had become clear that a strong counter-attack against the VIII Corps salient by tanks of the 9th SS-Panzer Division 'Hohenstaufen' was about to cross the XXX Corps front, along the Noyers–Cheux road to the south of Brettevillette. This counter-attack had been brewing since the early morning, but even though British air operations had yet again been hit by bad weather conditions, it had been severely delayed after a barrage from artillery and naval vessels out in the Channel had struck the assembled forces as they were manoeuvring into position for their advance. This terrific bombardment then continued throughout the day, and when the 'Hohenstaufen' attack did finally get going around 2000 hrs, described by Brigadier James Hargest, a New Zealand Army observer with XXX Corps, as being made by about twenty tanks and 200 infantry (CAB 106/1060), it was unable to build up enough momentum for a serious breakthrough and was eventually abandoned. Otto Weidinger describes the enormous stress

29 JUNE

this continuous pounding placed on the specialist teams who were trying to maintain communications during the attack, most of them being eliminated. This made it virtually impossible for the commanders to complete situation reports, and given that they were also starved of artillery and Luftwaffe support, their attempt to drive a wedge between the British XXX Corps and VIII Corps was beaten before it began. By late evening the enemy had been driven back amid the torrential rain of a thunderstorm. The 15th Division then began the job of 'mopping up' the small pockets of German forces which remained around Cheux and Gavrus.

By now, units from seven Panzer Divisions had been identified between Caumont and Caen: 2nd Panzer Division, Panzer Lehr, Kampfgruppe Weidinger (elements of the 2nd SS-Panzer Division 'Das Reich'), 1st SS-Panzer Division 'Leibstandarte SS Adolf Hitler', 9th SS-Panzer Division 'Hohenstaufen', 12th SS-Panzer Division 'Hitlerjugend' and 21st Panzer Division. In addition, the 10th SS-Panzer Division 'Frundsberg' was now being thrown into the fray south of the River Odon, with the intention of forcing the 15th Division out of Gavrus and securing Pt. 113 and Evrecy. However, although 'Frundsberg' had around seventeen combat-ready Mk IV Panzers and sixteen StuGs on 29 June, a lack of fuel meant that only a limited number were initially able to participate. Otto Weidinger mentions that although the 9th SS and 10th SS-Panzer Divisions were not at full strength, it had been hoped that having been severely combat-tested on the Eastern Front they would turn the tide for the German Army in Normandy.

Here is part of a resumé of the day's action given in the VIII Corps Intelligence Summary No. 4, 29.6.44 as mentioned in The Official Histories of WW2 (CAB44/248):

> *The enemy's general plan was to employ troops from the 1st SS and 2nd SS-Panzer Divisions (Kampfgruppe Weidinger) in a role of containing us (VIII Corps) and our neighbours XXX Corps, whilst the 9th SS-Panzer Division attacked through them . . . tomorrow's attack is likely to be stronger.*

In Lt Gen Dempsey's eyes, the enemy's counter-attacks of the 29th June had been a rehearsal for the following day.

30 JUNE

At 0600 hrs on 30 June, three Tyneside Scots returned from Brettevillette, where they had been for two days, and reported that some wounded were still lying in a farmyard in the village. Around mid-morning, the 4th Lincolns took over the 1st Tyneside Scottish positions and the Battalion moved to a concentration area behind the 11th DLI. At 1000 hrs, one squadron of Shermans from the 24th Lancers took over from the 4/7th Royal Dragoon Guards in their supporting role alongside the 10th DLI.

Cpl J.W.H. Tipler, Section Commander, 18 Platoon, 'D' Company, 1st TS:

We were pulled out, led by a piper, to a rest area a mile or so behind, where we had some food and sleep before moving to Rauray in the evening. As we marched in, we saw Pte J.J. Ross sitting on a box and being attended to – one of his arms was missing. He was deathly pale, but managed a smile. He died later the same day.

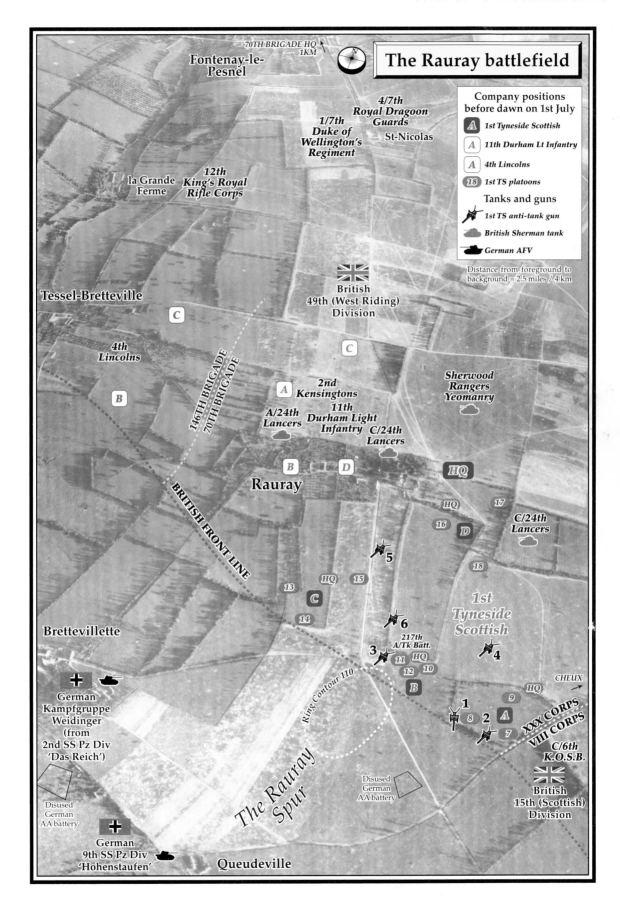

The Rauray battlefield

70TH BRIGADE HQ
1KM

Fontenay-le-Pesnel

4/7th
Royal Dragoon
Guards

1/7th
Duke of
Wellington's
Regiment

St-Nicolas

la Grande
Ferme

12th
King's Royal
Rifle Corps

Company positions
before dawn on 1st July

A 1st Tyneside Scottish

A 11th Durham Lt Infantry

A 4th Lincolns

18 1st TS platoons

Tanks and guns

1st TS anti-tank gun

British Sherman tank

German AFV

Distance from foreground to
background = 2.5 miles / 4 km

Tessel-Bretteville

C

British
49th (West Riding)
Division

4th
Lincolns

C

B

A

2nd
Kensingtons

11th
Durham Light
Infantry

A/24th
Lancers

C/24th
Lancers

Sherwood
Rangers
Yeomanry

B D

Rauray

HQ

HQ

16

17

D

C/24th
Lancers

18

5

13

HQ 15

C

14

6

217th
A/Tk Batt.

3

11

HQ

12 10

B

1st
Tyneside
Scottish

4

CHEUX

Brettevillette

Ring Contour 110

9

HQ

1

8 2 A

7

XXX CORPS

VIII CORPS

C/6th
K.O.S.B.

German
Kampfgruppe
Weidinger
(from
2nd SS Pz Div
'Das Reich')

The Rauray Spur

Disused
German
AA battery

Disused
German
AA battery

British
15th (Scottish)
Division

German
9th SS Pz Div
'Hohenstaufen'

Queudeville

At 1600 hrs, a conference headed by General Montgomery took place at HQ, 21st Army Group, after which Lt Gen Dempsey wrote in his diary, *First 100 days* (WO 285/9) that Second Army's task remained the same – to attract to itself (and to defeat) all the German armour and, when opportunity offered, to take Caen.

During the day, the enemy had probed the 'Epsom' salient, looking for weak spots. Once again, the road between Noyers and Cheux had formed an axis of attack, but VIII Corps had pulled in the perimeter of its forces and had managed to contain these dangers. They were greatly assisted in this task by intense artillery barrages and ferocious support fire from naval units. On their right, XXX Corps prepared its ground for the defence of Rauray. After three days of hard action without any sleep, during which they had struggled to secure the village against very stiff opposition, the two Durham Light Infantry battalions were relieved from their forward positions by the 1st Tyneside Scottish.

THE HOURS BEFORE STAND-TO

Lt C. Mitchell, Intelligence Officer, HQ Company, 1st TS:

On 30 June, we moved from our position in the line at Tessel-Bretteville to a concentration area behind the 11th Durham Light Infantry just south of Fontenay-le-Pesnel. For a few hours, rest and a wash were possible, but at 1400 hrs, the first 'O' Group was held in preparation for the take-over from the 10th DLI of their position at Rauray (Public Record Office WO171/1382).

During the afternoon and early evening of 30 June, parties of Tyneside Scottish reconnoitred the country around Rauray, but clear battlefield intelligence was difficult to gather owing to shortage of time and the awkwardness of the bocage. At the 1400 hrs 'O' Group meeting, the CO, Lt Col de Winton, gave orders for the Battalion to defend the fields around Rauray. Anti-tank gun emplacements were discussed and company positions decided according to the most suitable gun dispositions. Map studies revealed that the flat, open countryside forward of 'A' and 'B' Companies should provide the best killing ground for enemy tanks and it was clear that the four forward Detachments, Nos. 1, 2, 3 and 4, were the anti-tank guns most vital to the Battalion's defence.

While such 'O' Groups took place, it was regular practice for section rolls, containing blankets and groundsheets, to be collected up and taken by carrier back to 'B' Echelon. Short-term frontline slit trenches offered little more than a hole in the ground to lie in. Fortunately, the weather that evening was pleasantly warm and dry.

At 1930 hrs, four companies – HQ, 'A', 'C' and 'D', together with their supporting groups, moved into their carefully chosen defensive positions. This left 'B' Company with the task of moving up to its forward position on the Rauray spur just north of ring contour 110 after dark, this spot being visible to the enemy in daylight. As previously mentioned, this higher, open area was strategically very important as it was the only place

Lt Col R.W.M. de Winton, CO of the 1st Tyneside Scottish, 1 July 1944.

where a good field of view was possible, everywhere else being surrounded by tall bocage clumps and orchard trees.

Capt A. MacLagan, Platoon Commander, Anti-tank Platoon, 'S' Company, 1st TS:

In the early hours of 1st July, it is my recollection that I instructed my 2nd i/c, Lt Stewart, to visit 'C' Company area and check Nos. 5 and 6 guns linked up with 'B' Company and the DLI on our right flank, and then return to our small platoon HQ sited near to Bn HQ. I then made my way up to 'B' Company in the centre and examined the guns, being particularly concerned that their arcs of fire should link up with where I believed the 'A' Company position to be. I then retraced my steps back to my HQ, skirting a small copse near Bn HQ, and made my way forward again towards 'A' Company on our left flank.

Lt B.T.W. Stewart, 2nd i/c, Anti-tank Platoon, 'S' Company, 1st TS:

The night before the battle we were ordered to move to defensive positions in the Rauray area. The guns were positioned by map references (although to some extent we were committed to the DLI's dispositions) and ordered to dig-in in readyness for a possible attack by German armour at first light the next morning. I have a clear recollection of a sense of extreme urgency, and in view of the shortness of time available, I told the detachment commanders to blow themselves in with their anti-tank mines to ensure that they were thoroughly dug-in in the minimum of time. They accomplished this task successfully and the whole platoon was poised for action before dawn. It was important that the guns were adequately sited to provide the necessary opportunity to fire at the flanks of the enemy's tanks, not at the formidable front armour. Unfortunately, the siting was not done according to the drill book in all cases – some of the DLI guns being taken over in their existing positions; not at all where Capt MacLagan and I had decided from the map in the middle of the night, and as gun detachment commanders commented; some of the positions were not very good. However, it must be accepted that such infelicities are inevitable when the desire for stealth clashes with a desire for ideal siting.

Sgt S.C. Swaddle, 'A' Section Commander, Anti-tank Platoon, 'S' Company, 1st TS:

At approx 2200 hrs on 30 June, I went with Captain Stewart to the DLI anti-tank gun positions. He told me that if the DLI's guns were well sited, I was to take them over and give the DLI ours to save making any noise. This I did, giving the No. 2 gun detachment the first position and asking Cpl J. Drysdale what he thought. He said he was satisfied. Captain Stewart and I then went to the second position which my No 1 gun detachment took over OK. The Officer then went over to Sgt D. Watson's No. 3 gun, the next forward in the line.

Pte J.L.R. Samson, Bren-gunner, No. 4 Detachment, Anti-tank Platoon, 'S' Company, 1st TS:

During the night of 30th June, we were not on guard because our 6-pounder was close to the rifle company we were supporting ('A' Company). Our pits were dug and the gun emplaced under intermittent fixed line Spandau-fire. Occasionally the area was lit up by Verey lights and the odd star shell. The night seemed somehow unreal. However, eventually we finished our spade-work, the Loyd carrier went off back to 'B' Echelon and the five of us got into our slit trenches. Very tired, I soon fell asleep.

Pte T.J. Renouf, rifleman, 7 Platoon, 'A' Company, 1st TS:

'Come on Jock, here's a good slit trench for you'. These were the words that were spoken to me by a DLI soldier as we moved in to take over the front line positions from his battalion. It is strange that I should remember these words so clearly, but I have often thought of them and I believe the slit trench on offer helped me to survive the battle that was to come. I remember the track as we got near to the front line. For the last 200 yards we travelled along a typical bocage country lane, narrow and below field level with thick verges of hedgerows and trees. About 60 yards after an 'S' bend we moved into a field on our right. These were below a row of tall trees which grew on top of a three to four foot bank. The slit trenches were about four yards apart and most of 'A' Company were sited there. Another company ('B') was on our right flank and there was at least one of their platoons in the open fields on the extreme right. There was a streaky mist floating in the air and signs of a heavy dew, it was now after 8.30 pm. The Durham Light Infantry boys told us that things were quite quiet and that the Germans were in the woods across the open field about 200 or 300 yards to our front. They also mentioned hearing the sound of vehicles being moved around. The platoon sergeant came to inspect our positions and brief us on our duties. He commented on our slit trench but left it to us.

Lt J.T. Griffiths, Platoon Commander, 9 Platoon, 'C' Company, 2nd Kensingtons:

With our carriers, guns and numbers replenished, we made a night move to relieve another platoon which had been heavily engaged in supporting the 70th Brigade attack at Rauray. The relief was successful, the telephones working with lines intact, and so after my rounds we settled down for the rest of the short night.

Pte D.W. Jarvis, stretcher-bearer, attached to 'B' Company, 1st TS:

The fox-hole I got into was occupied by a Geordie (DLI) who said to me 'Nowt to worry about here Geordie'. I think he was joking.

He probably was; the 10th Durham Light Infantry had spent three days in close contact with the enemy, being relentlessly shelled and mortared, with virtually no sleep at all.

Capt J.S. Highmore, Company Commander, 'D' Company, 1st TS:

I was ordered to take over command of 'D' Company in the late afternoon of 30th June and almost immediately the battalion was ordered to relieve the Durham Light Infantry who were holding the Rauray area. We moved up and took over Company positions about dusk, and I remember when I was trying to find my left platoon's position (Lt I. Murray), I blundered into a small copse in the dark and found myself surrounded by 'ACHTUNG MINEN' signs erected by the previous occupants! However luck was with me.

Lt I.W. Murray, Platoon Commander, 17 Platoon, 'D' Company, 1st TS:

We took over from the DLI at Rauray on a bright summer's evening as June was slipping into July. 'What's it like here?' I asked my opposite number, a tall subaltern I had met only occasionally in the past on major training exercises. I'll never forget his reply, 'It's like a holiday,' he said, handing over a pile of paperbacks. I'm glad he enjoyed his. Actually, the portents had seemed unusually favourable – reserve platoon of a reserve Company ('D') tucked fairly well out of sight in a spot where the 'digs' had already been prepared for occupation.

Pte L.J.C. McLaren, Batman-Driver to IO, Intelligence Section, Battalion HQ, 1st TS:

The Intelligence Section was with the Battalion Command Post. We had no digging-in to do as we were able to use the slit trenches already there. Our vehicles were left behind us next to a fairly steep ditch which offered good protection.

Sgt E.A. Porterfield, Platoon Sergeant, Carrier Platoon, 'S' Company, 1st TS:

The Carrier Platoon, as far as I recall at the time of the Rauray battle, consisted of four sections of three carriers, each section commanded by a Sergeant or L/Sergeant and armed with a Bren gun, 2-inch mortar and PIAT to each vehicle. The usual role for the Carrier Platoon was to support the rifle companies by supplying additional firepower and, by their mobility, bringing this firepower to wherever it was required. Although usually attached to one of the companies ('D' at Rauray), the Carrier Platoon was supplied by Support ('S') Company and it was my job to keep them supplied with petrol, ammunition and rations.

Cpl G. Cowie, Section Commander, 18 Platoon, 'D' Company, 1st TS:

Each platoon sergeant would have previously indented (put in a written order) for arms and ammunition. These would have been delivered during the night. Both high-explosive and smoke bombs for 2-inch mortar, and about six to nine PIAT bombs were issued. Sufficient Bren gun magazines and ammunition were supplied in tin and cardboard boxes, and Bren teams (NCO and two others) had the *job of filling every mag with 30 rounds. They carried most of the mags, with one always on the gun of course, others being distributed among the rest of the section, usually two mags per man, stuffed in pouches. Each rifleman had to carry two cloth bandoliers, slung over both shoulders, each with five pockets containing ten rounds (two clips of five) – 50 rounds per bandolier. Normally, two grenades were issued to each man as well. Naturally, we already had most of all this, but we had to top-up as required. The chaps were responsible for cleaning their own weapons, unsupervised. It was worth their while to do so as an officer or NCO could carry out a spot check at anytime. Rifle barrels should have been spotless and bolts slightly oiled.*

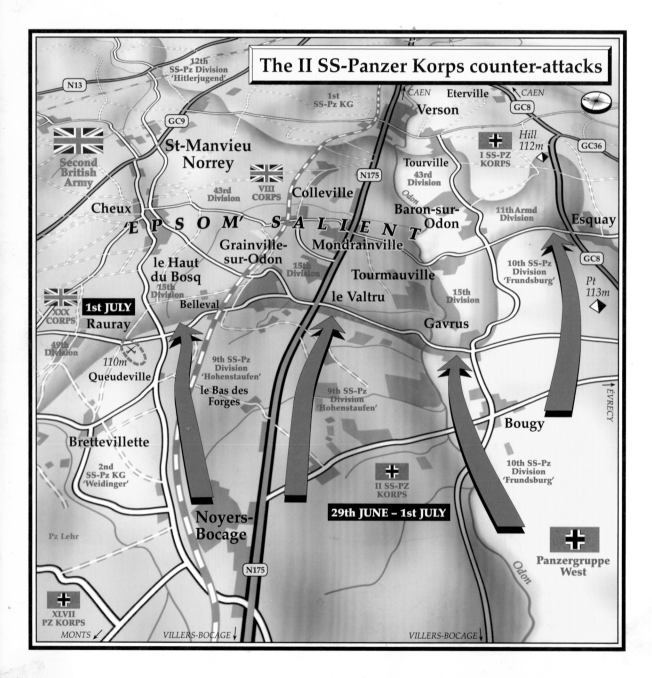

All along the 49th Division's front, from Juvigny-sur-Seulles to Rauray, expectant troops were getting well dug in. To the rear of the 1st Tyneside Scottish, the 11th Durham Light Infantry had defensive positions within Rauray and two companies behind the village forming a rear guard. West of the 11th DLI, the 4th Lincolns held the ground between Rauray and Tessel-Bretteville, with the Hallamshires, the 1/4th King's Own Yorkshire Light Infantry and the 11th Royal Scots Fusiliers in positions around Tessel Wood and Juvigny. South-east of Rauray, the 1st Tyneside Scottish were in touch with 'friends' from the 15th (Scottish) Division – the 6th King's Own Scottish Borderers, who had its 'C' Company dug-in on the other side of the road to le Haut de Bosq. This was the road along which the 9th SS-Panzer Division 'Hohenstaufen' had previously attacked VIII Corps.

In support of these infantry units, a considerable amount of firepower was on hand from artillery of the 69th, 143rd and 185th Field Regiments, tanks of the 24th Lancers, detachments of 6- and 17-pounder anti-tank guns from the 217th Battery of the 55th Anti-tank Regiment and machine guns of the 2nd Kensingtons. Two dummy 6-pounder anti-tank guns were also carefully positioned.

Operation 'Epsom' had by now been brought to an end. Radio messages from units of II SS-Panzer Korps, intercepted by British Intelligence, suggested a substantial build up of enemy tanks was taking place south of Noyers-Bocage – news which sent the RAF to work with a vengeance. While the 70th Infantry Brigade were taking up their positions around Rauray, Bomber Command dropped 1,300 tons on Villers-Bocage in twelve minutes, obliterating it completely. However, German records now show that this strike was aimed too far south of the enemy's main concentration of armour, and it is unclear how much damage, if any, this raid caused to the German Panzers as they advanced to the battlefront. What is certainly probable is that the massive artillery and naval gun bombardments which complemented the action severely disrupted the enemy's plans for a major night attack. On being notified about the enemy's build-up by SHAEF, Montgomery ordered VIII Corps to pull back, fearing that a marked increase in the number of SS-Panzer Divisions in the area would result in some of their far advanced units being cut off. The 11th Armd Division was subsequently withdrawn from Hill 112.

Lt Gen Dempsey claimed to have been aware of the need to revise his 'Epsom' plan and of the danger posed by II SS-Panzer Korps in counter-attacking the shoulder of the VIII Corps salient along the Noyers road towards Rauray, when he wrote:

Once we'd drawn armour in, no point in trying to bang on with 11AD. Essential to make sure we could take the shock of enemy c/a and give him a good hiding. Hence told O'Connor (Commander, VIII Corps) that vital spot was the Rauray gap.

According to Otto Weidinger, a last attempt to eliminate the deep British penetration was to be made by a large-scale night attack at 0300 hrs. The 9th SS-Panzer Division 'Hohenstaufen' arrived in the 'Der Führer' Regiment's sector after dark and a conference of all unit commanders took place. However, the CO of the 9th SS-Panzer Division, *SS-Obersturmbannführer* (Lt Col) Woith, who was due to deliver the attack order, had been wounded in an artillery barrage and failed to arrive causing total confusion as to the start time for the attack. In addition, the 'Hohenstaufen' Panzers were pulled back during the night, having found the terrain unsuitable. The 0300 hrs attack was therefore postponed. Eventually, battle orders arrived at the 'Der Führer' command post, and the 9th SS-Panzer Regiment, along with the Panzer-Grenadiers from Kampfgruppe Weidinger, began to move off to their start positions. The enemy's attack on Rauray was now set to begin at 0600 hrs.

THE BATTLE FOR RAURAY

AN ACCOUNT IN TWELVE STAGES

The following pages chronicle the day's action using signal reports made on the battlefield by the troops in action, interspersed with first-hand accounts from veterans of the battle.

Each stage of the battle has its own diagram giving the British viewpoint looking southwards from Rauray towards the German positions around the villages of Queudeville and Brettevillette. The distance between Rauray and Queudeville is about 1 mile/1.6 km.

Key to the regimental badges shown above each stage title:

Stages 1 and 7 – 1st Tyneside Scottish (Black Watch)
Stages 2 and 8 – 11th Durham Light Infantry
Stages 3 and 9 – 24th Lancers
Stages 4 and 10 – 4th Lincolns
Stages 5 and 11 – 6th King's Own Scottish Borderers
Stages 6 and 12 – 2nd Kensingtons (Princess Louise's)

British troops dodging enemy snipers at Rauray.

ORDER OF BATTLE

BRITISH FORCES

15TH (SCOTTISH) INFANTRY DIVISION

Infantry
44th Brigade: 6th King's Own Scottish Borderers, 6th Royal Scots Fusiliers

49TH (WEST RIDING) INFANTRY DIVISION

Armoured Corps
49th Recce Regiment, 141st Royal Armoured Corps (The Buffs)

Artillery
69th Field Regiment (RA), 143rd Field Regiment (RA), 185th Field Regiment (RA)

Anti-tank Guns
217th Battery, 55th Anti-tank Regiment

Machine Guns
2nd Kensingtons (Princess Louise's)

Infantry
70th Brigade: 1st Tyneside Scottish, 10th & 11th Durham Light Infantry
146th Brigade: 4th Lincolns
147th Brigade: 1/7th Duke of Wellingtons

8TH ARMOURED BRIGADE

Tanks
24th Lancers
Sherwood Rangers Yeomanry

GERMAN FORCES

2ND SS-PANZER DIVISION 'DAS REICH'

Infantry
Kampfgruppe 'Weidinger': I/SS-PzGR 3 'Deutchland', I/SS-PzGR 4 'Der Führer',
13th/III/SS-PzGR 4, 14th/III/SS-PzGR 4, 15th/III/SS-PzGR 4 and 16th/III/SS-PzGR 4

9TH SS-PANZER DIVISION 'HOHENSTAUFEN'

Infantry
SS-PzGR 19 and SS-PzGR 20

Tanks
SS-Panzer Regiment 9

1ST TYNESIDE SCOTTISH SENIOR OFFICERS
1 JULY 1944

BATTALION HQ
Commanding Officer – * Lt Col R.W.M. de Winton (Gordon Highlanders)
Second-in-command – * Major D.N. Nicol (Black Watch)
Adjutant – Capt H.W. Brown (Black Watch)
Intelligence Officer – * Lt C.B. Mitchell (Black Watch)
Medical Officer – Capt J.C.D. Mellor (Royal Army Medical Corps)

HQ COMPANY
Officer Commanding – * Capt W.G. Brennan (Black Watch)
Transport Officer – Lt T. Armstrong (Black Watch)
Signals Officer – Lt D.E. Salisbury (Duke of Wellington's Regiment)
Quartermaster – * Capt S. Manson (Cameron Highlanders)
Chaplain – CF. 4th Class C.W. Chesworth (RAChD)

SUPPORT COMPANY
Officer Commanding – Capt H.R. Alexander (Black Watch)
Officer Commanding Mortar Platoon – Lt K.D. Buchanan (Black Watch)
Officer Commanding Carrier Platoon – * Capt J. Dempster (Black Watch)
Officer Commanding Anti-tank Platoon – * Capt A. MacLagan (Black
Watch)
Second-in-command Anti-tank Platoon – * Lt B.T.W. Stewart (Black
Watch)
Officer Commanding Assault Pioneer Platoon – * Lt J.M.R. Hoare (Black
Watch)

RIFLE COMPANIES
Officer Commanding 'A' Company – * Capt D.C. Mirrielees (Black
Watch)
Officer Commanding 'B' Company – Capt K.P. Calderwood (Black Watch)
Officer Commanding 'C' Company – Major W.K. Angus (Black Watch)
Officer Commanding 'D' Company – * Capt J.S. Highmore (Black Watch)

SENIOR OFFICERS IN NORMANDY BEFORE 1.7.44
Officer Commanding 'A' Company – † Major W.L. McGregor (Black
Watch)
Officer Commanding 'B' Company – ‡ Major J.K. Dunn (Black Watch)
Officer Commanding 'D' Company – ‡ Major H.B. Boyne (Black Watch)

† wounded on 26.6.44

‡ wounded on 28.6.44

* wounded on 1.7.44

* killed later in Second
World War

* died before Major
Samson's dossier was
compiled

ARMOURED FIGHTING VEHICLES AT
RAURAY

In attempting to construct an accurate account of the Rauray battle, one is faced with the almost impossible task of trying to establish the number and type of German AFVs involved and subsequently destroyed or knocked out in the action. A considerable number of British sources, including official intelligence reports and veterans' accounts, mention the presence of Panzerkampfwagen Mk VI 'Tiger' tanks on the Rauray battlefield. The 24th Lancers record that one of their Shermans was destroyed towards the end of the day by a Tiger tank firing from the edge of Brettevillette, and a document in the 49th Division War Diary (Public Record Office WO171/500) states that one of the prisoners of war captured during the battle claimed that a number of Tigers had arrived at the front on the night of 30 June. However, despite all these reports, it is unlikely that Tiger tanks were used at all. The 9th SS-Panzer Regiment possessed no Tigers, only Panthers, Mk IVs and StuG III assault guns, and KG Weidinger was a Panzer-Grenadier force only. Certainly, the Imperial War Museum has film and photographic evidence of schwere SS-Panzer-Abteilung 101 Tiger tanks in and around Rauray in June (see photograph on page 45), but there is nothing to suggest that they were offering support to KG Weidinger on 1 July, therefore this theory cannot be successfully put forward as an explanation for Tiger sightings. In reality, it is most probable that British troops expected elite SS forces to have elite tanks and therefore confused Tigers with Panthers and Mk IVs; a very common mistake. Some have suggested that because the Tiger was practically unbeatable in close fighting, the discouraging effect this had on British tank crews led to the tendency for all enemy tanks to be classed as Tigers. As such errors in tank identification could apply to Panthers as well, this book only describes by type those enemy AFVs which were able to be irrefutably identified at the time. All others are referred to simply as tanks or AFVs.

PANZERKAMPFWAGEN MK V PANTHER

The German Panzer Divisions brought over 600 Panzerkampfwagen Mk V Panther tanks to Normandy. Although the Panther was highly respected by the British, they claimed its long 75mm gun made the turret heavy and slow to traverse, and therefore several shots could be fired at its flank before it could swing its turret round and return fire. Its frontal armour, a 35° sloping 'glacis', was 80 mm thick, which meant it could only be damaged from the front by a lucky shot hitting the joint between turret and hull. However, the side armour was a somewhat thinner 45 mm and could be successfully penetrated by a carefully aimed shot from a 17-pounder anti-tank gun, and sometimes even by a 6-pounder using high-velocity Sabot at close range. A Panther's total weight was 45 tons. At 54 tons, the Panzerkampfwagen Mk VI 'Tiger' was considerably more robust than the Panther, with side armour 80 mm thick. Its 88 mm gun was bigger as well. Although its greater weight made it slower (23 mph max.) than the Panther, when fully dug in, hull down, the Tiger was extremely

BRITISH ARMOURED VEHICLES

Sherman Mk 4

Loyd Carrier

Universal Carrier (Bren)

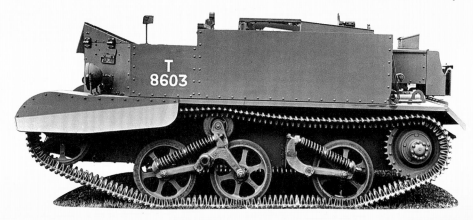

GERMAN ARMOURED VEHICLES

Panzerkampfwagen Mk V 'Panther'

Panzerkampfwagen Mk IV

Sturmhaubitze 42

difficult to destroy. The American Sherman M4 tank, as used by the 24th Lancers, was rather less resilient than the Panther. Its frontal armour was 76 mm thick and the side 51 mm. It carried a short 75 mm main gun and weighed around 30 tons. The fact that the 24th Lancers were able to outscore the enemy during the battle perfectly demonstrates how a defender could gain an advantage over an attacker in the Norman countryside.

PANZERKAMPFWAGEN MK IV

The most common German tank in Normandy, the Panzerkampfwagen Mk IV was the old warhorse in the Wehrmacht's stable of armour. Less of a threat than the Panther, the Mk IV was a much lighter tank and its 30 mm side armour could be penetrated much more easily. In this respect, it was weaker than the Sherman, but its firepower could achieve better results.

STURMGESCHÜTZ III

Capable of travelling at a speed of nearly 25 mph, the Sturmgeschütz III (StuG III) assault gun was very effective as a mobile anti-tank weapon. Although its gun was considerably shorter than that of the Panther and therefore had a slower muzzle velocity, it was the same 75 mm calibre and fired the same weight of HE shell. Its front and side armour was comparable to the Mk IV. In Normandy, some Panzer regiments had to employ the StuG III in place of battle tanks, but they were an inferior substitute as they lacked all-round traverse. The Sturmhaubitze (pictured left) was a varaition of the Sturmgeschütz.

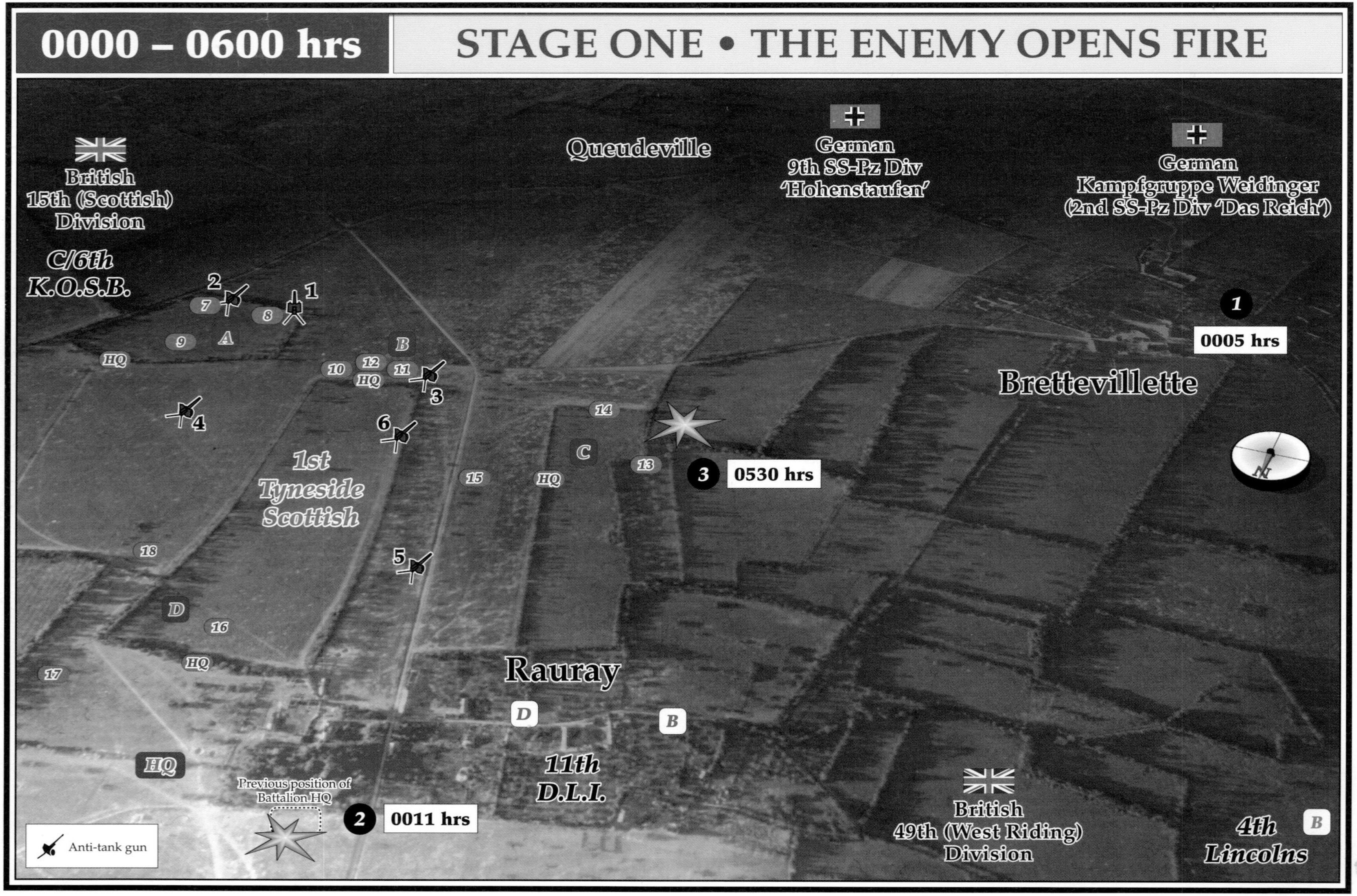

0000 – 0600 hrs   STAGE ONE • THE ENEMY OPENS FIRE

German
Kampfgruppe Weidinger
(2nd SS-Pz Div 'Das Reich')

1 0005 hrs

Brettevillette

German
9th SS-Pz Div
'Hohenstaufen'

Queudeville

3 0530 hrs

British
49th (West Riding)
Division

B 4th
Lincolns

Rauray

D

B

11th
D.L.I.

2 0011 hrs

Previous position of
Battalion HQ

1st
Tyneside
Scottish

British
15th (Scottish)
Division

C/6th
K.O.S.B.

Anti-tank gun

64

STAGE ONE

0000–0600HRS – THE ENEMY OPENS FIRE

I t is midnight. In the fields around the village of Rauray, the troops of the 49th (West Riding) Division are settling into their slit trenches, preparing themselves for the day ahead.

To the south-east of the village, about 800 yards away, lies a field roughly pentagonal in shape and measuring the length of two football pitches. One of its south-facing sides runs along the Noyers–Cheux road, the line of which forms the boundary between XXX and VIII Corps. Several military observers and historians would later refer to this enclosure as 'the five-sided field', and it is here that 'A' Company, 1st Tyneside Scottish, is positioned with its slit trenches nestling behind a tree-lined bank at right angles to the road. Two 6-pounder anti-tank gun detachments, Nos. 1 and 2, of the Battalion's Anti-tank Platoon are also dug-in at points along its length. To their left, across the road in the territory of the 15th (Scottish) Division, the men of 'C' Company, 6th Kings Own Scottish Borderers, prepare to defend their section of the British frontline, which curves away southwards along the 'Epsom' salient towards Grainville and beyond, to where the other fiercely contested small villages of le Valtru and Gavrus also await II SS-Panzer Corps.

On the right of the five-sided field, a gap in the bocage forms a natural breach in the Battalion's front, an ideal opening for the enemy to use as a breakthrough point for its tanks. As a counter-measure, the Anti-tank Platoon's No. 4 detachment has been positioned a short distance back to defend this area. On the other side of the gap stands the southern hedgerow of a long, oblong field which extends northwards back to the edge of Rauray. In the grassy outer margins of this hedge, uncomfortably free of any cover it might provide, lie the dangerously exposed slit trenches of 'B' Company, 1st Tyneside Scottish, the Battalion's central forward position. Helping them in their defence is the Anti-tank Platoon's No. 3 detachment. At the moment, 'B' Company is making the most of the shielding hours of darkness, but in the growing light of dawn its men will begin to survey the main prize of Operation 'Martlet': the wide, flat, open highground known to the British as the Rauray Spur. In front of them, from the map feature ring contour 110, long strips of corn will stretch their field of vision across to the villages of Queudeville and Brettevillette about 1,000 yards (914 m) away.

Defending the Battalion's right flank, 'C' Company's forward platoons are dug-in some 400 yards (366 m) to the west of 'B' Company, slightly behind them on the other side of the lane from Rauray to Grainville. Like 'A' Company, 'C' have the protection of hedgerows in front, but the surrounding bocage hampers their overall view of the battlefield. This could make their positions difficult to defend if the enemy manages to infiltrate the fields behind, cutting their platoons off from the units forming the second line of defence in Rauray itself.

Dug-in on the left-hand side of the village, the reserve troops of 'D' Company are spending the night wondering if the morning's work will involve them too, and in a field some way further back, Battalion HQ waits for the first sign of enemy movement. Similar scenes are being repeated among the ranks of the 11th DLI and 4th Lincolns in the orchards around the centre of Rauray.

1 • 0005 hrs • Five minutes into the new day, the first signal is pencilled into the log. 'C' Company has reported hearing enemy tanks moving around in Brettevillette. They appear to be limbering up and have fired off a few rounds from the right-hand edge of the village.

2 • 0011 hrs • A few minutes later, the enemy begins mortaring the area just north of the village, which had previously been occupied by the 10th Durham Light Infantry, and it is decided that Battalion HQ should move itself 200 yards to the left into another field next to some farm buildings behind 'D' Company's reserve position to avoid being pasted by mortar bombs. From its new position, HQ will also have a clearer view of the Battalion's rearguard. It is now 0100 hrs and the Battalion has been fed and is fully in position, with its main firepower, the Anti-tank Platoon, busy making sure that all its leading 6-pounders are facing the enemy with interlocking arcs of fire (anti-tank guns were most efficient when they were sited to support each other by firing across each other's front). Three Shermans and a German anti-tank gun set up as dummy, all destroyed in a previous encounter, will help to draw the enemy's fire away from Sgt D. Watson's detachment (No. 3).

Sgt S.C. Swaddle, 'A' Section Commander, Anti-tank platoon, 'S' Company, 1st TS:

We settled in to check the guns and ammunition. As I said before, 'A' Section guns (Nos. 1 and 2), on the left flank in 'A' Company's position, had taken over the DLI guns already there to save making any noise. No. 2 gun, with Cpl J. Drysdale as Detachment Commander, covered the road on the left, with my own gun, No. 1, to the right of it interlocking with its arc of fire. To my right came 'B' Section's guns, (Nos. 3 and 4) commanded by Sgt D. Watson.

Looking north across the large, oblong field towards the buildings where the 1st Tyneside Scottish HQ was situated.

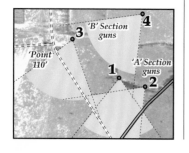

Pte T.J. Renouf, rifleman, 7 Platoon, 'A' Company, 1st TS:

During the night, the noise of moving vehicles continued but most of it appeared to be coming from a bit behind the enemy front line. I remember Verey lights being fired from time to time so as to illuminate the field ahead of us and expose any attempts at infiltration. A short time before dawn, I was one of four detailed to go back to the reserve companies and collect 'A' Company's rations.

Capt J.S. Highmore, Company Commander, 'D' Company, 1st TS:

I remember a patrol led by Lt J. Allan going out through 'D' Company positions to look for those wounded in a previous engagement in the Brettevillette area.

At 0100 hrs, Sgt A. Murray, 'C' Company, 6th KOSB, returns from reconnaissance patrol with a report of Germans assembling in numbers a short distance down the road from the 6th KOSB's position across the road from the five-sided field. A few hours later, a small 1st Tyneside Scottish patrol, consisting of an officer (Lt J. Allan) and three other ranks from 'B' Company, returns from Brettevillette at 0415 hrs and reports that, contrary to previous intelligence, there are no wounded men lying in the farmyard there. The patrol had encountered little opposition in Brettevillette, but did hear a considerable amount of tank noise to the south of the village, all of which confirms what intelligence had predicted, that the enemy is heavily occupied in forming up for a big armoured drive along the road running north-east from Noyers-Bocage. A sizable set-piece attack is about to explode right across the Battalion's front. A quarter of an hour later, the Tyneside Scots get the order to stand to.

Cpl J.W.H. Tipler, Section Commander, 18 Platoon, 'D' Company, 1st TS:

We stood to at first light and I recall going to the other slits making sure my men were awake. It was a fine morning and quite warm.

Sgt A.R. Esplin, Section Commander, Mortar Platoon, 'S' Company, 1st TS:

The Mortar Platoon was commanded by Lt K.D. Buchanan with Platoon Sgt J. Horne, the other section commander being Sgt W. Johnson. In the semi-gloom of that morning, we got well dug-in with our base plates on firm ground (as we thought), the six mortars with Observation Post slightly forward. Our commanders kept us busy, getting our mortars settled in, firing on pre-arranged targets. As the daylight came, we knew we were going to have a fight and that we would be staying for a while, for the ammunition trucks were by this time unloading more mortar bombs than I ever thought we would need.

Capt A. MacLagan, Platoon Commander, Anti-tank Platoon, 'S' Company, 1st TS:

I finally reached 'A' Company's position shortly before dawn. During this time I was very much aware of enemy activity – tank engines etc. revving and moving about, warning us that an attack was imminent. I recall being near Major Mirrielees as he gave orders for his company to stand to. I remember making a small alteration to the position of No. 2 gun and getting Cpl Drysdale to set up a dummy gun position some 30 yards to his left using a Verey pistol tied to a small bush and the gun's side shields.

0501 hrs • Sunrise (calculated from astronomical tables and adjusted for BST). The first light of a fine summer's day is now given an unusually dull cast as a wave of smoke is laid down by the enemy in an attempt to mask his attacking forces as they line up for action.

Pte A. Corris, rifleman, 7 Platoon, 'A' Company, 1st TS:

The weather the previous day had been lovely and having dug-in in the dark and done the usual two on two off, I did think it odd as dawn broke that we were in a mist so intense that visibility was down to a few yards. My partner in crime that day was a lad from Somerset way named Reeves and when we climbed out of our slitty to stretch our legs, to our surprise the mist lifted in a matter of seconds and realising it had been a smoke-screen, we both peered over the hedge. In the field immediately to our front and at about 500 yards were rows of tanks, silent and motionless, presumably they had crept up in the night. Reeves's first observation was 'This is going to piss on the chips'. A sentiment that I completely agreed with.

3 • 0530 hrs • A message from 'C' Company gives the first serious warning of what is to come. Major Angus reports that the enemy are peppering the company's position with mortar bombs, and machine gun fire is coming in thick and fast from Queudeville, about 800 yards directly in front of them. The artillery is informed of this intensification, and four miles back from the front, the 25-pounders of the 185th Field Regiment make their preparations. Having pinpointed the enemy's position by constructing a tri-section of bearings using their own compass readings along with those sent in by the infantry companies, Forward Observation Officers will relay the resulting co-ordinates to the gunners who will open fire on the designated point. From his position slightly to the rear of 'C' Company's forward platoons, Major Angus sweeps the fields in front of him with his binoculars, looking for the first signs of an enemy attack.

Major W.K. Angus, Company Commander, 'C' Company, 1st TS:

The view from my Company HQ was restricted by the typical tall double hedges of the bocage country. I could see the hedges in front of which my two forward platoons were situated. The platoon on the right (13) was commanded by Lt D. W. Wallace, with the left platoon (14) commanded by Sgt J. MacMillan, no officer being available.

L/Cpl N.E. Waters, Section Commander and LMG No. 1, 14 Platoon, 'C' Company, 1st TS:

At early light, the position came under heavy fire. My Platoon, which was little more than a section in strength, was dug-in against a large hedge from where we came under direct small arms fire.

The hedgerow which formed the front line along which 'A' Company was positioned in the five-sided field. In 1944 the height of the bund would have been much greater.

From 'C' Company's position, the barrage searches its way along the front line to the left flank, where the occupants of the five-sided field now start to feel its effect.

Pte T.J. Renouf, rifleman, 7 Platoon, 'A' Company, 1st TS:
We got back and I deposited the platoon rations at platoon HQ which was in the left hand corner of the field adjacent to the lane. I had just got back to my slit trench when a German barrage opened up. This would be around dawn. It was not heavy and not too near our positions, it was mainly mortar shells that were falling. After a lull it started up again but this time it was nearer. The process was repeated and by then the shells were dropping around our position. It seemed as if for the first half-hour or so the enemy were ranging more and more accurately on to our positions.

Capt A. MacLagan, Platoon Commander, Anti-tank Platoon, 'S' Company, 1st TS:
I did not know which unit was positioned to the left of 'A' Company (it turned out to be the K.O.S.B. who were further forward than I anticipated), but while I was moving about in the area trying to make some contact with them, the enemy opened up with very heavy mortar fire.

Capt J.S. Highmore, Company Commander, 'D' Company, 1st TS:
About dawn, or shortly afterwards, things started to happen. A cascade of Verey lights went up over the German held area to the south-west and the ominous sound of tanks on the move grew louder. Heavy fire came down on the Battalion front and literally the fog of war rolled over the battlefield.

The enemy's first furious barrage is now at its height. This shelling will continue and be joined by returned fire from the defenders, building up to a storm of artillery and mortar fire that will last throughout the day.

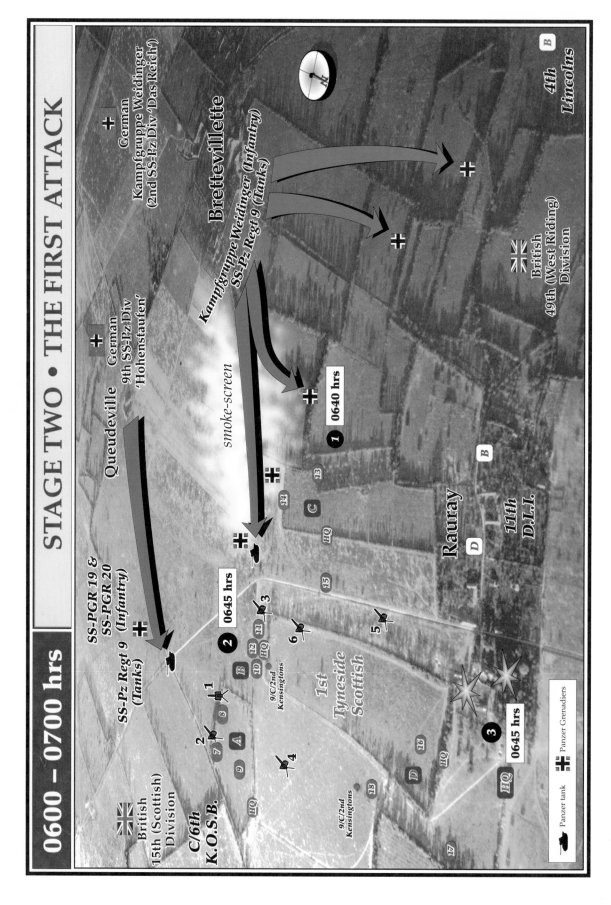

STAGE TWO • THE FIRST ATTACK

0600 – 0700 hrs

German
Kampfgruppe Weidinger
(2nd SS-Pz Div 'Das Reich')

Bretteville lette

Kampfgruppe Weidinger (Infantry)
SS-Pz Regt 9 (Tanks)

German
9th SS-Pz Div
'Hohenstaufen'

Queudeville

SS-PGR 19 &
SS-PGR 20
(Infantry)

SS-Pz Regt 9
(Tanks)

British
15th (Scottish)
Division

C/6th
K.O.S.B.

smoke-screen

1   0640 hrs

2   0645 hrs

B

4th
Lincolns

British
49th (West Riding)
Division

Rauray

11th
D.L.I.

13

14

C

HQ

15

1st
Tyneside
Scottish

3   0645 hrs

1

8

2

7

A

9

4

HQ

18

9/C/2nd
Kensingtons

B

12

11

HQ

10

3

6

5

16

D

HQ

17

HQ

9/C/2nd
Kensingtons

Panzer tank

Panzer Grenadiers

STAGE TWO

0600-0700 HRS – THE FIRST ATTACK

The air is now full of the sound of heavy gunfire as the Germans try to soften up the defenders of Rauray before unleashing their first assault. Kampfgruppe Weidinger, with supporting AFVs from SS-Pz Regt 9, will attack 70th Brigade's right flank, while 9th SS-Pz Div Hohenstaufen units SS-PzGR 19 and 20, with supporting AFVs from SS-Pz Regt 9, will advance towards Cheux along the road between the 15th and 49th Divisions, their intermediate objective being the Ferme des Cigognes, a farm by the side of the road, just south of le Haut du Bosq. A château just north of Grainville will be another objective. The German troops move off at 0600 hrs and advance rapidly, the Weidinger Panzer-Grenadiers confident that they can reach their objective.

1 • 0640 hrs • FIRST ATTACK • The battle begins. 'C' Company is first to report that it is under attack from both tanks and infantry. The enemy, just visible in the dim light of the early morning, is rapidly advancing across the fields from Brettevillette, taking full advantage of the cover being provided by the drifting smoke-screen and artillery barrage. They appear to be fighting in small attack groups, each group having around five tanks. On reaching the Tyneside Scottish lines, the Hohenstaufen Panzers provide covering fire, pounding the Battalion's slit trenches with shells and strafing machine gun fire, while the Weidinger Panzer-Grenadier snipers and Spandau teams take up strategic positions. Once these are established, the attackers quickly mount their machine guns and rake 'C' Company at close-quarters. The Panzers meanwhile keep moving, rumbling on through the smoke past 'C' Company's front towards ring contour 110, where 'B' Company and the Battalion's anti-tank guns wait for the attack to impact on them.

The two forward platoons of 'C' Company now engage in a violent and chaotic fire fight with the Panzer-Grenadiers as they try to push deep into 1st Tyneside Scottish territory. Similar Weidinger groups are entering the fields in front of the 4th Lincolns on the Battalion's far right, and along the whole 49th Division front line from Tessel-Bretteville to Rauray, the news is spreading that the enemy is attacking in force.

Pte A. Henderson, rifleman, 13 Platoon, 'C' Company, 1st TS:
My mate John Laing and I were in a dug-out in the middle of a hedgerow which we had covered with branches and bracken,

leaving space for a field of vision of the area we were to defend. The Germans had begun plastering us with mortar and artillery fire and this seemed to last for ages, but as soon as it lifted, I spotted German soldiers across the other side of the field in another hedgerow who were trying to work their way down past our dug-out. We started firing our rifles at them. Soon their heads went down and we never saw them again.

This view looking west from ring contour 110, taken during a post-war tour of Rauray, is as close as one can get to a contemporary view of the July 1944 battlefield (see map on page 74).

On the right, 13 Platoon's position is taking the brunt of the firepower covering the enemy's infiltration into 'C' Company's area, their slits being adjacent to a long shielding hedgerow which the attackers are using as their line of entry as they creep northwards in their bid to take Rauray. The defenders are trying to hang on, but the enemy's machine guns are ripping into them and they are taking heavy casualties.

Eventually, the bursts of blazing Spandau fire cut too deep, and some sections give ground as two of their leaders are killed.

Major W.K. Angus, Company Commander, 'C' Company, 1st TS:
In the course of this attack, Lt D.W. Wallace and his platoon sergeant were killed. After this unhappy event, the enemy overcame 13 platoon's resistance and overran its position.

Pte J. Capaldi, Gun Number, No. 5 Detachment, Anti-tank Platoon, 'S' Company, 1st TS:
We were positioned just off the road, with 'C' Company just in front. We were on stand to at daybreak, and there was the sound of heavy gunfire from the 'C' Company positions. Carriers were moving up and down the road, some taking back wounded from 'C' Company. Sgt Day (No. 5 Detachment Commander) saw about four

Germans going along the side of a hedge and threw a hand grenade in their direction. We then had a fright when the grenade hit a tree and rebounded, but we were all OK.

Having been immediately informed of the attack, the 24th Lancers are responding accordingly, their 75 mm guns bellowing out a defiant reply from positions in Rauray. 'C' Squadron has two troops on the eastern side of the village, and two troops situated in its western orchards. Their HQ is situated by the road which runs south to ring contour 110. The 1st Tyneside Scottish mortars are also in action, firing their 3-inch bombs on pre-arranged targets, and a few miles back in the small villages around Audrieu, the 143rd and 185th Field Regiments are also opening up with defensive artillery fire.

M. J. Wood, 507th Battery OP, 143rd Field Regiment:

One of my main tasks was maintaining telephone communications to forward infantry positions and to our own forward Troop Commander's Observation Post. These lines were vital – many lives depending on information and firing orders being passed back to our gun positions by day and night – and they were being constantly cut by German shell and mortar fire, and by the odd tank. One, I remember, made itself a real pest by firing a few rounds before retreating, leaving telephone lines really 'chewed up', and of course there were several lines at one point – all the same colour! Sorting them out took time, and as they ran along the open sunken lanes it was not very healthy to stay too long. The 507th Battery's OP's half-track and crew's dug-outs were on the north edge of a copse on the eastern side of Rauray, by the lane which ran north/south through the village. Our forward Troop OP was on the other side of the lane, and only approachable through an orchard which was chest high in stinging nettles. The lane was the site of some vigorous shelling, and I remember once mending the telephone lines by it with a relief signaller when an enemy 88 mm opened up. I was well used to the noise it made – the signaller was not! The look on his face has stayed with me over the years.

Looking northwards along the main road through Rauray. The building on the left appears in the photograph on page 45.

Sgt H. Cooke, 185th Field Regiment:

Observation Post teams in forward positions, observing 'fall of shot' etc, had a greater percentage of casualties than those serving the guns. Whilst I, as a Gunner, am proud of the various plaudits about our artillery, when I look back at the infantry doing their dangerous job I think we were very lucky – they were in direct contact with the enemy and bore the brunt of everything. 'Thank God for the infantry' was a well used expression by us.

Sgt A.R. Esplin, Section Commander, Mortar Platoon, 'S' Company, 1st TS:

When hell did break loose, no order from the Observation Post was less than three round rapid fire with 'repeat – repeat' being on order most of the morning.

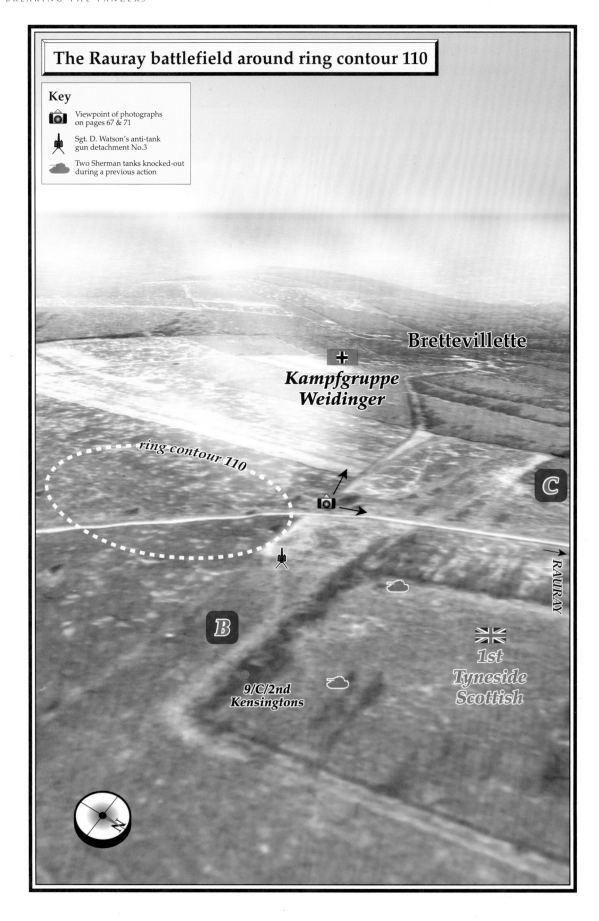

The Rauray battlefield around ring contour 110

Key

📷 Viewpoint of photographs on pages 67 & 71

⚓ Sgt. D. Watson's anti-tank gun detachment No.3

🛡 Two Sherman tanks knocked-out during a previous action

Brettevillette

✠ **Kampfgruppe Weidinger**

ring contour 110

C

RAURAY

B

9/C/2nd Kensingtons

🇬🇧 *1st Tyneside Scottish*

2 • 0645 hrs • Five minutes after 'C' Company's WT call, 'B' Company, under the command of Capt K. P. Calderwood, report that the enemy is in its position. The Panzers have continued their advance past 'C' Company and are now entering the area within ring contour 110. Panthers and Mark IVs rumble out of the smoke-screen and open up on 'B' Company who try to return fire from the cover of their slit trenches. Calderwood is told to hang on while the machine guns of the 2nd Kensingtons are called up for support, and as groups of Weidinger Panzer-Grenadiers begin to emerge from behind the advancing tanks, 9 Platoon, 'C' Company, 2nd Kensingtons engage them at ranges down to 150 yards.

Lt J.T. Griffiths, Platoon Commander, 9 Platoon, 'C' Company, 2nd Kensingtons:

Early that morning just after stand to, we were alarmed by the bursting of shells around us. I could now see our situation for the first time. The platoon HQ was at the edge of a large field in a ditch that gave some protection. One section only slightly forward of us and some eighty plus yards to our left, was well hidden at the edge of a badly knocked about little copse. The other section was several hundred yards forward and some twenty left at the far edge of the field, shallowly dug in behind a hedge and just beside a knocked out British tank leftover from the earlier attack. The infantry was well dug in to our front, and now beyond them emerging from the smoke were German tanks with infantry in support.

Lt J.F. McLaren, Platoon Commander, 12 Platoon, 'B' Company, 1st TS:

The first sighting of the Germans was their tanks appearing through the mist or haze. The platoon on my right (11), commanded by Sgt L. Furlong, engaged with a PIAT but this did not appear to be effective.

Pte D.W. Jarvis, stretcher bearer, attached to 'B' Company, 1st TS:

Jerry sent a smoke-screen over and opened fire on our position with everything he had. I watched Jerry tanks coming through the smoke-screen, followed by the infantry.

Pte P. Birkett, Intelligence Section, Battalion HQ, 1st TS:

The first signs were from 'C' Company, then in very quick time practically all the rifle companies were sending WT Calls. I can remember the CO asking for mortar and artillery support, and in what seemed to be seconds all of us at Battalion HQ knew we were in the centre of one hell of a battle.

3 • 0645 hrs • Heavy enemy Nebelwerfer rocket-mortar fire falls on Battalion HQ. Luckily, the wood on the edge of the village receives most of it and HQ fortunately avoids being wiped out, having been moved from this position during the night.

L/Cpl A. Richardson, Regimental Police Officer, Police Section, Battalion HQ, 1st TS:

I remember being joined by Lt C. Mitchell, the Intelligence Officer at the time. Having asked him what the situation was, he replied the companies were having a tough time, but with the aid of the attached armoured unit and artillery we should keep the enemy in check. At this time, the Battalion HQ was being heavily mortared by those 'Moaning Minnies' as we called them. There was a lot of comings and goings of Army personnel to the Command Post.

Pte (A/Cpl) J.W. Barnes, Section Commander, 18 Platoon, 'D' Company, 1st TS:

My first recollection of the day in question is associated with the irreparable loss of six sausages, properly known in those days as 'soya links'. They had just 'come up' and were shared out two to a man. My trench mates, there were usually three of us in the trench, were not sausage lovers and so I got theirs. Part of the trench was covered by an old door and that in its turn was covered over with the spoil from the trench, as was normal practice. I sat down on the bottom of the trench under the covered part, with my back against the end of the trench. At that moment the German barrage opened up. The barrage was obviously no ordinary 'stonk', firstly because of its intensity and secondly because there was heavy calibre stuff coming over in some quantity. I hadn't gotten through the first sausage when the trench took a direct hit. The shell must have been a fairly hefty one because it blew in the whole of one side of the trench producing a considerable crater, burying me in the process. The door over the end of the trench was reduced to firewood, but fortunately some of the larger pieces fell across my chest, taking part of the weight of the spoil which had collapsed on top of me. I thus had just enough relief from the weight to be able to breathe. By a stroke of luck, the other two occupants of the trench, who were standing up at the opposite end, were miraculously blown out of the trench unscathed. They took cover behind a hedge. Subsequently they told Sgt Ernie Parker (Platoon Sergeant, 18 Platoon, 'D' Company) what had happened. Luckily for me, he insisted they go back to the trench and dig me or my bits out and make definite by examination my departure for 'Abraham's bosom'. By the time they got back to me I was

A view looking north from ring contour 110 taken on a post-war tour of the Rauray battlefield (see map on page 74).

beginning to panic. I couldn't move and was having difficulty breathing as the mass of earth settled. However, they dug me out and in celebration of my resurrection, some tank men, or Vickers machine gunners, sent me a collection of cigarettes they had made.

L/Cpl A. Richardson, Regimental Police Officer, Police Section, Battalion HQ, 1st TS:

When the battle started, the Police Section was instructed to dig-in around the Command Post and be in readyness for any order or task given to us.

0655 hrs • 'B' Company reports that five tanks and a company of infantry are attacking it. The men on the edge of ring contour 110 are firing non-stop in a frantic attempt to withstand the enemy's onslaught, and the Carrier Platoon is warned to stand-by and await orders to supply them with more ammunition. Braving the scything bursts of incoming fire, Platoon Commander, Lt J. McAllan, wearing rubber shoes to give him greater agility, leaps from slit trench to slit trench to see that his men are all right. Meanwhile, other enemy tanks situated in front of Brettevillette shoot high-explosive shells at 'C' Company and the 11th DLI positions in Rauray.

0700 – 0800 hrs   STAGE THREE • ANTI-TANK GUNS RESPOND

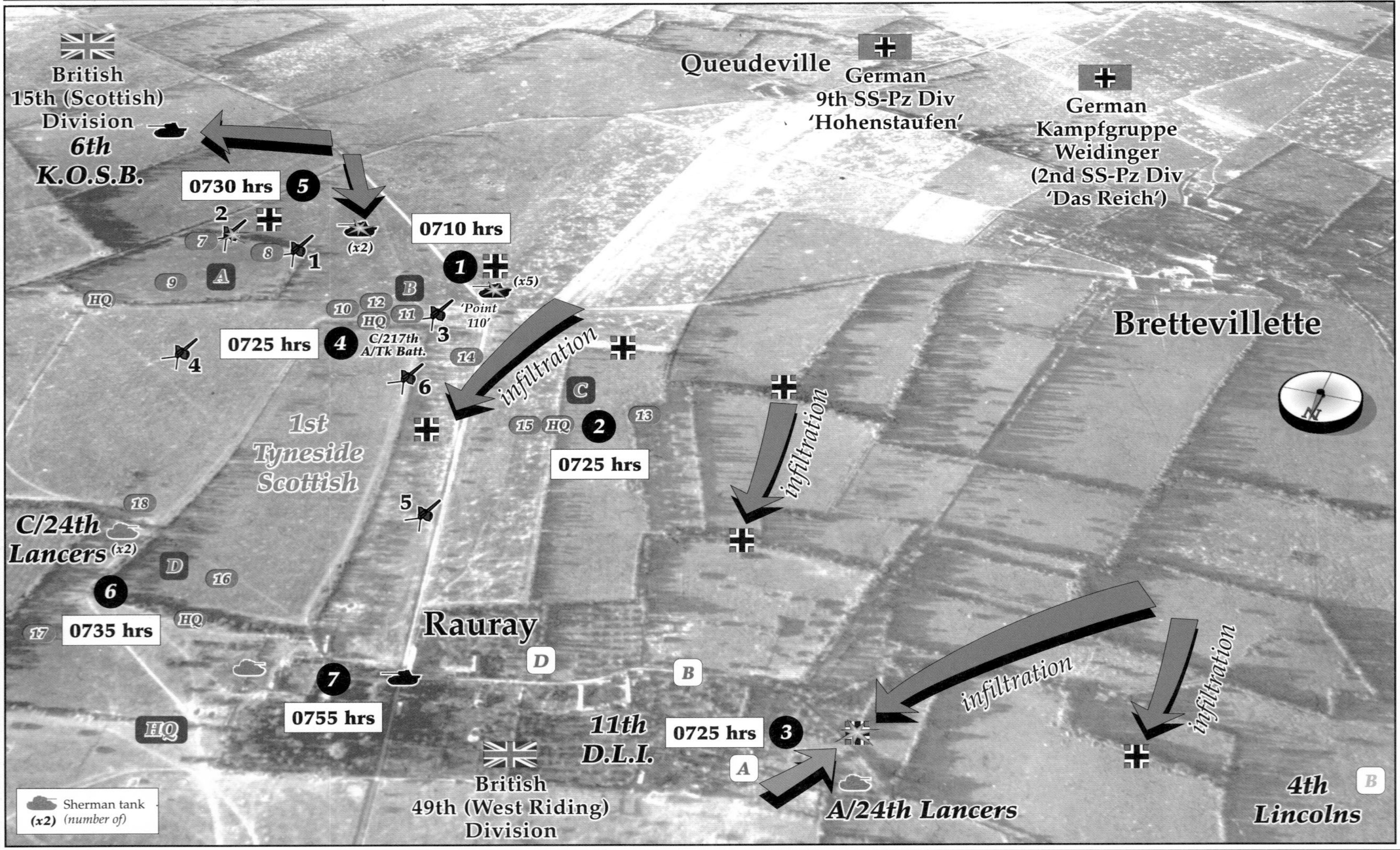

German Kampfgruppe Weidinger (2nd SS-Pz Div 'Das Reich')

German 9th SS-Pz Div 'Hohenstaufen'

Queudeville

Brettevillette

infiltration

infiltration

infiltration

4th Lincoln

A/24th Lancers

11th D.L.I.

0725 hrs

British 49th (West Riding) Division

Rauray

0755 hrs

1st Tyneside Scottish

0710 hrs

Point 110

C/217th A/Tk Batt.

0725 hrs

0730 hrs

6th K.O.S.B.

British 15th (Scottish) Division

0735 hrs

C/24th Lancers (x2)

Sherman tank (x2) (number of)

STAGE THREE

0700–0800 HRS – ANTI-TANK GUNS RESPOND

Just twenty minutes have elapsed since the first reports of an enemy attack, but in that brief time the front line troops of the 1st Tyneside Scottish have been severely mauled. Artillery fire from both sides has been colossal. However, the enemy have not managed with their first effort to achieve their primary objective of bursting right through the British front. The defenders of Rauray are refusing to be brushed aside. Above the continuous rip and crack of small arms fire, ring contour 110 intermittently resounds to the thunderous exchange of German tank shells and British anti-tank rounds. Although hard pressed by five tanks, 'B' Company are putting up a spirited fight, and one of the Tyneside Scottish 6-pounders, Sgt D. Watson's No. 3 detachment, is pitching everything in against the tanks which are being engaged in turn as they come into range.

Lt J.F. McLaren, Platoon Commander, 12 Platoon, 'B' Company, 1st TS:

The anti-tank gun on my right was in action and casualties appeared among the enemy's tanks.

Sgt D. Watson, 'B' Section Commander, Anti-tank Platoon, 'S' Company, 1st TS:

At daybreak, someone shouted 'Tanks!' and everyone got to their positions. My Bren gunner, Pte J. Walker, got severely wounded in the hand and I sent him back to the RAP. We kept on firing at the tanks, but then my aimer (Pte C.D. Tierney) got struck in the face and I got him away and sent him back too. I took on the job of aimer and with the speed that the loader kept pushing the shells in we managed to take a few of the tanks. I noticed that we were

Sergeant David Watson.

running short of ammunition and as Sgt O'Brien was attached to me, I sent him to the nearest company to get them to phone 'B' Echelon for more shells. When he came back, he told me that he could not get through to anyone and I told him to go back and keep trying. Then I was hit in the knee by a piece of shrapnel and my loader (Pte W. Cook) was hit on the back of the hand. His hand kept on bleeding, but we just carried on until we had no more ammunition left. As my loader and I were now both wounded, we had nothing else to do but leave the gun. Sorry I can't give any times, I never had time to look at a watch (Sgt D. Watson was awarded the Military Medal for this action*).*

Pte W. Cook, Gun Number, No. 3 Detachment, Anti-tank Platoon, 'S' Company, 1st TS:

I was on guard with Charlie Tierney when the bubble burst, from then on it was a matter of head down and shoot straight. Our first casualty on the gun was Jim Walker, a Montrose chap. He was hit on the hand as he fired the Bren, a short distance away from the gun. Then Charlie Tierney was blinded by a near shell burst, and Dave Watson and I were left to carry on for a while before we were both hit. Dave was hit in the leg and I in the right forearm. My arm wound was minor, but my left hand was blistered with the shell cases not ejecting properly.

Sgt T. O'Brien, Anti-tank Platoon, 'S' Company, 1st TS:

We had a go at them all, one after the other. As one caught fire, others came forward. (M. O. I. No. 6021/A744).

Aiming through the smoke and flames at what they believe to be the source of Sgt Watson's Sabot darts, the Panzers slam their shells into the knocked-out Shermans and the old German anti-tank gun being used as a dummy. Far from aiding their attack, the enemy's smoke-screen is hindering them.

1 • 0710 hrs • As the confused battle rages on, a hurried report is sent in from an uncertain source which states that three tanks have been knocked out and that a gun is damaged. Five minutes later, there is news of more success. Although his team is now wounded and the Battalion's No. 3 gun out of ammunition, Sgt D. Watson's detachment has managed to put out of action the five tanks within the perimeter of 'B' Company's position, successfully blunting the enemy's initial attack on ring contour 110.

We must pause here to consider the evidence concerning the number of AFVs destroyed or knocked out by Sgt D. Watson's anti-tank gun, No. 3. There are two separate documents: Immediate Report No. 26, dated 31.7.44, CAB106/963, and an account given in a letter to Major-General E.H. Barker, held by the Imperial War Museum, which describe the action involving Sgt D. Watson's detachment. Both credit his gun with having knocked out a total of nine tanks. The Immediate Report No. 26 was later included in a War Office Overseas Report prepared under the direction of the CIGS as follows:

On 1 July at Rauray, a 6-pdr anti-tank gun belonging to a battalion of a Highland regiment was ordered to occupy a very forward position near three knocked-out Shermans. It was not possible to move up until dark when the detachment manhandled their gun forward and started to dig it in. The enemy kept on putting up flares and firing at these men, so that it was extremely difficult to work. These difficulties increased as the night went on, and the detachment was eventually compelled to lie flat and dig with their hands. At first light they noticed a blown up 6-pdr nearby. They put this gun in position again, and camouflaged it so as to look as though it was in action.

At 0650 hrs, enemy tanks were seen approaching from the village of Brettevillette. Someone excitedly shouted 'Tanks – look out', to which the gun detachment replied, 'That's all right—we can see them – keep quiet'. Gradually about 20 tanks came into view and the detachment commander gave 'Engage!'. At that moment, the layer was wounded so the detachment commander took over his duties.

The leading tank was now getting uncomfortably close, but as it kept head-on to the gun, it was allowed to continue. Two other tanks, farther off, offered their flanks, and they were promptly shot up. Then, when the leading tank was only 150 yds away and still closing, the detachment fired at its front and set it on fire.

Altogether the detachment killed nine tanks from this position – one head on at 150 yds, and the remaining eight sideways on at an average range of about 400 yds. The gun had only 24 rounds of Sabot shot, and ran out of ammunition after getting its ninth tank. More ammunition had been sent for but had not arrived. It was therefore decided to withdraw and join a gun detachment of a nearby anti-tank battery. Some hours later, the detachment took over another gun and succeeded in killing a tenth tank, thereby reaching double figures in one day. On the other hand, owing, presumably, to the careful siting of the first gun, not a single shot was fired at it. All the enemy fire was directed at the three derelict Shermans and the decoy 6-pdr.

It is likely that this figure of ten tanks derives from a statement given by Sgt T. O'Brien after the battle was concluded, in which he claimed nine tanks for Sgt Watson's gun and one other, the latter having been knocked out when he brought forward another anti-tank gun some time later. So, we have a total of ten tanks from Sgt O'Brien – exactly the number given as a total for the 1st Tyneside Scottish by Lt Col A.E. Warhurst in his Immediate Report No. 25 – CAB106/963, and by the Anti-tank Platoon in its 0949 hrs report mentioned in the Battalion's War Diary intelligence log, WO171/1382.

However, Sgt S. Swaddle clearly describes his own gun as having knocked-out two tanks, and Capt J. S. Highmore's account claims that Sgt Day's gun knocked out another two. Therefore if we deduct these claims, plus Sgt O'Brien's single claim, from Warhurst's total of ten tanks knocked out by the Battalion's anti-tank guns, we are left with a figure of five tanks for Sgt Watson's gun. Indeed, Lt C. Mitchell, the Battalion IO, stated in his final report that one gun alone knocked out five tanks, and *Harder than*

Hammers, the Battalion's own history, states that five tanks were knocked-out in a very short space of time with his gun crew's first six shots, two of them at point-blank range. This figure would certainly make more sense, as timed signal reports suggested that the Panzers were attacking 'B' Company in groups of five, not twenty as O'Brien suggested. The truth is, we will never be able to say for sure just how many AFVs Sgt Watson's detachment put out of action, and in conclusion one could perhaps say that figures are irrelevant. Regardless of numbers, one fact remains indisputable – nobody could deny that Sgt Watson and his gallant team showed a great deal of cool determination and bravery when faced with a head-on SS-Panzer attack, and their achievement in halting the enemy's first assault on ring contour 110 should be seen as the perfect representation of men doing their duty in battle.

> ### Lt B.T.W. Stewart, 2nd i/c, Anti-tank Platoon, 'S' Company, 1st TS:
> *Visiting the guns, it appeared to me that not only were we set out in text book fashion, but also that the detachments were firing in exemplary text book manner. Perhaps the reason why we were doing so well was that the enemy's tanks were so close! I moved back to Battalion HQ looking for information and ammunition and learned that we were under heavy attack on all sides. When I returned to 'B' Section, commanded by Sgt D. Watson, I found that he and his two guns were in a sort of no man's land, surrounded by an extraordinary number of wrecked German tanks which he had destroyed since the beginning of the attack. Watson's gun had fired all its ammunition, so I doubled off to see how Sgt Swaddle and 'A' Section were faring.*

Defiladed in the hedgerow bank just to the north of 'B' Company's position, the guns of 'C' Troop of the 217th Battery, 55th Anti-tank Regiment, are also trying to halt the enemy. For the moment, Sgt Watson's anti-tank gun has stopped any tanks approaching 'B' Company's position from advancing towards the left, and so the next group deploy rather hesitatingly to the right, heading for the gap between 'B' and 'C' Companies. As they creep down the gap, the Panzers fire on 'C' Troop and destroy one of its guns. Now dangerously exposed, Sgt W. Hall of 'C' Troop decides to move his gun away from the hedgerow bank, manhandling it 350 yards away to a fresh position near an artillery OP. From here, Sgt Hall and his aimer, Bdr L.W. Sparrow, achieve a limited arc of fire at a range of 450 yards. As soon as he is in position, a tank in hull-down position creeps out from behind the smoke of another, burning tank. Visibility is very poor, but guided by the artillery OP which is situated on a higher level in a house in Rauray, Hall and his team lay and fire two rounds. Both rounds enter the turret, the second causing it to 'brew up'. A few minutes later, another tank does the same thing and as it clears the two burning tanks it is destroyed with a single round, the shot entering just above the track. However, success comes at a price. A tank moves out from some trees over on the right and advances across the gun's front and fires at it, killing one man and wounding several others. Undaunted, the remaining gunners fight back, laying more rounds. Eventually, the tank is forced to withdraw and soon after it is seen in flames (Sgt W. Hall was

awarded the DCM and his layer, Bdr L.W. Sparrow, the Croix de Guerre. Lt W.S. Vaughan, 'C' Troop Commander, received the MC).

0711 hrs • 'B' and 'C' Companies both request more ammunition and the Carrier Platoon sets off on its way to the front line for the first of the many trips it will make during the course of the battle.

Lt T. Armstrong, Motor Transport Officer, HQ Company, 1st TS:

About 0700 hrs, the Brigade Transport Officer of 70 Brigade, Capt D. Elrick, arrived at 'B' Echelon from Brigade HQ. He told me of the attack on the Battalion and instructed me that I should prepare to move forward the reserve ammunition trucks. At about the same time the RSM arrived stating that three-inch mortar and anti-tank gun ammunition was urgently required and he took this forward.

Sgt J. D. Wright, Section Commander, Carrier Platoon, 'S' Company, 1st TS:

I was that day employed with my carrier ferrying ammunition to the forward positions and bringing back wounded, often under heavy enemy fire. We made four such trips in all. One of the casualties I took back was a young Lance Corporal of another unit, probably DLI, who we found lying on the road. He was badly hurt, both his arms were in a very sorry state. I strapped them to his chest before we put him on to our carrier and conveyed him to our RAP.

Sgt D. Watson, 'B' Section Commander, Anti-tank platoon, 'S' Company, 1st TS:

When we got back beside one of the platoons (12 Platoon, 'B' Company), the RSM arrived with a carrier full of ammunition but by then it was too late. Lt McLaren then told the carrier driver to take me down to the RAP to have my knee seen to and I was soon on my way to hospital.

Over on the right flank, 'C' Company is fighting hard to remain in position, but Kampfgruppe Weidinger appears to be steadily gaining ground here and it cannot be long before some sections of 'C' Company will have to fall back towards the village.

Major W.K. Angus, Company Commander, 'C' Company, 1st TS:

So far as I could judge, the enemy were advancing in a north-easterly direction across my front. On the left, 14 platoon continued actively to engage the enemy, replenishing its ammunition stocks on several occasions. Sgt J. MacMillan, who was awarded the Military Medal, continued to give effective leadership, though wounded, until a second wound caused him to seek medical aid. After this, his platoon's resistance was no longer so effective.

L/Cpl N.E. Waters, Section Commander and LMG No. 1, 14 platoon, 'C' Company, 1st TS:

We had to pull out of our position on the left to what I recall was a wide path or lane and for the next couple of hours or so we were using the hedge bank on the lane as a firing position.

2 • 0725 hrs • 'C' Company is now finding itself short of men, its forward platoons are in serious danger of becoming boxed off by Weidinger Panzer-Grenadiers creeping in behind them. On the right, 13 Platoon appears to be completely surrounded, while on the left, 14 Platoon has been pushed sideways over towards the Rauray/Grainville road just north of ring contour 110.

Pte A. Henderson, rifleman, 13 Platoon, 'C' Company, 1st TS:

I heard a crashing noise and a soldier's leg came through our dug-out roof, but he kept on running. I thought at first it was a German soldier, so I said to John Laing 'Let's get out of here, we must be surrounded'.

3 • 0725 hrs • From their position on the edge of Rauray, the 11th Durham Light Infantry counter-attack the enemy with 'A' Troop, 24th Lancers in support. A platoon from 'A' Company (11 DLI) led by Capt R. Ellison, along with two carrier sections under Capt J.B. Nicholson,

successfully break up a Weidinger group as they attempt to infiltrate the fields between the Durhams and the 4th Lincolns to their right, and the mortar platoon manages to drive off an enemy tank.

4 • 0725 hrs • The remnant of 'B' Company is now also surrounded, but with remarkably determined optimism they send a report signalling that they are 'doing well'. One big advantage on the side of the defenders is now beginning to tell; the artillery appears to be finding the range of its targets, having had considerable success in dispersing enemy AFVs as they approach, and several have been 'brewed up' by well ranged shells. Unless it can withstand the pulverising effect of this continuous bombardment, SS-Pz Regt 9 will fail in its attempt to drive a large enough wedge between the 15th and 49th Divisions. However, it does appear to be having some success on the Battalion's left flank in 'A' Company's position – the five-sided field.

5 • 0730 hrs • The first report received from Capt D.C. Mirrielees of 'A' Company calls for urgent assistance. An enemy tank is in the area, firing into its lines. The German attack reached 'A' Company's position a little time after 'B' and 'C' were hit, but the charge of Panzers and Panzer-Grenadiers of the 9th SS-Panzer Division on the five-sided field was equally savage. Lying as it does alongside the road which 'Hohenstaufen' is using for its main thrust, 'A' Company's position is probably one of the hottest places in Normandy at this moment, and it will take some extremely brave support by the Shermans of the 24th Lancers on the eastern side of Rauray village if some of the Panzers supporting the main drive are to be held off from breaking through and fanning out across open fields.

Pte T.J. Renouf, rifleman, 7 Platoon, 'A' Company, 1st TS:

At some time before 0800 hrs, the shelling suddenly increased in concentration and accuracy into a barrage of deadly ferocity. It seemed as if the entire firepower of the enemy was directed on to our positions as the ground around us shook to the rapid succession of shells. During this time we were pinned in our slit trenches by the intensity of shrapnel above ground level, and seldom were we able to move out to our observation position looking over the bund. The positioning of the slit trenches was unfortunate, not only because there was no observation to our front directly from the trenches, but because of the additional hazard introduced by the tall trees on top of the bund. Some of the shells directed at our position were exploding in the trees and showering shrapnel downwards into our trenches. The memorable feature of our trench which now emerged was that it was partly roofed with logs cut to size, giving us considerable extra protection against the flying shrapnel.

During this time, casualties were mounting and soon there was a continuous stream of wounded crawling back past our slit trenches, some suffering further injury as they went. Many of these men were bleeding badly and had to get back while they still had strength, but to do so they knew they had to run the gauntlet of deadly shellfire. All of a sudden the shelling stopped, it seemed to be lifted off the forward companies and laid on the reserve. The reason for this was to

A 6-pounder anti-tank gun emplaced in a hedgerow.

become immediately apparent. When we climbed up the bund to our observation position, we saw that the enemy was attacking. There were four tanks fairly near our position and these were followed by advancing infantrymen. It was around this time that the order to evacuate reached our section. We travelled for about 100 yards inside the hedgerow along the road. This meant that we were visible neither from the roadway, which was now a line of enemy fire, nor from their tanks advancing into the field. It also meant that we were scratched and torn by a multitude of thorns. It was necessary to abandon our small packs as we struggled through the thickets.

Pte A. Corris, rifleman, 7 Platoon, 'A' Company, 1st TS:

The silence was shattered by a battery of those 'Moaning Minnie' rocket launchers, that familiar high-pitched 'Whow, Whow, Whow' we knew so well. We also knew from experience that if you saw the first and second rocket explode, you could be sure that the following rockets from the salvo would come in an increasing straight line. They passed overhead some 100 to 200 yards to our rear where the remainder of 'A' Company was dug in. This lasted about five minutes, then stopped and immediately the tanks to our front started up and moved forward. Some went left, some right, and the remainder headed our way. About 30 yards to our right, I saw Sgt Thompson and a couple of lads get off two rockets from a PIAT, but as usual they bounced harmlessly off the first tank without exploding and for their gallant effort the lads received a tank shell which blew them to pieces. We crawled to the rear as the tank gun layers and machine gunners took over from the 'Moaning Minnies'.

Lt J.T. Griffiths, Platoon Commander, 9 Platoon, 'C' Company, 2nd Kensingtons:

The field telephone was out of action, the line probably cut by the shelling. I was trying to raise the forward section by phone, when the abandoned British tank near it was hit and a large explosion resulted. We could see that the effect was to cause the men of the section to leave their meagre shelter and swan about. I decided to dash over to them. I realised at once that the debris from the tank, so near the poorly dug-in unit, had caused considerable damage. Pte H. McNulty, an eighteen year old who had joined us as one of the replacements only two days earlier, was badly injured and our two Vickers guns were apparently out of action. The men were all very shocked so I decided that we should withdraw since we were of no use where we were. We got back to the HQ area of the field carrying the injured McNulty and suffered no more casualties. Leaving the platoon sergeant to organise the men into a defensive line along the ditch, I then visited my second section which was already in action. It was in good shape and was able to help repulse the attack and continue in the action. Back at HQ I found Major Pinks had arrived and was organising replacement guns and ammo, and soon we had both sections in the action again. Despite the efforts of our medical orderly and other para-medics; poor McNulty died.

Capt A. MacLagan, Platoon Commander, Anti-tank Platoon, 'S' Company, 1st TS:

Alternately seeking some cover and then running, I began to make my way back to my HQ. During a lull and looking back, I was aware that the line of the attack appeared to be diagonally across 'A' and 'B' Company's positions, towards that of the Kings Own Scottish Borderers. Heavy enemy mortar fire continued, and when I reached a point some 50 yards short of my HQ, I was hit and severely wounded. I lay for some time, passing out and coming to, until I eventually saw Lt D. Salisbury, the Signals Officer, retiring in his carrier towards Battalion HQ. I attracted his attention with a short burst from my Sten and he and his men heaved me aboard, saving me and carrying me to the RAP.

Sgt S.C. Swaddle, 'A' Section Commander, Anti-tank Platoon, 'S' Company, 1st TS:

As the battle started we stood by our guns, most of the trouble coming in on Sgt D. Watson's position (No. 3). I was listening to the gun shots but could not help to see the tanks off Sgt Watson.

The road from Queudeville along which the Hohenstaufen Panzers made their attack. On the right is the entrance gate into the five-sided field.

Universal (Bren) carrier.

Everyone was on alert first as riflemen until tanks appeared on our front. Five tanks came along the road, three carried straight on and the other two came through the fence of the field in front, towards my gun. No. 1 gun team then took up position. I gave instructions for the two tanks to be allowed to get within about 100 yards of us. They appeared to be moving across towards Sgt Watson's gun on our right. We attacked the second tank first. On firing our first shot, we found although we could see the tank through the sights, the shot went into the embankment 5 feet in front of us, so as a team we pushed the gun forward placing the barrel over the embankment. Our second and third shots killed the second tank. We then turned to the first tank and hit the target with two shots. It stopped dead. We had fired five rounds of Sabot. I then began to wonder about the other three tanks and if they had troubled the other gun, so I left my team with instructions to stay in their trenches and use the gun if needed, I was going to see what we could do from our No. 2 gun.

On approaching the gun, I found that it had taken a direct hit on the barrel, ripping the slide right off. One man was wounded in the legs (Pte H. Allen). I told him to make his way back down the hedge as there was bound to be some first aid behind, but he could not walk or crawl and he asked me to take him out. With the help of L/Cpl W. Barclay, we took him to safety, running all the time under small arms fire with Hughie on our shoulders. When we got to the bottom of the *field there was nobody there, so I left Bill Barclay with Hughie and went in search for help. This I could not find, and when I returned to the other two they were no longer there (Barclay had carried Allen back to the RAP). Later, I saw Barclay in a trench and joined him there. It was not long before a platoon went past us towards the front and we were told to go back and rest a bit. I never saw my two gun teams anymore. Our Platoon Sergeant saw us and said that one man was missing, the rest wounded – only Barclay and myself alive for another day.*

Pte H. Allen, Gun Number, No. 2 Detachment, Anti-tank Platoon, 'S' Company, 1st TS:

Early that morning we came under heavy mortar fire and all our detachment were hit, the Detachment Commander (Cpl J. Drysdale) being the first one. I jumped into a slit trench and was almost immediately caught by a mortar bomb, being wounded in the left leg and right knee so badly that I couldn't move. Some time later our Section Commander, Sgt S. Swaddle, came to our position and with help from L/Cpl W. Barclay, took me to safety. Taking turns, they carried me over their shoulders all the way back to the RAP (one and a half miles). Our gun was damaged by the enemy fire and we never fired a shot with it (a crucial factor, as this gun covered the road and formed a major part of 'A' Company's protection against the 9th SS-Pz Regt attacks).

Cpl J. Drysdale, No. 2 Detachment Commander, Anti-tank Platoon, 'S' Company, 1st TS:

At dawn, the Jerries attacked and my gun crew, including myself, were hit. I was in the slit trench and some of the lads put me out in the open. They said they would send a Bren carrier down for me, but alas the Jerries came up to our positions. I tried to get back into the trench, then there was a bang and I was lifted up bodily and dropped into the trench. I was shot at all the time I was on top.

Pte J.L.R. Samson, Bren-gunner, No. 4 Detachment, Anti-tank Platoon, 'S' Company, 1st TS:

Soon I heard the full-throated roar of tank engines and some 200 to 300 yards in front, between the two woods facing us, I saw about half a dozen tanks. The Detachment Commander, Cpl S Cummings, ordered 'Take post!' and the crew dashed up to the gun, some 25 yards from the pits. I began to look over my Bren. Being the Detachment Bren gunner, I had to remain in my slit trench. The tanks seemed to be lying out there without any movement and I found myself thinking, hoping and praying that they would not discover our position before we could get the first shot in. I sat there awaiting the order to fire on either the enemy infantry when they became visible, or on the Panzers to make them close their lids. Unluckily, our gun was dug-in deeply in a shell hole, so that it was impossible to get our sights on to the tanks. But fortunately on the other hand, the tanks had not seen us. A few minutes later, the platoon 2nd i/c, Lt B.

Stewart, arrived and said that we were the only gun not in action, but that we would be so shortly as we were with the far left-hand company of the Division (49th Division). Some 100 yards to our left over a road lay the far right-hand company of the 15th Division and it was believed that Jerry was attempting to drive down the road between the two Divisions

Troops digging in beside Sherman tanks, Rauray, 29 June 1944.

Lt B.T.W. Stewart, 2nd i/c, Anti-tank Platoon, 'S' Company, 1st TS:
When I reached Sgt Swaddle's position, I found that he had already knocked-out two Panzers with his gun when the Germans had tried to come round our left flank. I found both detachments in good heart, despite the hail of shot, shell and mortar bombs, and justifiably

proud of their marksmanship. But Corporal Drysdale, commanding No. 2 gun, was badly injured. Somewhere along the line I had discovered that Capt MacLagan was 'hors de combat', and so I was acting Anti-tank Platoon Commander and using the HQ carrier instead of my motorcycle. I now sprinted back to this carrier, found a medic and returned to try and improve Drysdale's situation. We dared not move Drysdale without a stretcher, but I took away two other wounded men from his detachment. As I returned to the RAP with the two wounded men in my carrier, I met the Support Company Commander in the middle of an open field. He too was in a carrier, and stopped to discuss the situation, standing up! At which point, a Panzer ranged on us and a large splinter from a shell hit my leg, nullifying all my earlier efforts to avoid enemy fire by sprinting and dodging. I felt nothing; there was no serious pain, although when I looked down I saw to my surprise that the sharp stab had made a large hole in my left thigh. I slapped on a field dressing and continued on my journey. On delivering the casualties at the RAP, I was told to submit to medical orders and removed from my carrier. The wound was beginning to be painful and I was losing a lot of blood. My legs were bound together, sulphur powder was poured into the hole in my thigh, and I was ordered out of the action and sent to hospital.

Capt J.S. Highmore, Company Commander, 'D' Company, 1st TS:
I heard over the No. 18 radio set from the CO, Lt Col de Winton, that 'A' and 'B' Companies were heavily engaged but holding and that some 'Big Bears' (tanks) were coming to help out.

6 • 0735 hrs • 1st and 3rd Troops from 'C' Squadron of the 24th Lancers have moved across to the orchard about 500 yards behind 'A' Company's position to reinforce 2nd and 4th Troops. Their job will be to stop the Panzers from advancing beyond the five-sided field. From the hedges here it is possible to fire forward about 800–1,000 yards, straight at the gap between 'A' and 'B' Companies where the enemy's tanks are attempting to force a breakthrough. Targets in 'B' Company's area are also being successfully engaged by the Shermans. For the men of 'D' Company, sheltering in their slit trenches positioned in the field immediately in front, the deafening report from the salvo of fire from the Lancers is shatteringly loud.

Pte P. Lawton, PIAT No. 1, 18 Platoon, 'D' Company, 1st TS:
I remember that the Sherman tanks of our support troop were firing from positions only a few feet behind us, but because of the height of the corn we had no idea what or where their targets were.

Gnr J. Mercer, 185th Field Regiment Observation Post:
On the left, some Sherman tanks were moving up to reinforce our troops. One was struck by an AP shell fired from an 88 mm gun. It 'brewed up', its crew jumped out in haste and it caught fire and exploded. One man was in flames (from Mike Target by John Mercer).

The American Mk 4 Sherman tank was notorious for the ease with which it caught fire. Gruesomely nicknamed 'Tommy Cooker' by the Germans, flames could sweep through the body of the tank in about three seconds. With such a short time available for escape, tank crews had little or no chance of escaping the conflagration, and this difficulty was added to by another problem. The Sherman's front hatch was positioned below the gun barrel when it was pointing ahead, therefore the tank's drivers could only escape when the gun was at right angles to this position, left or right.

7 • 0755 hrs • Despite all the hard work done by the anti-tank guns, a few enemy AFVs have penetrated the 70th Brigade's outer defences and it is clear that some elements are about to enter the outskirts of Rauray itself. A German tank, with infantry close behind, has burst through and is setting itself for action in hull-down position 150 yards from the tanks of 'C' Squadron, 24th Lancers. Immediately, Major B. Luddington manoeuvres his Shermans into positions where they can harry the incursive Panzer.

STAGE FOUR

0800–0900 HRS – SURROUNDED

The full light of day brings with it both clarity and confusion. There is little doubt that the 1st Tyneside Scottish are caught in the press of a resolute attempt by the enemy to burst through at the point between XXX and VIII Corps. However, the leafy cover of orchards and tree-filled hedgerows make it very difficult to gauge how effective the enemy's initial attack has been and there is a great deal of confusion as to what is developing around the surrounding bocage. Although anti-tank guns have prevented the Panzers from slicing through the Battalion, small groups of KG Weidinger Panzer-Grenadiers have infiltrated between 'A', 'B' and 'C' Companies and snipers are setting up positions in the orchards between the 11th DLI and the 4th Lincolns.

Lt B.T.W. Stewart, 2nd i/c, Anti-tank Platoon, 'S' Company, 1st TS:
Each gun detachment had two Loyd carriers. These were small, tracked vehicles, steered by levers which applied breaks to the tracks, slewing the carrier around as need be. Accurate and efficient double declutching of the gears, and practise with the levers, made for considerable manoeuvrability. When tracks became dislodged, practised Jocks could get them back on fairly fast – but repairs in the open in front of an enemy tank force, were unpleasantly exposed and fraught. I observed that track repair under these conditions was much faster than usual!

Pte J.L.R. Samson, Bren-gunner, No. 4 Detachment, Anti-tank Platoon, 'S' Company, 1st TS:
One of our Loyd carriers with ammunition was driven up to our position and we left our action posts to unload a few boxes of AP and HE shells. At this time, we were under light mortar fire and we had hardly taken one box off the carrier when it received a bomb straight on the engine. The carrier burst into flames and the driver, who was handing out

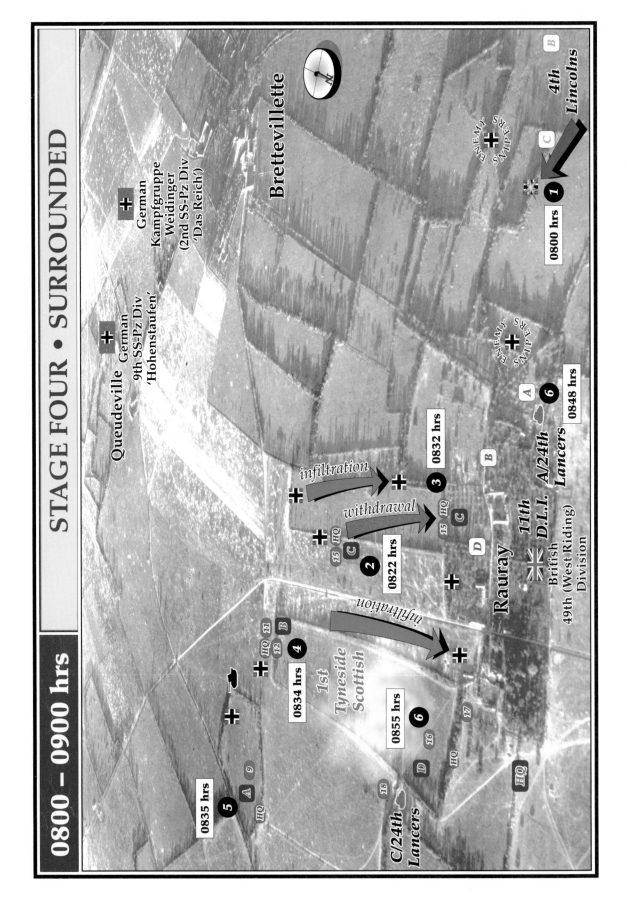

STAGE FOUR • SURROUNDED

0800 – 0900 hrs

Brettevillette

Queudeville

German
Kampfgruppe
Weidinger
(2nd SS-Pz Div
'Das Reich')

German
9th SS-Pz Div
'Hohenstaufen'

ENEMY SNIPERS

ENEMY SNIPERS

4th
Lincolns

B

C

0800 hrs

1

0848 hrs

6

A/24th
Lancers

A

6

0832 hrs

3

infiltration

withdrawal

HQ

15 C

B

D

11th
D.L.I.

Rauray

British
49th (West Riding)
Division

0822 hrs

2

HQ

15 C

infiltration

0834 hrs

4

HQ 11
12 B

1st
Tyneside
Scottish

0835 hrs

5

HQ
A 9

0855 hrs

6

D 16

HQ

17

HQ

18

C/24th
Lancers

the ammunition, jumped out. The petrol tanks of this type of vehicle were in front with the engine at the back, therefore it was only a matter of minutes before the fire would reach the petrol. The driver and Detachment Commander tried to put out the flames with fire extinguishers, but it was a losing battle and the carrier soon looked like a 'Brock's Benefit', with 2-inch mortar bombs, 6-pounder and small arms ammunition all exploding. The Jerry mortar observers must have spotted the blaze, for the mortar bombs seemed to come over far too fast for our liking. The 'strafing' was such that our gun numbers were obliged to leave the gun-pit and take shelter in the slit trenches. In doing so, the Detachment Commander was hit in the hand by a fragment from a mortar burst. We were now feeling pretty unhappy, being helpless to do anything. However, things were moving far too fast to be actually terrifying, especially seeing the good example of our Detachment Commander.

Sgt J.D. Wright, Section Commander, Carrier Platoon, 'S' Company, 1st TS:

I went forward with a Bren gun and an officer to try to pinpoint a sniper, and as I was creeping forward past a gun-towing vehicle, it was hit by a mortar and set on fire and all the small arms ammunition and shells on board it started exploding.

On the 4th Lincolns' front, 'B' Company (4th Lincolns), under the command of Major W. E. Pattin, have put up a stout defence in the fields directly to the south-east of Tessel-Bretteville, but a group of Weidinger Panzer-Grenadiers have managed to fight their way further into the Lincolns' area.

1 • 0800 hrs • A swift counter-attack by 'C' Company (4th Lincolns) successfully halts the enemy's penetration between them and the 11th Durham Light Infantry, plugging the gap that was appearing between the 70th and 146th Brigades and making the 49th Division's western flank considerably firmer. Artillery support for the 4th Lincolns is being provided by the 69th Field Regiment.

0800 hrs • Four German prisoners are brought in. They prove to be men from I/SS-PzGR 4 'Der Führer', Kampfgruppe Weidinger. One is an Alsatian and not a volunteer.

Lt C. Mitchell, Intelligence Officer, Battalion HQ, 1st TS:

These were pretty miserable specimens of Hitler's picked troops (Public Record Office WO171/1382).

L/Cpl A. Richardson, Regimental Police Officer, Police Section, Battalion HQ, 1st TS:

A company truck arrived, and I was ordered to take them to Brigade HQ.

Lt I.W. Murray, Platoon Commander, 17 Platoon, 'D' Company, 1st TS:

We did capture a few of our assailants who, far from being subdued and resigned to their fate, demanded cigarettes and 'feuer'. They were just laddies in their mid-teens.

0812 hrs • 'C' Company is claiming that the first enemy soldiers to reach its position were wearing British uniforms (the 1947 history of the Battalion, *Harder than Hammers*, claims that British POWs were being driven on in front of the Panzer-Grenadiers as the first attack went in, the possibility of which had been previously mooted by the Intelligence Officer, Lt C. Mitchell, in his July 1944 War Diary account).

2 • 0822 hrs • On the Battalion's right, 'C' Company's situation, although not altogether clear-cut, is starting to look pretty hopeless. The two forward platoons of 'C' Company (13 and 14), appear to be completely cut off and are judged to have been overrun. Major Angus, together with 15 Platoon, is holding on, but the enemy, who has been infiltrating round his right side for some time, is now beginning to press from the left. Some of his men have been taken prisoner by the Germans, and for them, the battle has taken on a new and disheartening aspect.

Pte G.J. Malone, rifleman, 13 Platoon, 'C' Company, 1st TS:
Our trench was well forward and we had not received any word to retreat. Pte A. Pryde, who had joined me in my trench during the night, was wounded in the arm that morning and we were taken back behind the German lines. There were another three chaps in a barn there and one said that they were from 'B' Company, but I did not know any of them. Pte Pryde and I were put on an armoured vehicle and taken to a first aid station where we were separated.

(Private Malone was attached to Stalag 8 at Sagan and sent to work at a sugar factory outside Breslau, where he remained until January 1945. When the Russians started to advance from the east, he was moved out of the factory and marched 800 kilometres to the province of Hanover, where he was liberated on 16th April 1945).

Pte A. Henderson, rifleman, 13 Platoon, 'C' Company, 1st TS:
I crawled over into the next field which was covered with long grass or straw and bumped into a German tank. I said to Pte Laing, 'Keep down beside me and crawl close to the hedgerow'. We reached the bottom of the hedgerow where there was an anti-tank gun, and a soldier, whom I did not recognise, said to me, 'Are you staying Jock?', and I said, 'Yes'. When I looked back at the tank, it seemed to have stopped. A head was sticking out of the turret. I fired a shot and it disappeared into the tank. There was a dead soldier lying by his Bren gun at the side of a gate. I moved him to one side and began firing across the open field at some movement.

3 • 0832 hrs • Major Angus and the remains of 'C' Company, who have been fully stretched for the last hour or so, are now being compelled to give ground by their assailants, and HQ gives Angus permission to fall back and form a link with the 11th DLI immediately behind. This he does, and his group establish a firm base on the southern side of an orchard on the edge of Rauray village. With their backs protected, it should be possible for them halt any further advance by enemy infantry.

Major W.K. Angus, Company Commander, 'C' Company, 1st TS:

My Company HQ was not well situated for front line defence, and with the survivors from my forward platoons, I withdrew to a south facing hedgerow about 100 yards north of my previous position. I continued to engage such of the enemy as were visible in the area formerly occupied by my left platoon (14 Platoon). The enemy tried to move along the hedge running north-west from that platoon's former position. We were able to hold them up about 25 yards from our position and they later withdrew after killing a stretcher bearer engaged in evacuating wounded.

4 • 0834 hrs • 'B' Company, like 'C', has now been fighting solidly for two hours, and amid the smoke and clamour of battle some platoons have become disjointed, 12 Platoon moving back to the field behind the Company's slits to regroup. However, Capt Calderwood is still in position and now reports that his group is holding firm and has the situation in hand.

Lt J.F. McLaren, Platoon Commander, 12 Platoon, 'B' Company, 1st TS:

All the Jocks I could see were banging away, but the visibility was poor and apart from 11 Platoon I couldn't really see anyone else. Fire from our people seemed to die down and enemy tanks were more or less on our position. I had no contact with Company HQ, either verbally or by wireless. At some time, a Jock, I think Major Calderwood's batman, fell into my slit trench and gave me to believe, wrongly, that the Company Commander had been killed. By this time the anti-tank guns were out of action and I could see no sign of life other than some of my own platoon. At this point I took the decision to order the few troops I was in contact with to fall back, in the first place, to the hedge in our rear and then to the reserve company position at the bottom of the next field.

Pte J. Quigley, rifleman, 12 Platoon, 'B' Company, 1st TS

Early on, 'B' Company pulled out of its positions but soon returned to them. I was then hit by a mortar bomb splinter in the thigh and evacuated.

5 • 0835 hrs • Capt Mirrillees, the commander of 'A' Company, is now told by the 70th Brigade HQ to link up with the 6th KOSB on his left and to watch the Battalion's flank (one imagines this would have been difficult to accomplish given that the forward company of the 6th KOSB, 'C' Company, was also severely hard-pressed at this time). Those scattered sections of 'A' Company, whose slits ran along the left side of southern hedgerow of the five-sided field, have now drifted in a north-easterly direction towards an area south of le Haut de Bosq, to the north of the 6th KOSB.

6 • 0848 hrs • Once more, the 11th DLI sets about dealing with enemy infiltration on the western side of Rauray. While its companies have found it difficult to ascertain the wider picture of the battle from

their positions around the village's orchards, each man appears to be content with doing his own job, and the Durhams are refusing to be uprooted or unsettled by Spandau fire, mortar bombs or tank shelling, the latter reported to be 'most unpleasant'. Like their Tyneside Scottish neighbours, the Durhams are being well supported by their Mortar Platoon, who have on two occasions driven off an enemy AFV that was shelling their lines.

7 • 0855 hrs • On the eastern side of Rauray village, 'D' Company, 1st Tyneside Scottish, report smoke being put down in front of its position. Around the perimeter of its long oblong field, the Battalion's reserve company has engaged in several small-scale skimishes with the enemy and No. 5 Detachment of the Anti-tank Platoon has knocked out two AFVs.

Pte G.E. Rolle, rifleman, 18 Platoon, 'D' Company, 1st TS:
Three tanks approached, crossing our front. The leading tank was knocked out by our anti-tank gun (No. 5), the other two withdrew.

Capt J.S. Highmore, Company Commander, 'D' Company, 1st TS:
During the course of the battle I visited the anti-tank gun detachment (No. 5) which was located in the area of my right-hand platoon (18 Platoon). The detachment commander (Sgt W. Day) was delighted with his crew's and gun's performance, claimed two tanks destroyed and pleaded for more Sabot ammunition which was then very secret and in short supply.

Pte J.R. Hodgkyns, rifleman, 18 Platoon, 'D' Company, 1st TS:
My platoon advanced down the road to Rauray and as we proceeded a Spandau gun opened fire at the end of the road. I dived for cover, as everyone else did, but we engaged the enemy and knocked out the Spandau with our 2-inch mortar and the enemy retreated across a field at the end of the road, into a small wood. I saw one of our section wounded and realised he could not walk. I carried him to the RAP and then rejoined my section, which by then had crossed the field to the hedgerow on the edge of the wood. The enemy had retreated to the other side of it and we all dug in the best way we could. After some 'Moaning Minnie' fire, the enemy came out of the wood, but soon took cover as we opened fire. We were told we must hold this position because of the road.

Capt J.S. Highmore, Company Commander, 'D' Company, 1st TS:
About mid-morning, my right-hand platoon (18 Platoon) reported German infantry working their way down a typical bocage hedge towards the anti-tank gun position (No. 5) and Company HQ. They were engaged with small arms fire which would have been pretty ineffective because of the valley between the high banks topped with trees and thick hedging. I remember climbing on top of the Sherman tank parked in the Company HQ area (another one here had been knocked out by this time I think) and asked the

Commander if he could fire a few rounds of HE to explode in the branches of the trees above the ditch and stop the enemy infiltration. He obliged effectively because nothing further developed from that hedge. I remember the view of the battlefield from the top of that tank and recall seeing at least half-a-dozen burning German tanks. They were mainly in the area where I imagined 'A' and 'B' Companies to be located.

CF C.W. Chesworth, Battalion Chaplain, Battalion HQ, 1st TS:

The only time we were able offer some assistance to each other was of course in the lull which took place between the shelling. It was then that we emerged out of our slit trenches and went to the aid of anybody who was in desperate trouble. As Chaplain, I did everything I could to help those who were wounded or dying and gave them what spiritual, as well as physical, assistance I could manage to offer, which always seemed to be very poor at the time.

Pte S. Leedale, Medical Orderly, Medical Platoon, Battalion HQ, 1st TS:

We were busy all the time with first aid dressings for wounds from bullets and shrapnel. The Medical Officer and Padre covered for morphine, tallies, blessing and supplies. Boys from 'brewed up' tanks

A computer-generated model of a Panzerkampfwagen Mk V 'Panther'.

Major Luddington was awarded a Military Cross for his achievements at Rauray. His leadership was later described as being a great source of strength and inspiration not only to his own squadron but also to the 1st Tyneside Scottish infantry he was supporting, and was largely instrumental in Rauray being in British hands at the end of a day of difficult and confused fighting.

Infantry passing Sherman tanks, Rauray, 26 June 1944.

were a very sorry sight, most of their clothes scorched off their bodies. We made them comfortable with sulphamide and gauze pads for their arms and chest, and masks for their faces – burnt grey with eyes red. We were located in a cow byre, the gable end of which faced the rear of the CO's point.

In Rauray village, the 24th Lancers' business with the hull-down Panzer has now been concluded and the German tank has withdrawn, its threat having been eliminated by Major Luddington and 'C' Squadron of the 24th Lancers.

STAGE FIVE

0900-1000 HRS - PINNED DOWN BY GUNFIRE

Although the enemy's initial attack has failed to force a breakthrough, Kampfgruppe Weidinger Panzer-Grenadiers have infiltrated deep into the territory being defended by the 1st Tyneside Scottish. The response by British artillery and tank fire, supplemented by naval guns firing from warships lying off the Normandy coast, has checked any serious penetration by AFVs of SS-Panzer Regiment 9, but determined snipers and Spandau teams have managed to take up strong positions on the edge of Rauray.

Despite taking some casualties, the 2nd Kensingtons have got in some good shooting. The remaining machine guns, joined by the Brens and rifles of 9 Platoon HQ, are now supporting 1st TS 'D' Company. In reserve, 11 Platoon, 'C' Company, 2nd Kensingtons are with the Durham Light Infantry behind the village.

Pte T.H. Clark, Batman driver to 2nd i/c, 'C' Company, 2nd Kensingtons:

There was plenty going on behind a huge wall some two to three hundred yards ahead. I took up a position by a large opening in our field – to my left, a grass verge on which many Durhams lay side by side whilst others were regrouping to return to the fray, led by a major.

Sgt A. Greenland, Platoon Sergeant, 11 Platoon, 'C' Company, 2nd Kensingtons:

A vivid recollection, even after all these years, is of some tanks behind us (possibly Sherwood Rangers Yeomanry) being torched by

STAGE FIVE • PINNED DOWN BY GUNFIRE

0900 – 1000 hrs

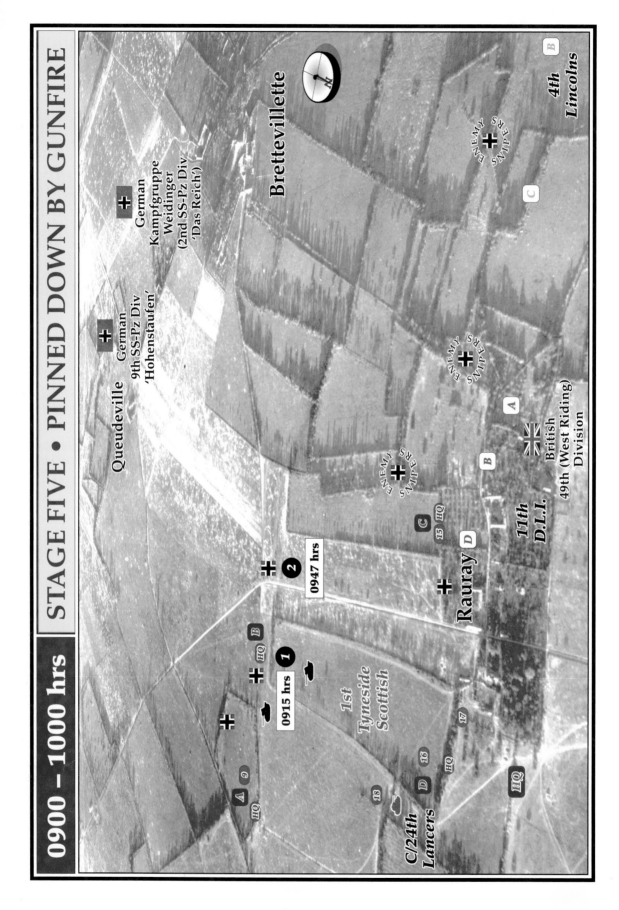

Brettevillette

Queudeville

German
9th SS-Pz Div
'Hohenstaufen'

German
Kampfgruppe
Weidinger
(2nd SS-Pz Div
'Das Reich')

ENEMY SNIPERS

ENEMY SNIPERS

ENEMY SNIPERS

A

B

C

British
49th (West Riding)
Division

4th
Lincolns

B

C

11th
D.I.L.

Rauray

D

C

15

HQ

2
0947 hrs

1st
Tyneside
Scottish

B

HQ

1
0915 hrs

17

16

HQ

9

A

HQ

18

D

HQ

C/24th
Lancers

enemy guns. There were snipers about, and it must have been from one such that I received a wound in my left arm as I was getting out of my trench to make my way back to Company HQ for a meal.

0903 hrs • 'A' Company report an enemy tank moving north behind 'B' Company's position. The Shermans of the 24th Lancers are unable leave the protection of the leafy orchard to the east of Rauray as two tanks are dominating the ground from positions on each flank, but they hold their position within the cover of the trees.

0904 hrs • In Rauray village, the 11th DLI report that it has consolidated and its position is now firm.

1 • 0915 hrs • 'B' Company reports that it is being subjected to machine gun fire from its left.

0930 hrs • Enemy Spandaus now have what is left of 'B' Company completely pinned down, and as they crouch in their slits listening to the familiar ripping sound of the Mk 42, the small band can only wait and hope for reinforcements. Behind them, the carriers are having to fight their way up to ring contour 110 to supply the defending group with ammunition.

Cpl J.W.H. Tipler, Section Commander, 18 Platoon, 'D' Company, 1st TS:

The bombardment continued and at approximately 0900–0930 hrs, CSM 'Paddy' Shanks organized a hot drink which we went for in turn. I remember he was his usual debonair self, laughing and joking about being 'bomb-happy' and so on – good for morale.

Pte (A/Cpl) J.W. Barnes, Section Commander, 18 Platoon, 'D' Company, 1st TS:

As the morning wore on, there was a small diversion from the otherwise grim prospect. This was provided by CSM Shanks, or 'Paddy' as he was more generally known. He turned up on a battered 'Don R' motorcycle. He made the rounds of the Company area on it, distributing bandoliers and offering anyone who was interested a swig of some unspecified fluid from a large stone jar balanced on the tank of the bike. The rear tyre of the machine was flat and it bore the marks of a hazardous life, bits of the engine finning obviously having had the attention of passing shrapnel. I suggested to CSM Shanks that perhaps it wasn't the safest way to spend the day. His only reply was that he had noticed several dirty mess tins that morning! No 'pibble pubble' in Paddy's camp.

Word was passed on that 'they' had smashed up 'B' Company with tanks and infantry, partially overrun some of 'A' Company's perimeter and were heading our way, and we could expect to be engaged soon. By 0930 hrs, concentrated mortar, artillery and rocket fire was falling directly on our positions. In addition, small arms fire from automatic weapons began to arrive from some source on our left front. Sometime between 0930 and 1000 hrs, a KOSB lance-corporal asked me if I could help him with some wounded. I went with him and found several dead KOSB but no wounded. Whilst searching for wounded, we were fired upon by German infantry at a range of perhaps 80 yards. They were approaching through the trees. We took cover in a gun pit containing a German MG42 (Spandau) on a mount with three dead crew. The lance-corporal turned the gun mount round, but the gun would not fire. The Bren gun he was carrying also chose this moment to become non-operative. Thus we had to resort to rifles, with which we returned fire. At this moment, I saw a group of, presumably, KOSB approach on our left front and engage the enemy with heavy automatic fire. As no more fire came in our direction, I assume that the Germans were either eliminated or withdrew. I shook hands with the KOSB 'lance jack' and left to return to my own trench. This proved to be a somewhat protracted process, the whole area being subject to heavy bombardment.

On 'C' Company's front, Major Angus looks through his binoculars and wonders if any members of his other platoons could be holding out, still in position and waiting to be relieved. He leaves his remaining platoon in its position on the south side of Rauray and goes forward, searching his way along the hedgerows in a desperate attempt to try and locate and rally as many of his front line men as he can.

Major W.K. Angus.

> ### Pte A. Henderson, rifleman, 13 Platoon, 'C' Company, 1st TS:
> *Major Angus came out of nowhere and ordered us to follow him.*

0942 hrs • It appears that Major Angus has been suprisingly successful in his quest for survivors, as he now reports that he has managed to collect together two officers and twenty-five other ranks, and they are now all back safely with the rest of 'C' Company and are in touch with the 11th DLI in Rauray. Other members of the company have not been so fortunate. Back in the area of 14 Platoon's slits, many still lie dying and wounded and it will be hours before they can be reached and brought to safety.

> ### Pte A.J. Stephens, LMG No. 1, 14 Platoon, 'C' Company, 1st TS:
> *I was the cut-off Bren, with my No. 2, covering 14 Platoon falling back on Rauray. A German tank with infantry support broke through on my right and I and my No. 2 engaged them. Our position then came under mortar fire. They later found me lying wounded and my No. 2 dead. I regret that due to the nature of my injury brought about by the explosion, my memory is extremely hazy.*

2 • 0947 hrs • The 11th DLI seem to have located the source of the machine gun fire that is pinning down 'B' Company, as it now reports that an enemy Spandau team has been observed in a damaged tank north-west of ring contour 110.

> ### Sgt T. O'Brien, Anti-tank Platoon, 'S' Company, 1st TS:
> *We went back and picked up another gun and knocked out another tank. We fought our way forward with this gun and got to within two yards of the position of the first gun (No. 3).*

0949 hrs • A report comes in that anti-tank guns have knocked out fifteen tanks. Ten are claimed by the 1st Tyneside Scottish gunners and five by the 217th Battalion, 55th Anti-tank Regiment. However, most of the anti-tank guns are now damaged and out of the battle. From now on, the defence of Rauray will mainly depend on the brave efforts of the 24th Lancers and static artillery firing from positions further back.

Lt B.T.W. Stewart, 2nd i/c, Anti-tank Platoon, 'S' Company:, 1st TS:
By this time the Anti-tank Platoon had done its duty, and whether the total number of enemy tanks destroyed by its 6-pounders was ten, twelve or fourteen, it was a magnificent performance and the exchange was certainly cost effective – a tank was worth a lot more than a gun!

Bretteville

Brettevillette

German
Kampfgruppe
Weidinger
(2nd SS-Pz Div
'Das Reich')

Queudeville

German
9th SS-Pz Div
'Hohenstaufen'

ENEMY SNIPERS

ENEMY SNIPERS

ENEMY SNIPERS

B

4th
Lincolns

C

A

British
49th (West Riding)
Division

B

11th
D.L.I.

C   HQ

D

15

Rauray

HQ

1005 hrs

B

HQ

1

2

1049 hrs

17

16

HQ

18

D

A   9

HQ

HQ

C/24th
Lancers

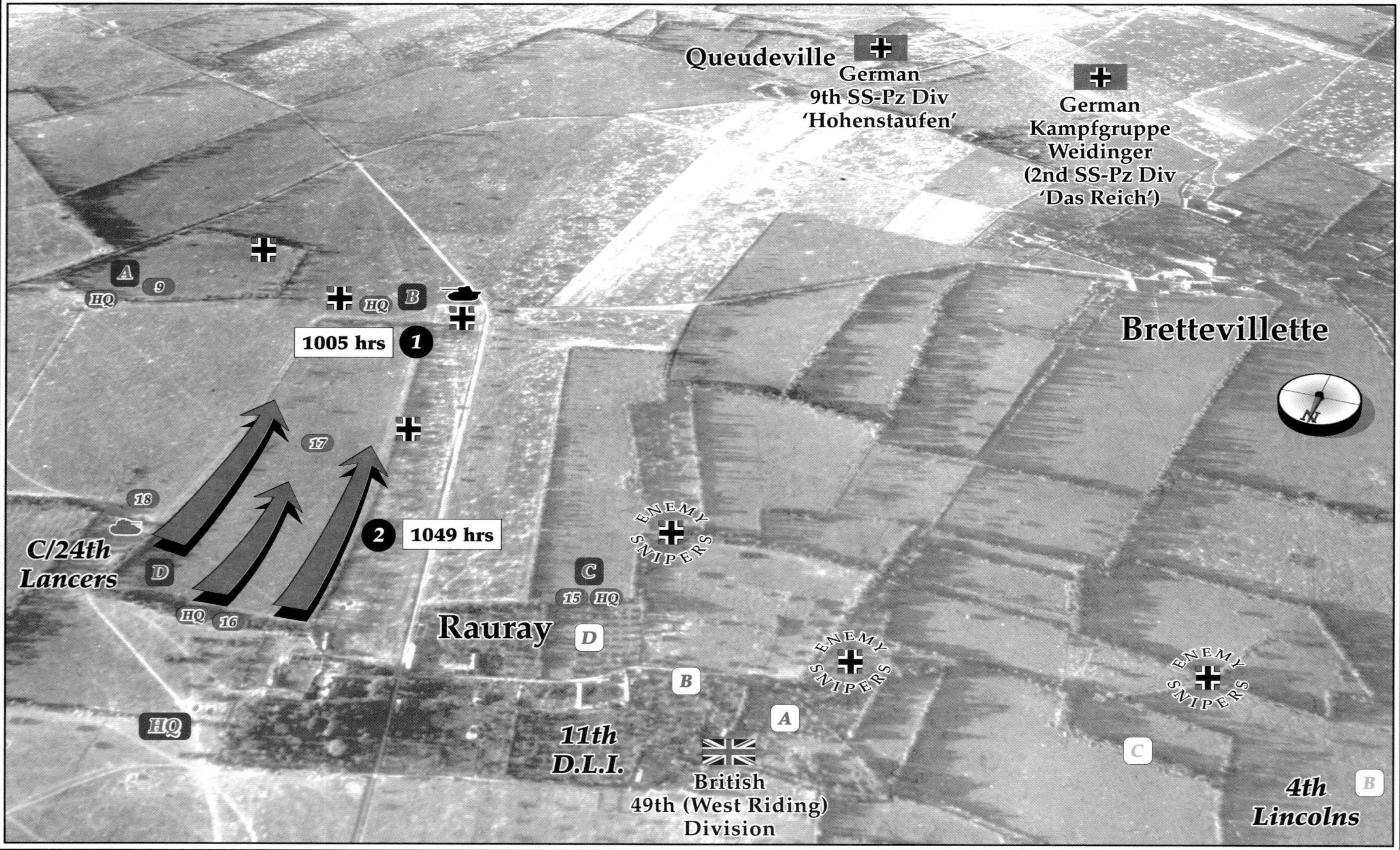

STAGE SIX

1000–1100 HRS – 'D' COMPANY ON THE MOVE

With the first phase of the battle now over, the 11th Durham Light Infantry and 4th Lincolns are busy 'mopping up' in the fields to the west of Rauray. Although snipers are still giving trouble in the orchards around the village, the situation is reasonably under control. However, on the eastern flank the state of affairs is less certain. The very few that remain dug in on the edge of ring contour 110 are still holding on, but 'A' Company's condition is unclear. Meanwhile, the overall German aspect is already beginning to look grave. General Speidel, Rommel's chief of staff, has telephoned von Rundstedt's OB West HQ stating that the renewed counter-attacks by II SS-Pz Korps have been stopped by very strong artillery concentrations.

A great deal of credit for setting up and directing this formidable display of artillery firepower must go to two members of the 185th Field Regiment. During the first few hours of the battle, Lt Col K.F. Mackay-Lewis, the Regiment's CO, arrived at its observation post in Rauray and took command when the situation looked very serious for the 70th Brigade (Mackay-Lewis, also known as 'Squirrel' on account of his distinctive moustache, was awarded the DSO for his coolness and determination and for showing the utmost disregard for his personal safety. Another member of the 185th to be decorated for his efforts was the Commander of the 274th Battery, Major F.R. Lucas, who received the Military Cross for directing most of the 185th Regiment's DF shoots, once the likes of Capt Calderwood had sent in their shell reps).

Sgt H. Cooke, 185th Field Regiment:
Lt Col Mackay-Lewis was the best officer I have ever known; a strict disciplinarian, but very fair and one who cared greatly for his men and their requirements. A member of the OP party once recalled to me the moment when the Lt Col arrived at the OP in Rauray at a

Looking south from Rauray along the main road up to ring contour 110. In 1944 the view across the field would have been obscured by trees and damaged hedgerows.

critical time in the battle. He remembered the CO saying to his officer that the infantry was being very hard pressed, but not to worry, things were being sorted out. Apparently, his carrier driver then asked, 'Is it OK Sir, if I turn the carrier around facing the rear?', to which the CO replied, 'If you like, but we are all staying here. We came to advance, not retreat'.

1003 hrs • 'A' Company report an enemy tank dug-in on the left flank. There is no news of the state of the men left in the five-sided field or their number.

1 • 1005 hrs • 'B' Company is once more being encircled on the right. Virtually isolated, its position is now very serious and it is ordered to hold firm while a platoon from 'D' Company attempts to fight its way up to join the handful of men that are left. Artillery and mortar platoons are contacted and increased firepower is called for in order to support the 'D' Company platoon in its venture.

Capt J.S. Highmore, Company Commander, 'D' Company, 1st TS:
I received orders from the CO to send a platoon to reinforce 'B' Company. I decided to send Lt I Murray with 17 Platoon to work their way up the left side. They set off but met with stiff opposition and returned. Being unable to get through on the left, I sent them off to try via the hedge on the right.

Lt I.W. Murray, Platoon Commander, 17 Platoon, 'D' Company, 1st TS:
We were to reinforce 'B' Company with manpower and ammunition, so it was a heavily laden platoon that was to advance down the field to the beleaguered company. To assess our chances, which were at best dismal, I recall slowly standing up on the start line to ascertain the volume of fire we were likely to attract from hidden marksmen. Not a round, nothing. I sent one section of the platoon down one side of the field, another down the opposite and the third section with Platoon HQ down the centre – the object being that each side section could support the other, if necessary, with diagonal fire across the field. Any gaps could be plugged by the third section and Platoon HQ.

L/Cpl D. Huxstep, Section Commander, 18 Platoon, 'D' Company, 1st TS:
I remember quite clearly Lt Murray and his platoon going up round the side of the field in front of us to reinforce 'B' Company. We gave covering fire to this advance, along with 3-inch mortars from Support Company.

1040 hrs • Impatient for relief from 'D' Company, Capt Calderwood calls for tank support as well.

2 • 1044 hrs • The 'D' Company platoon led by Lt Murray is meeting resistance on the road up to the spur. Supported by a squadron of the 24th Lancers, 17 Platoon is gradually inching its way towards 'B' Company's position, but progress is frustratingly slow.

1055 hrs • 'A' Company report two enemy tanks moving on the left of the 6th KOSB front.

Infantry under fire from enemy snipers on the edge of Rauray, 28 June 1944.

Pte (A/Cpl) J.W. Barnes, Section Commander, 18 Platoon, 'D' Company, 1st TS:

During a respite in the barrage, a carrier came up to our positions containing Lt J. McAllan, a Platoon Commander from 'B' Company. I told him that there was enemy infantry in the vicinity, that they had tank support and that it would be dangerous to go any further in a carrier. I think perhaps it was his intention to try and contact his company, but whatever the reason, Lt McAllan proceeded forward of our positions and along the side of a hedge. The carrier had gone approximately 200 yards, when I heard what sounded like an AP strike and a few moments later a large plume of smoke went up. I went forward with Pte S. Bryden of 18 Platoon and found Lt McAllan's carrier burning and immobilized, having been hit by an AP shot. The driver of the carrier was very badly injured or dying and Lt McAllan was seriously wounded. We carried Lt McAllan to the rear and returned for the carrier driver. As we were putting him on a stretcher, Pte Bryden drew my attention to a German tank approximately 100 yards away and standing in what I remember as a field of corn. As we attempted to staunch some of the blood flow of the carrier driver, I saw the tank commander climb out of the turret and sit down on the front of the tank apron. He then lit a cigarette and continued to watch us through binoculars as we carried our wounded man away.

Capt J.S. Highmore, Company Commander, 'D' Company, 1st TS:

A young captain or lieutenant from the Middlesex or Manchesters or somewhere, I forget which, reported with three Vickers machine guns and crews desperately anxious to get into the war and begged to be given a target! (5 Platoon ,'A' Company, 1st Middlesex Regiment were supporting the 6th KOSB on 1 July, see page 119). Our targets, such as they were, were short range and unsuited to Vickers and I remember choosing from the map with him some likely German assembly areas to the south-west and he happily set up his guns and blasted of thousands of rounds over the heads (I hope) of 'C' Company. I then went forward from Company HQ to see if I could see 17 Platoon on the move to 'B' Company. On my way back I was hit in the abdomen by a burst of machine gun fire and evacuated from the battlefield, leaving 'D' Company under the command of Capt R.J. Gelston, a Canadian CANLOAN Officer.

STAGE SEVEN

1100–1200 HRS THE SECOND ATTACK

The battle has now reached a crisis point for the 1st Tyneside Scottish. It is crucial that 'B' Company's position is reinforced soon. The party of 'D' Company who are attempting to fight their way along the hedgerows to get to them are doing well, but they are not yet in contact. Without Lt Murray's men, the lonely group on ring contour 110 cannot realistically hope to hold out. Somehow, 17 Platoon must quickly find a way of reaching the end of the long oblong field between 'B' and 'D' Companies.

Pte P. Birkett, Intelligence Section, Battalion HQ, 1st TS:

About 1100 hrs, the Padre (CF C.W. Chesworth) came over and asked if someone would try to get through to 'B' Company and bring wounded back who were unable to walk. A reserve Bren gun carrier with driver and myself, hoisted a white flag up front and moved to a gap in the hedge facing towards 'B' Company. Immediately, shellfire was narrowly missing the carrier. The driver tried another two or three times and then gave up.

Pte (A/Cpl) J.W. Barnes, Section Commander, 18 Platoon, 'D' Company, 1st TS:

Later in the morning I was asked by Lt Gelston to take off my equipment and carrying a Sten gun only, find 'A' Company and secure information about its situation. I was told to run all the way. This proved to be easier said than done because of the quantity of shell and small arms fire. En route along the direction I had been given, I came upon a small group who were setting up a Vickers machine gun on its tripod. The men were not TS nor were they Kensingtons, which unit they belonged to I never discovered. I found 'A' Company's area

STAGE SEVEN • THE SECOND ATTACK

1100 – 1200 hrs

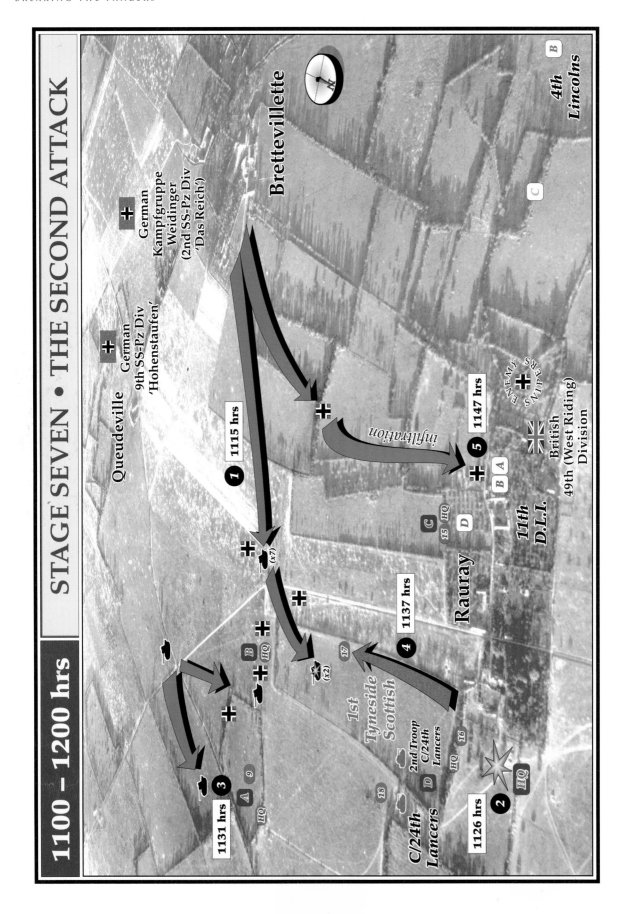

Brettevillette

German
Kampfgruppe
Weidinger
(2nd SS-Pz Div
'Das Reich')

German
9th SS-Pz Div
'Hohenstaufen'

Queudeville

1 1115 hrs

infiltration

ENEMY SNIPERS

5 1147 hrs

British
49th (West Riding)
Division

11th
D.L.I.

1137 hrs

Rauray

4

1st
Tyneside
Scottish

2nd Troop
C/24th
Lancers

1131 hrs

3

C/24th
Lancers

1126 hrs

2

4th
Lincolns

*and it was immediately evident that there had been heavy fighting and many casualties. I came upon the remnants of a platoon with a lance-corporal in charge, they were digging in. The lance-corporal directed me to where he thought the Company HQ might be. I subsequently found Capt Mirrielees behind a hedge accompanied by a private who had a 38 wireless set. The Captain, who appeared to be in a state of exhaustion, received Lt Gelston's request for information and replied, verbatim: 'Tell them we are holding'. Before leaving 'A' Company's area, I met and spoke briefly with a friend of mine, Pte B.W. Holligan, Battalion Sniper. His uniform was very bloodstained and I asked him if he had been hit. He told me he hadn't been, but when the battle began he had taken up a position with one of the forward sections and when the German attack came in, their infantry, backed up by tanks, had virtually overrun their trenches. Panzer-Grenadiers had suddenly appeared on their trench line and he personally had been confronted by a Feldwebel (*a kind of technical sergeant, a rank not applicable in the British Army. In a Waffen-SS unit, this would actually have been an SS-Oberscharführer). *They had shot it out and the German had fallen on Holligan bearing him to the ground and bleeding all over him, hence the state of his uniform. He said he was alright and asked me how things were with 'D' Company. Before I left, he expressed the opinion that if we could hold on till nightfall we should make it.*

WS-38 Mk II, portable wireless set.

Returning to my company by the same route as I had come, I passed by the place where the group had been setting up the Vickers. They were all dead, having sustained a direct hit from a shell, the Vickers totally destroyed. By this time, there was quite an increase in the amount of small arms fire in the area. Sprinting as best I could over some open ground, I saw a Tyneside Scottish lance-corporal step out of cover about fifty yards away from me. He was waving his arms and shouting something in my direction. Almost immediately, he was shot in the head. I recognised him as I passed by but I can no longer recall his name. He had obviously been trying to warn me to take cover. I often think about him.

1 • 1115 hrs • SECOND ATTACK • As if 'B' Company's problems were not deep enough, a second enemy attack is now under way. Once more, infantry and AFVs are advancing across from Brettevillette and Queudeville. As in the first attack at 0640 hrs, KG Weidinger Panzer-Grenadiers, with AFVs from SS-Pz Regt 9, will attack 70th Brigade's right flank, while 9th SS-Pz Division 'Hohenstaufen' units SS-PzGR 19 and 20 (dug in just near the crossroads, about 300 yards south of ring contour 110), with supporting AFVs from SS-Pz Regt 9 attack the left. Artillery

and mortar fire from both sides is intense. 'B' Company reports that seven enemy AFVs are 300 yards north-east of ring contour 110, and the 24th Lancers respond to this immediately, their Shermans having covered this area previously. The characteristic and calm voices of the British tank commanders send their troopers into action with well polished efficiency and once more the enemy is prevented from breaking through the gap in the bocage. The 24th Lancers' operations are being brilliantly handled by their CO, Lt Col W.A.C. Anderson (he was awarded a DSO for his efforts on 1 July – see photograph opposite).

1122 hrs • 'B' Company reports that 'D' Company are not yet in contact.

2 • 1126 hrs • The 1st Tyneside Scottish HQ suddenly comes under heavy enemy mortar bombardment in an attempt to throw the Battalion's command centre into confusion, and several casualties are sustained as the whole area to the east of Rauray village is stonked.

3 • 1131 hrs • 'A' Company report that enemy tanks have gone through the 6th KOSB, and that they have seen another tank due east of ring contour 110. The forward company of the 6th KOSB, 'C' Company, is now in a similar plight to its Tyneside Scottish neighbours and it too is in grave danger of becoming surrounded. The Borderers have also lost the majority of their anti-tank guns, only one being left in the fight.

4 • 1137 hrs • Enemy AFVs are shooting at the 'D' Company party as they edge their way towards 'B' Company's position, but these are being engaged by the 24th Lancers. The lush, leafy mid-summer vegetation is making the observation of groups of infiltrating Germans extremely difficult, but conversely, it is also helping to hide the 49th Division's armour, making it a little easier for the 24th Lancers to defend Rauray. By disguising his tank as part of a hedgerow, L/Sgt W. Wilcox, a 24th Lancers troop sergeant from 'C' Squadron, slowly creeps his Sherman away from the safety of the orchard where his fellow tanks are sheltering and manages to reach a point out in the open from where he can observe the German tanks as they form up for their attack. Once the tanks are fully committed to their attack, he calls up the rest of his troop and they all get in a furious 30-second burst of fire. They then return to their original positions behind the cover of smoke before the enemy's tanks can get a fix on them. Wilcox meanwhile stays put. To remain in an exposed position like this takes a great deal of coolness and patience, and one mistake could leave him a sitting target. Throughout the morning, this brave performance manages to stop the enemy from advancing down the large field in front of 'D' Company – a major contribution to the defence of Rauray.

There is also an enemy machine gun firing along the road ahead of Lt Murray's group as they draw near to the burnt-out Shermans at the southern end of 'D' Company's field.

L/Sgt W. Wilcox was awarded a Military Medal for his courageous actions.

Lt I.W. Murray, Platoon Commander, 17 Platoon, 'D' Company, 1st TS:

Unfortunately, the Germans did not remain so charitably-minded as we progressed towards 'B' Company, and at the first attempt,

I succeeded in only getting the right-hand section on to its objective. En route, we passed an anti-tank gun with a burnt-out Sherman tank behind it, peppered with holes.

Lt J.F. McLaren, Platoon Commander, 12 Platoon, 'B' Company, 1st TS:

I seem to remember this tank was in fact deserted, having been hit in some previous incident, but it did have petrol for there was a 'brew up' in it.

Gnr P. Moss, Gun aimer, 'B' Troop, 217th Battery, 55th Anti-tank Regiment, 1st TS:

We saw a young Tyneside Scottish soldier crawling along a hedgerow. His hand was severed and hanging at the wrist. I carried him back to the Aid Post on my shoulders. He seemed more bothered about his Bren gunner pal who he had left behind than himself.

1145 hrs • Capt Calderwood yet again shouts into his 18 wireless set for defensive artillery fire as enemy tanks once more roll into 'B' Company's area. His bearings are noted and further artillery and mortar strikes are laid on. Soon after, the ground shudders as the resulting hail of shells and mortar bombs rain down on ring contour 110.

Cpl G. Cowie, Section Commander, 18 Platoon, 'D' Company, 1st TS:

Every platoon had a 38 wireless set. It was carried slung across the chest, and had earphones and a throat mike which allowed the hands to be free when transmitting. These platoon 38s were 'netted' to a 38 control set located at the company HQ. The 38 set's aerial rod only had a range of about a mile, but this was generally sufficient as the company HQ was rarely farther away than that. If a wood or copse was in the way it usually neutralized the transmission. At company HQ, an 18 set relayed messages to Battalion HQ and artillery OPs (the 18 set could transmit up to a distance of ten miles, see pages 113 and 129).

Lt Col W.A.C. Anderson, CO of the 24th Lancers, 1944.

5 • 1147 hrs • 'C' Company reports that groups of enemy infantry are putting in an attack on the 11th DLI in the orchard on the western edge of Rauray. Shortly afterwards the commander of 'D' Company, 11th DLI, Major J. Brewis, is very seriously wounded while trying to deal with an enemy Spandau, and Capt D.M. Grant takes over.

1148 hrs • The 24th Lancers send in an excited report. With his Sherman still dressed in its arborescent camouflage, L/Sgt Wilcox has knocked out two of the enemy AFVs which were attempting to infiltrate between 'A' and 'B' Companies.

1155 hrs • Less than ten minutes have gone by since 'C' Company reported the new attack on its 11th DLI friends, but they now send in news about a further developing action involving more enemy Weidinger Panzer-Grenadiers in a movement to try and infiltrate round the Company's right flank. If successful, the Germans will have managed to split the two parties and gained important ground in Rauray.

1157 hrs • Two tanks are reported destroyed just north of ring contour 110.

STAGE EIGHT

1200–1300 HRS – THE THIRD ATTACK

Although hard pressed, the defenders of Rauray have so far managed to withstand a second serious German attack, but the enemy is already forming up its Panzers and infantry for another effort.

From his post on the roof of Belleval farm, near the 6th KOSB's HQ, Captain Shaw, a forward artillery observer, has been keenly monitoring the progress of the Panzers on the 15th Division front. Scanning the German positions through his binoculars, his attention suddenly focuses on the small hamlet of Queudeville. He instantly realizes that the enemy is actively forming up for the next phase of the battle and immediately sends the information down the line to his RHQ. Meanwhile, in Rauray, similar activity in Brettevillette is also being noted by the 185th Field Regiment's OP, where Lt Col Mackay-Lewis takes control of the situation. Within a short space of time, the air resounds with the cry 'Victor target!', and all the guns in VIII Corps have their line of fire directed on to Queudeville, and every available gun in XXX Corps is brought to bear on the enemy in Brettevillette. The resultant massed artillery DF pours hundreds of shells into the area, seriously disrupting the northernmost elements of II SS-Pz Korps and its plans for a successful counter-attack on the Second British Army's front at Rauray.

1200 hrs • In response to this colossal 'stonk' on Queudeville and Brettevillette, German tank commander *SS-Obersturmbannführer* Otto Meyer, sending in his midday report to the 9th SS-Panzer Division 'Hohenstaufen' HQ, finishes his message with a quotation from Dante – 'Abandon hope all ye who enter here'.

However, the Germans who have survived 'Hell on earth' up till now and infiltrated deep into the 70th Brigade's territory have not yet abandoned hope altogether. Enemy sniping from trees and clumps of overgrown hedgerow in the countryside around Rauray remains as deadly as ever.

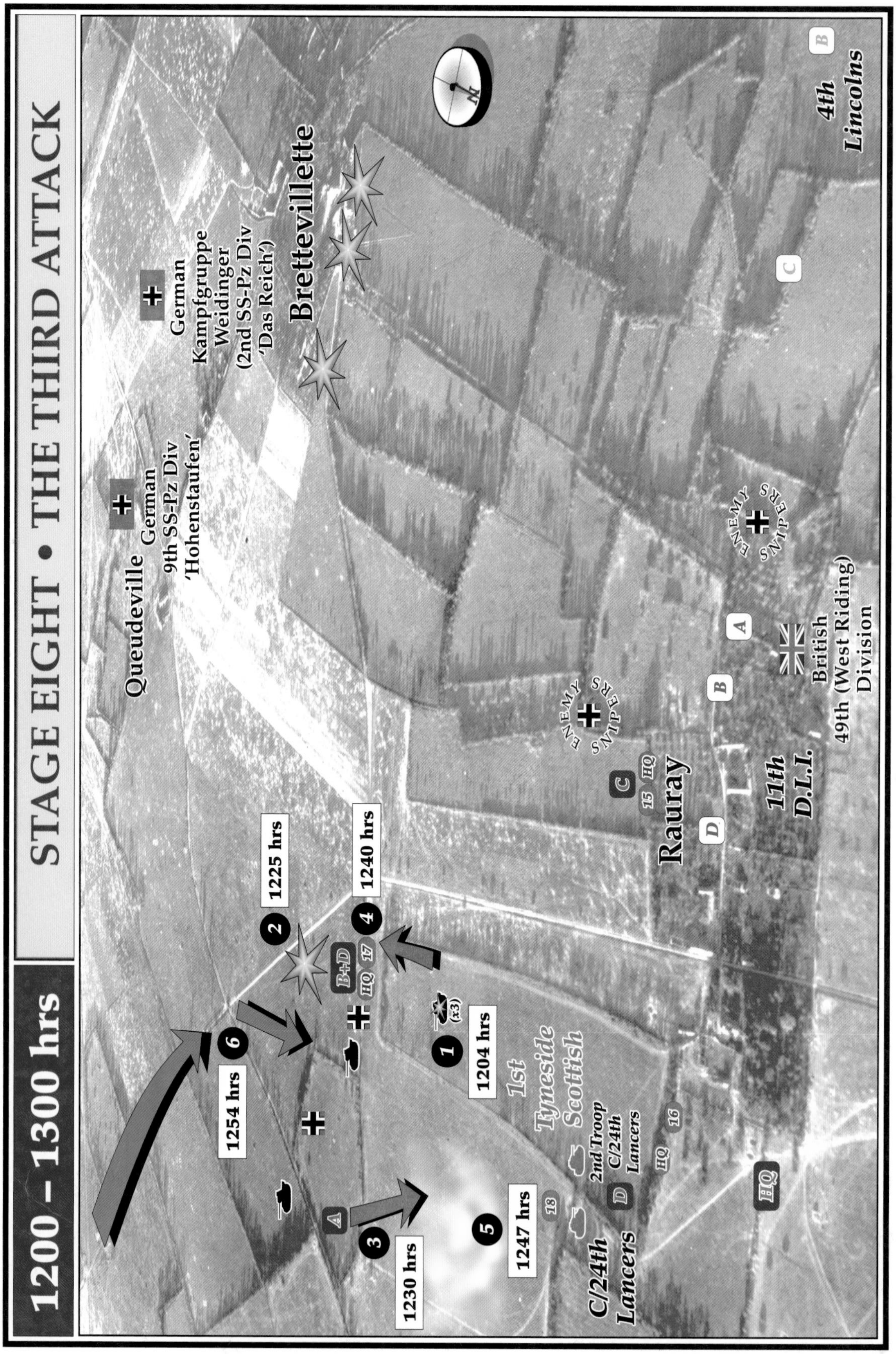

STAGE EIGHT • THE THIRD ATTACK

1200 – 1300 hrs

4th
Lincolns

B

C

German
Kampfgruppe
Weidinger
(2nd SS-Pz Div
'Das Reich')

Brettevillette

Queudeville German
9th SS-Pz Div
'Hohenstaufen'

ENEMY PANZERS

ENEMY PANZERS

A

B

British
49th (West Riding)
Division

11th
D.L.I.

Rauray

C HQ

15

D

1225 hrs **2**

1240 hrs **4**

HQ 17

6 1254 hrs

1 1204 hrs

1st
Tynesfde
Scottish

2nd Troop
C/24th
Lancers

D

HQ 16

3 1230 hrs

A

5 1247 hrs

18

C/24th
Lancers

HQ

L/Cpl N.E. Waters, Section Commander and LMG No. 1, 14 Platoon, 'C' Company:, 1st TS:

I was told to go forward with two men to see if the enemy was still in the area we had pulled back from. This we started to do, but after only 20 yards we were all hit. One of us I think was killed, myself and the other man wounded. I received two severe wounds in the groin and stomach, but managed to crawl back to the path where I was helped on to a Bren carrier for removal to the RAP. This carrier was then hit and we (three or four of us) were transferred to Loyd carrier and made a run for it under heavy fire. We made it back to be part of the stream of wounded waiting for treatment and, in my case, evacuation.

1 • 1204 hrs • 'B' Company reports three more tanks knocked out and that the handful of men left on the edge of ring contour 110 are sitting tight in anticipation of 'D' Company's arrival.

1217 hrs • Six tanks are now burning in 'B' Company's area. The combined efforts of accurate artillery, mortar fire and Shermans appear to have contained the enemy's second attack and prevented the Panzers from advancing northwards towards 'D' Company's main position near Rauray village.

2 • 1225 hrs • There is still plenty of action going on around 'B' Company though, and Capt Calderwood again calls on the artillery for a renewed 'stonk' of the area in front of his slit trench.

3 • 1230 hrs • Disaster for 'A' Company. The Battalion's left flank is about to crumble as more 'Hohenstaufen' Panzers thunder across no man's land and up to the edge of the five-sided field. This time, any hope of resisting them is immediately smashed as the encircling tanks suddenly swing the barrels of their 75 mm guns round and blast 'A' Company's slits from the side. Cut off from their 6th KOSB friends on their left, the shell-shocked remnants try to stagger back towards Rauray in a confused state. Over the road, the other 'forlorn hope', 'C' Company, 6th KOSB, are now virtually surrounded themselves, only one of their anti-tank guns remains in action and they have taken severe casualties. Supporting machine guns of 5 Platoon, 'A' Company, 1st Middlesex Regiment, under the command of Lt Bayman, have been in continuous action since the first attack began, and one section was forced to leave their guns and throw in their lot with the Borderers once the enemy had begun to penetrate the perimeter of their field. The 6th KOSB CO, Capt Rollo, is given permission by the 44th Brigade HQ to withdraw his forward 'C' Company, and it falls back to Belleval farm to rally around its Battalion HQ.

Pte J.L.R. Samson, Bren-gunner, No. 4 Detachment, Anti-tank Platoon, 'S' Company, 1st TS:

Capt Mirrielees ('A' Company CO) passed us at the double, only stopping to say that the Panzers had pretty well decimated his company and that he was on his way to the Battalion Command Post for reinforcements. Soon after this we saw the remnants of 'A' Company coming back, some without weapons, some without steel helmets and practically all without any webbing. I noticed that among the score or so I could see, there were no NCOs and no one was carrying a PIAT (each company carried three of these weapons). We attempted to rally the boys

The side lane shown in the photograph below, as it appeared in April 2002.

Vehicles sheltering by a farm entrance, Rauray, 28 June 1944.

to join us in our slit trenches, but even the threat of being fired upon by us could not halt them. They were 'finished', and I for one could not blame them seeing that our gun was their only support against the enemy and that we could not assist them, the mortar fire being too heavy for us to move the gun from its pit without any carrier and bring it to bear on the tanks.

The 1st Tyneside Scottish pipers have been right in the thick of the action since the first action at Tessel Wood on 26 June, sometimes leading the troops into an attack, on other occasions acting as stretcher-bearers. In the heat of battle, attending to the wounded and removing them from the field is a job which demands great courage and a cool head. Often the stretcher-bearers are called on to operate in dangerously exposed positions, and time and again their red cross insignia fail to offer them any protection from snipers or raking Spandau fire.

Piper R.S. Forrest, stretcher-bearer, Band (mid-section), attached to 'A' Company, 1st TS:
'A' Company, to whom I was attached, took the force of the attack, splitting it up. We, the four stretcher-bearers, were cut off from the

company and spent some time with the 15th (Scottish) Division and it was said we were missing in action. Our casualties were I believe heavy, as we had quite a few wounded to attend to.

Pte J. Munro, Intelligence Section, Battalion HQ, 1st TS:
I knew many of the Pipe Band as I played chanter with Piper Forrest back in the UK. One of my good friends, Piper Jock Simpson from Aberdeen was shot by a sniper while he was tending a wounded man – he did wear the red cross insignia.

Pte L. Newton, Carrier Driver, Carrier Platoon, 'S' Company, 1st TS:
I was detailed along with Pipe Major T. Imrie to ferry wounded to the RAP, until I was kept in myself with exhaustion and taken to hospital.

Lt I.W. Murray, Platoon Commander, 17 Platoon, 'D' Company, 1st TS:
A recollection of that day which lingers, is the sight of three stretcher-bearers going round with a cart rather like a pre-war Boy Scouts' trek-cart. I can remember thinking that this must have been a painful mode of transport for any casualties. It was also pretty painful for the stretcher-bearers, several of whom, I'm told, were killed or wounded. I am almost certain that it was because of this that our pipers were, under CO's orders, to be no longer employed for stretcher-bearing, but to stay behind the lines to play for the troops.

One of the 'D' Company sections trying to reach ring contour 110 has found that the rear of 'B' Company's position is covered by the enemy with automatic weapons. Several of the Weidinger Panzer-Grenadiers manning these weapons have been eradicated, but the reinforcements have been temporarily forced back. However they are now making another attempt.

4 • 1240 hrs • Relief at last for the men dug-in at the front. 'B' Company reports that the party from 'D' Company have finally arrived on the edge of ring contour 110, and that the reinforced party can now hold on, providing that tanks come and support it.

Lt J.F. McLaren, Platoon Commander, 12 Platoon, 'B' Company, 1st TS:
I rejoined 'B' Company with the Jocks I had, up the line of the hedge in company with Lt I. Murray, I think. I seem to remember very considerable mortaring at this point and I know German infantry were in the slit trenches previously held by 11 Platoon.

Lt I.W. Murray, Platoon Commander, 17 Platoon, 'D' Company, 1st TS:
We all eventually reached our objective, having tried umpteen ways to get down the length of the field and when we did finally succeed with the last group of men, we turned the corner of the hedge to face three Germans, armed with rifles and stick grenades, who incredibly didn't see us. I then made a mistake. I took a Bren gun from its 'official' handler and at about ten yards range I missed all the

members of the trio, who took to their heels. By this time, ring contour 110 was under fire again and we leapt into the first available slit trenches and sat back to survey the scene. This could be done by leaning against the back 'wall' and gradually raising one's head. The sight was hardly encouraging. To the left of centre and within range of a well-hit brassie shot were four tanks which, apart from all else, were really spoiling our day. One false or careless move and they opened up at what was really point-blank range.

It's strange (or is it?) the things one thinks about in that situation. My companion, a corpse, concentrated my mind wonderfully. Only days before, I had received a gold ring from my parents for my twenty-first birthday, inscribed with the crest of The Black Watch. I was convinced that my fighting days were done. At worst, I would be dead or wounded – at best, I would be a prisoner. We would all be dead, wounded or prisoners. 'The ring', I thought. 'They're not going to get the ring or my watch.' I placed them both in a small cellophane envelope, in which I carried a spare watch face, and buried them in the bottom of the trench. And so, on we sat in a hail of shells, bombs and bullets. At intervals, we watched the four German tank crews come up and out for air. They smoked cigarettes and chatted. No one dared fire at them for fear of counter-fire.

5 • 1247 hrs • A smoke-screen is being laid by the enemy over on the left flank.

'C' Company reports that a German self-propelled gun (Sturmgeschütz III) has been knocked out on its left.

6 • 1254 hrs • THIRD ATTACK • Despite all the casualties he has sustained from artillery bombardment, the enemy is attacking yet again with tanks and infantry on 'B' Company's left, and in order to counter this, the artillery is now asked to focus its attention on the eastern flank. A 217th battery 6-pounder anti-tank gun, positioned in a hedgerow on the left, is confronted by an enemy tank at a range of 700 yards. The tank approaches slowly and for some time the detachment's crew displays considerable restraint. According to the rule book, they should wait until it turns, but eventually their patience runs out and although the enemy tank is still several hundred yards away, they open fire. The first shot, by luck or judgement, hits the ring just below the turret. The tank immediately proceeds to reverse, still head on, and the gun's crew fire two more which glance off the frontal plate. The detachment commander, Sgt R. Sturgeon, then tells the aimer, Pte P. Moss, to go for the track, which a fourth shot hits. The tank then slews and faces broadside on, fatally miscalculating its position in relation to the gun. A fifth shot penetrates through the side and the tank 'brews up'. This brings the tally of enemy tanks destroyed by the 217th Battery up to six.

Gnr P. Moss, Gun aimer, 'B' Troop, 217th Battery, 55th Anti-tank Regiment:
I thought my second and third shots had missed, but on visiting the tank later in the day, I noticed that both shots had bounced off the tank leaving score marks on the frontal plate.

STAGE NINE

1300–1400 HRS – MORE PANZERS ARRIVE

A morale-boosted 'B' Company, now reinforced with the extra firepower of the group from 'D' Company, is once more doggedly defending ring contour 110 in the face of a renewed attack. Having overrun 'A' Company's position, the enemy is now making a determined strike at the Battalion's left flank.

Pte J.L.R. Samson, Bren-gunner, No. 4 Detachment, Anti-tank Platoon, 'S' Company, 1st TS:

Our Detachment Commander stripped the firing mechanism from our gun, dropping its parts haphazardly about, and ordered our withdrawal across the road to the 6th KOSB positions. We made our way across the field towards the road which had a thick hedge on its far side. All our kit was left behind in the slit trenches, we took our personal weapons only, although I carried a box of magazines as well as my Bren gun. Crossing the road, we found a 15th Division RA 17-pounder anti-tank gun pointing directly towards our own gun, with a Quad Tractor close to it (the 97th Anti-tank Regiment were attached to the 6th KOSB on 1 July). This gun had no crew with it except a sergeant and the detachment's Bren gunner. Looking southwards across the KOSB field we could see a 6-pounder anti-tank gun in the hedge which bordered its southern edge, this being about 400–600 yards from the 17-pounder. Halfway down the hedge along the road, there were some vehicles burning fiercely, including a jeep, near which were two figures kneeling beside some recumbent ones. The RA sergeant said that the position had come under German mortar and tank fire, which had caused casualties to the KOSB company ('C' Company) his gun was supporting. He had tried to move

STAGE NINE • MORE PANZERS ARRIVE

1300 – 1400 hrs

Brettevillette

4th Lincolns

German Kampfgruppe Weidinger (2nd SS-Pz Div 'Das Reich')

Queudeville

German 9th SS-Pz Div 'Hohenstaufen'

1350 hrs

3 (x12)

1343 hrs **2**

B

ENEMY 1345 hrs

A

ENEMY 1345 hrs

British 49th (West Riding) Division

ENEMY 1345 hrs

C

B

C

HQ 15

D

11th D.L.I.

Raury

B+D 17

HQ

1st Tyneside Scottish

D 16

HQ

1338 hrs **1**

C/24th Lancers 18

HQ

his gun to the left to engage the enemy armour but this had proved to be impossible as most of his detachment had left him, and the Quad had been made unserviceable by a direct hit. The four of us, with the RA sergeant and his Bren gunner, then made several attempts to shift the 17-pounder, but failed to do so.

For the next half an hour or so, a flurry of reports are sent in by Capt Calderwood, providing the following information:

1300 hrs • Yet again, the magnificent ammunition carriers successfully get through to 'B' Company.

1303 hrs • About 700 yards away on the battalion's left flank, a squadron of the 15th Recce Regiment has now entered the battle and is adding its supporting fire to that the 24th Lancers.

1306 hrs • 'B' Company calls for a continuation of the artillery 'stonk' on its front.

1310 hrs • Despite the carriers getting through, 'B' Company report a shortage of two Bren guns. 70th Brigade calls up more supplies.

1320 hrs • Five enemy tanks are seen approximately 1000 yards south of ring contour 110.

1329 hrs • 'B' Company asks if tanks can clear machine guns on the left. The 24th Lancers are ready and their Shermans boom out their noisy response to 'B' Company's request.

1337 hrs • The 6th KOSB report that thirteen Tyneside Scots of 'A' Company have been picked up and are being returned to the Battalion.

1 • 1338 hrs • 'D' Company's main position is mortared. Although some way back from the forward companies, the men of 'D' Company have suffered a number of casualties from mortar bomb and tank shell.

Pte P. Lawton, rifleman, 18 Platoon, 'D' Company, 1st TS:

Each time someone brought a Bren magazine to your trench, the man at the front of the trench had to climb out with it and run to the next trench. I was in a trench with Pte Hamer when Pte Holt brought a magazine to us. I climbed out of the trench and carried it to the next one. Within minutes, a shell came over and hit the trench I had just left. We went to see what could be done and found that Pte Hamer had been virtually cut in half by the shell. Pte Holt didn't appear to have suffered any physical damage at all, but he was taken off to hospital suffering from shock and I never saw him again. I have no doubt that he has felt the effects of that moment ever since.

2 • 1343 hrs • We now see a change in the enemy's movements on ring contour 110. The Panzers now pass 'B' Company front on its right, heading towards 'C' Company's front.

3 • 1350 hrs • Apparently thwarted by the Shermans of the 24th Lancers from advancing towards the eastern side of Rauray, the enemy seems to be preparing to make an attempt from a different angle. Twelve tanks are now forming up on the track west of ring contour 110, just south of 'C' Company's original forward position.

1355 hrs • Five minutes later, another twelve are observed waiting to move forward, 1,000 yards behind.

Pte J.L.R. Samson, Bren-gunner, No. 4 Detachment, Anti-tank Platoon, 'S' Company, 1st TS:

A KOSB subaltern came up to the 17-pounder and on finding that we were all anti-tank specialists, said that he would like a volunteer or volunteers to join the KOSB 6-pounder which was short of gun numbers and was trying to knock out a tank which had given them a great deal of trouble. I must add that the noise of shells exploding and the steady rain of mortar bombs all the time was often quite deafening and that this must have numbed my senses for I quickly said I would go to the KOSB gun. I asked the subaltern what I should do with my Bren gun and he said he would use it himself and took it from me. None of the others from our detachment offered their services, and indeed, Pte G. Penman told me I was mad and ever since the end of that day I have agreed with him. The subaltern and I walked across the field to the 6-pounder, and when we had got halfway there, I could see more clearly the kneeling men near the roadside hedge attending to wounded and hear the crackling flames from the burning vehicles. Upon reaching the gun, I could see that it was placed in a gap in the hedge, not dug-in at all and had no slit trenches for the protection of the crew, which consisted of a corporal and private only. The subaltern told the corporal that I was an anti-tank gun number, and the latter told me to load and repeat his fire orders. The other private would lay, and he would go out to the left flank to control our fire, which would be at the enemy tank we could see, hull-down, behind the hedge directly opposite. The subaltern also went to the left taking my Bren gun, and I believe that I later saw that he and it had suffered a direct hit from a shell or mortar bomb, but anyway I never bothered to recover my Bren gun. I can however definitely state, even now forty years later, that apart from the KOSB subaltern, corporal and private on the 6-pounder, the two stretcher-bearers by the roadside, the two RA people and our own TS anti-tank gun detachment, I saw no one else on their feet in that field.

(The 6th Kings Own Scottish Borderers War Diary for 1 July, PRO WO171/1322, states that the attack began on 'C' Company's front at 0700 hrs. Eventually all the anti-tank guns were knocked out and 'C' Company was forced back, but the remnants made a gallant stand on the line of the Company HQ. 'C' Company HQ was positioned in the field to the rear of the 17-pounder, approximately 300 yards behind. The other 6th KOSB companies were positioned to the left, continuing the British 15th (Scottish) Division front on a line running south-east towards Grainville-sur-Odon).

The 6-pounder had plenty of ammunition near it, and so I loaded one of the recently issued Super Velocity Discarding Sabot rounds into the breach and passed on the corporal's fire order which was, I believe: 'Enemy tank, 12 o'clock, range 400, fire!'. If my memory as regards the range is faulty, it is not respecting the rest of the order. We fired this round, which obviously missed its target as the tank began firing its machine gun or guns at us, the bullets passing all round us and rattling against the gun shield. I now realise why we missed and

carried on missing our target, as we set a range on the gun's range scale which should not have been done with this Sabot ammunition. Indeed, when the 1st Tyneside Scottish anti-tank platoon was given its first issue of the Sabot rounds in early June 1944, we were not instructed, as we should have been, to fire them with our range scales at 'T', i.e. no range, and I think the same must have happened with the 6th KOSB, thus the corporal should have ordered us to set the range at 'T'.

Infantry edging their way forward, Rauray, 28 June 1944.

Lt B.T.W. Stewart, 2nd i/c, Anti-tank Platoon, 'S' Company, 1st TS:

The 'miracle' Sabot rounds were much, much faster in flight, and the tungsten 'dart' which emerged was able to penetrate much thicker armour. However, the extra velocity seriously affected our range finding and the need to lay off for speed. The new ammunition had a different trajectory, which is of course self-evident – flatter trajectory with a greater speed – but we were not told this when the Sabot ammunition was first issued and there were no instructions to accompany it. We simply knew that it was more effective, which it proved to be, but we should have taken note of the effects of vastly increased velocity in the art of the aimer. It was unfortunate that we had no opportunity before we left the UK to practice with this new, highly effective ammunition or there would have been more damage done to the enemy.

Pte J.L.R. Samson, Bren-gunner, No. 4 Detachment, Anti-tank Platoon, 'S' Company, 1st TS:

The machine gun fire must have killed the corporal, as we heard no more from him and saw his body huddled down. We carried on trying to hit the tank, whether we fired three or four times more I cannot remember, but I do remember that by now the tank had started to use its own gun at us, and after two or three shells, one exploded just in front of the left hand side of our gun shield. The gun's sights were damaged, the layer badly wounded and I was bowled over by the blast. I must have lost consciousness for some seconds, for I only noticed the damage to the gun and the state of the layer when I got to my feet. I then found that I was the only person standing and was beside a useless 6-pounder with a wounded man I could not help, and I suddenly thought of self-preservation. Yelling 'stretcher-bearers!' I left the gun, picked up a rifle lying nearby and began to make my way back to the 17-pounder. The noise never seemed to cease, and how I got back to the 17-pounder I will never know, but I did, and I am certain that I never broke into a trot! At the 17-pounder, I found only Pte Penman with the RA sergeant and Bren gunner, and after a very brief discussion we decided to make our way to the rear, thinking that with three rifles, a Bren gun and a 17-pounder we could not move, we had no further part to play where we were. We proceeded northwards down the road, and after going half a mile or so came upon an RAF corporal and airman calmly and steadily reeling out signal cable towards the way we had come. We asked them if they realized that there was nothing between them and Jerry, but they just carried on with their work and we still went to the rear. After more or less another mile, we saw two Military Police NCOs from 49th Division beside a sign marked 'Straggler Collection Point' and Pte Penman and I were directed to our Battalion Command Post.

STAGE TEN

1400-1500 HRS – THE FOURTH ATTACK

The 9th SS-Pz Regt's AFVs are queueing up to attack what remains of the 1st Tyneside Scottish, but all their efforts so far suggest that they will be unable to survive the intense British shell and mortar fire long enough to achieve a breakthrough. It appears that the tanks are inclined to crowd at a certain point and therefore a code-word for this area has been devised. Within a minute of it being uttered by Capt Calderwood into the mike of his 18 wireless set, the artillery observers relay his message to the 185th HQ and a highly concentrated barrage of 25-pounder artillery is brought down on the enemy.

1400 hrs • Capt D.C. Mirrielees takes over command of 'D' Company.

1405 hrs • An extra 2nd Kensingtons machine gun platoon arrives to add its much-needed firepower.

1 • 1408 hrs • FOURTH ATTACK • Seven and a half hours have elapsed since the enemy was first seen racing across the smoke-covered fields from Brettevillette in the early morning light. Since then his forces have made the dash a further two times with mortar bombs and shells from Shermans and medium field artillery blasting and burning the earth all around them. So far, they have succeeded only in setting up sniping positions among the hedgerows and orchards on the outskirts of Rauray village. Their main objective on the 49th Division's front, to plough a wide gap along the Corps boundary, sweeping aside the defenders in Rauray with a series of bulldozing Panzer attacks, has up till now been held up on the edge of the village by almost continuous fire of all kinds. True, the 9th SS-Panzer Division has driven a line of tanks up the Noyers–Cheux road as far as le Haut de Bosq, but they have suffered too many losses and become perilously outnumbered as they have tried to penetrate deeper into the shoulder of the British salient. Many are now cut off and at the mercy of the rearguard of the 15th Division.

Now, having formed up their tanks for a fourth attempt, the Germans are on the move again and the battered and bruised surviors of 'B'

WS-18, portable wireless set.

STAGE TEN • THE FOURTH ATTACK

1400 – 1500 hrs

Bretteville

German
Kampfgruppe
Weidinger
(2nd SS-Pz Div
'Das Reich')

German
9th SS-Pz Div
'Hohenstaufen'

Queudeville

4th
Lincolns

B

C

ENEMY SNIPERS

ENEMY SNIPERS

British
49th (West Riding)
Division

A

B

ENEMY SNIPERS

Rauray

C

HQ 15

D

2

1420 hrs

11th
D.I.I.

1408 hrs

1

B+D

HQ 17

1st
Tymeside
Scottish

D

HQ 16

HQ

18

C/24th
Lancers

1422 hrs

3

British
15th (Scottish)
Division

C/6th
K.O.S.B.

Company are being attacked once more from the south-east and south-west and Capt Calderwood radios in a message stating that he urgently requires reinforcements.

1415 hrs • The enemy's fourth attack is met by yet another massive artillery defensive barrage.

1416 hrs • On the edge of ring contour 110, 'B' Company is being troubled by an enemy MG42 which has established a position in a hedge on the left.

2 • 1420 hrs • Incredibly, several hours after Major Angus rallied his last party of survivors in the hedgrows south of Rauray, 'C' Company now reports that some of its forward platoons did after all manage to sit tight and Major Angus has managed to gather together about thirty men who had been cut off from the rest of the company.

3 • 1422 hrs • The 6th KOSB report that they have managed to recover some ground on the Battalion's left.

1430 hrs • 'B' Company report that they can see some enemy tanks milling around in front of 'C' Company's position.

1445 hrs • The 24th Lancers report that no enemy tanks are now in view.

Sgt R.S. Thomson, attached to HQ on special duties with IO, Sniper Section, Battalion HQ, 1st TS:

To the right hand side of the Battalion HQ position there was a road leading into Rauray village which was protected by a small sandbagged position with, at most, four Durham Light Infantry in it. In the afternoon, I was in this area when an attack was made on this position from the first houses in the village. This attack was beaten back leaving German dead behind. One of them was lying in the road, flat on his back with two stick grenades on his body. If he had managed to throw them it could have been goodbye DLI position and the way would have been open for the enemy to attack the rear.

Following the enemy's fourth attack, the Battalion's situation is now even more unstable. Its rifle company losses have been appalling and it needs to muster as many troops as it can from any source available. If the Battalion can remain firm until dusk, the danger of further enemy AFV strikes will be reduced as in the dark the Panzers will become sitting ducks for British infantry attacks, forcing them to stay back from the front line.

L/Cpl E. Taylorson, i/c Petrol, 'A' Echelon, Admin Platoon, HQ Company, 1st TS:

I was at 'A' Echelon, issuing petrol during the battle, and we all knew that it was something big by the number of wounded that were coming back. At one point there was a rumour that all cooks, clerks and drivers not really needed were to be sent up the line.

Pte R. McGowan, MT Driver, 'A' Echelon, Admin Platoon, HQ Company, 1st TS:

I was based at 'A' Echelon, which was near Ducy-Ste-Marguerite, and my duties were to deliver rations and supplies to the Battalion.

The senior NCO at 'A' Echelon was CQMS J. Collins. On occasions we were shelled and mortared, and under these conditions we had to dig slit trenches for ourselves and camouflage the vehicles with scrimm netting. When it was confirmed that the Germans had attacked, the alert was given and we at 'A' Echelon were all told to stand to. Shortly afterwards, Major D.N. Nicol arrived. He had been detailed to round up every possible soldier. He collected everyone – storemen, cooks, drivers, even the postie – and moved us up to Battalion HQ. We were all armed and our orders were to help hold the line.

Cpl G. Cowie, Section Commander, 18 Platoon, 'D' Company, 1st TS:

I was at our Divisional Field Hospital having just recovered from a severe form of enteritis, when orders were received that all Black Watch men were urgently required by the Battalion. One of our own 3-tonners came to collect us. I was the senior NCO in the party, which consisted of a draft of fifteen newcomers, all of whom had just completed training in the UK, and about four from the Battalion who had been evacuated sick, like myself. On arrival at 'B' Echelon, we had just had time for a mug of tea when a jeep came hurtling down a small track leading towards our position. The jeep's occupant, Major Nicol, our 2nd i/c, ordered every available soldier into the nearest 3-tonner, saying something like 'every man is required NOW!' As well as my party, some others joined us including the Battalion tailor. We were definitely scraping the barrel for reinforcements. We went up a track for a mile or so, the sound of battle now almost deafening. It was a very hot day and in the back of the truck with the tarpaulin on there was a peculiar sweet smell. It may have been from the dead cows lying in the fields nearby, or maybe this truck had been used to convey some dead soldiers to the rear, although normally these were left where they had been hit and buried on the spot when the opportunity arose.

STAGE ELEVEN

1500-1700 HRS THE ENEMY BROKEN

After nearly nine hours of continuous fighting, the enemy seems to be flagging. However, more SS-Panzers are being rushed to the front. Behind the 1st Tyneside Scottish lines, similar efforts are being made to bring every available man forward to help reinforce the Battalion's battered defences.

1550 hrs • 'B' Company yet again asks for defensive fire. Radio etiquette has been abandoned as Capt Calderwood repeatedly shouts the desperate plea – 'For mercy's sake, give us fire!' (Capt K. P. Calderwood was awarded the Military Cross for remaining at his post throughout the battle).

1 • 1600 hrs • 'D' Company reports four tanks are moving to the left of ring contour 110.

2 • 1605 hrs • FIFTH ATTACK • The enemy are preparing to make one last attack. 'B' Company reports that Panzer-Grenadiers can be seen debussing from troop-carrying vehicles at Queudeville, where twelve tanks are forming up. At once, a great barrage of artillery and mortar fire is brought down on the whole area, and from his dug-out, Capt Calderwood reports with satisfaction that it appears to be doing great execution. The fifth and final German attack has failed before it has started.

Lt I.W. Murray, Platoon Commander, 17 Platoon, 'D' Company, 1st TS:

Immediately to our front, Germans were climbing out of lorries and forming up to attack. A frantic radio message went back to HQ for defensive fire and to our delight it duly came. It was a tremendous 'stonk', a large proportion of which landed on ourselves, but at least we were dug-in.

Capt K.P. Calderwood.

STAGE ELEVEN • THE ENEMY BROKEN

1500 – 1700 hrs

German
Kampfgruppe
Weidinger
(2nd SS-Pz Div
'Das Reich')

German
9th SS-Pz Div
'Hohenstaufen'

Queudeville

Brettevillette

4th
Lincolns

B

C

C/141th
RAC

A

3

1640 hrs

British
49th (West Riding)
Division

C/141th
RAC

B

2

1605 hrs

C   HQ
15

Rauray

11th
D.I.I.

D

4

1650 hrs

B+D
HQ 17

1

1600 hrs

1st
Tymeside
Scotish

D

16

HQ

C/141th
RAC

British
15th (Scottish) Division

C/6th
K.O.S.B.

18

HQ

C/24th
Lancers

Crocodile

(This could go a long way to explaining the reason why such a small band of men were able to hold out for so long in such an exposed position. By calling for defensive fire to be brought down virtually on top of his position whenever the enemy came close, Capt Calderwood would have created a pocket of destruction on ring contour 110 in which his well dug-in party would have been too hot to handle).

It deserves to be put on record that we couldn't have sent the message seeking support fire if Lt D. Salisbury, the Signals Officer, hadn't gone back earlier to bring up a spare battery. In the meantime, the German infantry now caught in murderous fire, began to disperse, slowly at first and then with increasing alacrity. In short, it became a rout. For the first time for hours our own riflemen and LMGs could fire without fear of hellish retribution. But truth to tell, the fire was desultory. The enemy was patently defeated.

Sgt A.R. Esplin, Section Commander, Mortar Platoon, 'S' Company, 1st TS:

We were getting very worried as our base plates had started to sink into clay soil so badly that if the enemy attacks carried on we would have to stop firing. It was so serious, that my No. 1 was lying on his stomach trying to lay sights. The barrels by this time were only a foot above the ground. The No. 2s were dead beat lobbing in bombs and I had a go myself to give them a break. To my horror, most of us were getting so much blast from the barrels being so far into the ground that our eardrums were at bursting point and it was getting more dangerous every round. Our ammunition was also getting short and we were now firing off only a few rounds at a time to try and make them last.

1625 hrs • Despite the latest blow to the enemy's forces, 'B' Company sees yet more armour moving up on the right.

3 • 1640 hrs • Six flame-throwing Churchill tanks, known as 'Crocodiles', from 'C' Squadron, 141st Royal Armoured Corps (The Buffs) are attached to 70th Brigade. Three Crocodiles of 11 Troop, 'C' Sqn, 141 RAC, roll into the eastern side of Rauray to help the 1st Tyneside Scottish, while three from 14 Troop, under the command of Lt Grundy, make their way to the area in front of the 11th DLI positions. With pressure up, the Crocodiles move off from their start lines, hauling their vulnerable, fuel-filled trailers behind them, followed by their supporting infantry. Hidden in the undergrowth, German snipers watch with horror as these ungainly dragons crawl along the sides of the hedgerows searching for their prey and offering covering fire to the infantry with their BESA machine guns. When positioned in front of an area where snipers are believed to be hiding, the Crocodiles suddenly belch a long, curling ribbon of fire which consumes great swathes of vegetation, engulfing the bocage in clouds of acrid smoke. The Crocodiles wait for any movement in the surrounding hedgerow and then move on, flaming their way through the outskirts of the village. On the Durham's front, they manage to flush out about five snipers, all other infiltrators having withdrawn,

A 3-inch mortar team prepare to fire.

repelled by the ghastly threat of incineration. The three Crocodiles of 14 Troop fire 45 flame shots each. After this, things become a little easier in Rauray and the danger from sniping decreases. However, on the Tyneside Scottish front, disaster has struck 11 Troop. As they formed up at the start of their fire-breathing mission, one of the three Crocodiles was suddenly hit and immediately burst into flames. Tragically, it is believed that 'friendly' fire has destroyed the Commander's tank, killing three men and badly burning two others.

> **Pte L.J.C. McLaren, Batman-Driver to IO, Intelligence Section, Battalion HQ, 1st TS:**
> The RAC entered Rauray and certainly put to rout any foot soldiers that remained in the area.

> **Pte J. Munro, Intelligence Section, Battalion HQ, 1st TS, 1st TS:**
> As the day wore on, everyone was tired and flaky. Our initial relief came in the form of 'Crocodiles' – Churchill tanks equipped as flame-throwers. These proceeded to flush out any pockets of enemy activity.

The flame-throwing Churchill Mk V tank had a flame nozzle replacing its hull-mounted BESA machine gun which was repositioned in the turret. Fuel for the flame was carried in an armoured trailer behind, consumption being four gallons per second. Each burst of fire usually lasted around a second or so, the fuel being pressurized by nitrogen and passed through a pipe fitted under the tank's hull. It took 30 minutes to raise pressure, which could not be sustained owing to leaks. Tongues of flame could be projected up to 120 yards, although the standard range was about 60–80 yards. The sweep of the flame was only possible in a short arc of about 30 degrees and from the front of the tank only the Crocodile could not flame from the side. The target therefore had to be directly in front, which could be problematic as manoeuvrability was very difficult, especially when backing up with the trailer in position. Operators were urged to remember that they were not defensive weapons and should not be used against enemy armour, but only as a means of clearing infantry positions. These would include field defences on the edge of woods, isolated buildings, concrete emplacements, hedges, ditches and slit trenches. In an attack situation, it was important that the Crocodiles went in and fired in an angled position, away from the infantry and into the wind. The smoke generated by the flame and the subsequent fire, would then be blown back in a protecting curtain through which the infantry would attack.

A Churchill flame-throwing tank in action.

4 • 1650 hrs • 'B' Company reports that the men have seen 'C' Company, 11th DLI moving over to the left to support the Battalion and this heartens them.

1651 hrs • 'D' Company report enemy machine gun fire from left, and the 24th Lancers return fire.

1700 – 2300 hrs | STAGE TWELVE • ALL POSITIONS RESTORED

Queudeville
German
9th SS-Pz Div
'Hohenstaufen'
German
Kampfgruppe
Weidinger
(2nd SS-Pz Div
'Das Reich')
3
British
15th (Scottish)
Division
C/6th
K.O.S.B.
C/141th
RAC
C
B+D
HQ
17
18
D
1
1810 hrs
C/24th
Lancers
(x2)
11th
D.L.I.
1st
Tyneside
Scottish
Brettevillette
N
C/141th
RAC
C
B
2
1810 hrs
1st
Tyneside
Scottish
11th
D.L.I.
D
HQ
Rauray
D
A
HQ
British
49th (West Riding)
Division
C
4th
Lincolns
B

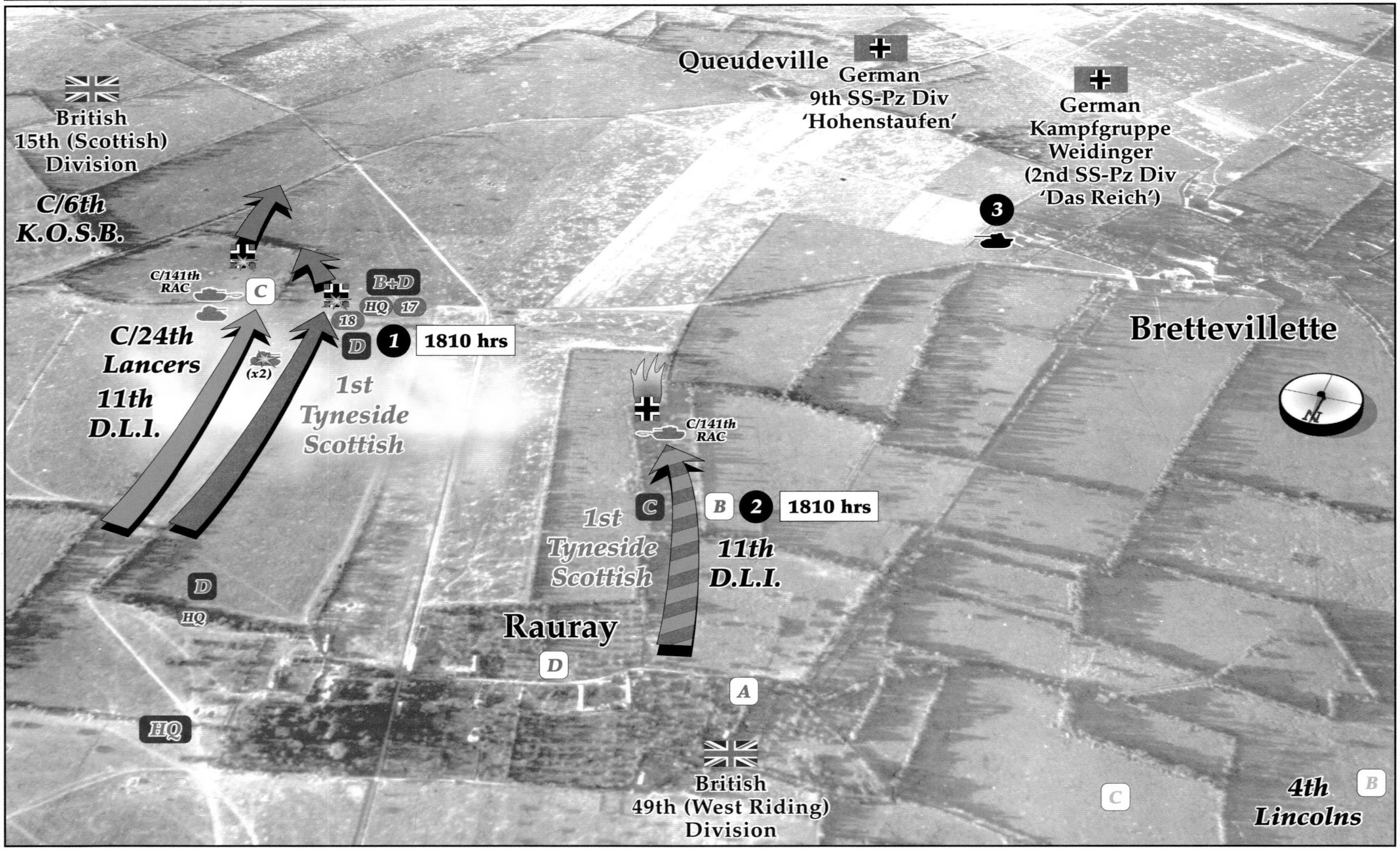

STAGE TWELVE

1700–2300 HRS – ALL POSITIONS RESTORED

It is now late afternoon, and 'D' Company, 1st Tyneside Scottish, together with 'C' Company, 11th Durham Light Infantry and tanks of the 24th Lancers, has begun the job of clearing enemy snipers and Spandau teams from the fields and bocage between Rauray and the forward positions. Fire-breathing Crocodiles have been busy flaming the hedgerows, forcing any remaining enemy troops to give themselves up or be shot, and a counter-attack is being planned by Brigade HQ for early evening which should remove any remaining enemy forces and restore all the Battalion's defensive positions.

Cpl G. Cowie, Section Commander, 18 Platoon, 'D' Company, 1st TS:

The truck drove into a large field, actually in view of the enemy as I discovered later. We had arrived at our Battalion reserve positions. We quickly de-bussed and were ordered to make our way forward to 'D' Company just ahead of us. As we walked forward in loose tactical formation, I noticed on our right a group of officers lying on the ground, quite dispersed, each with their own map case. The CO, Lt Col de Winton, was one of what appeared to be a Battalion 'O' group. The noise was terrific. Shells were screaming over in both directions, mortar bombs were cramping all over the shop and small arms fire could be heard all the time, the steady rat-tat-tat of Brens and the ripping noise of enemy Spandaus. Further to the right on a larger field surrounded by low hedgerows, were a number of tanks, all disabled as far as I could see with many on fire. A couple of hundred yards in front was a high bank with a hedge. On the left of the bank, a double hedgerow at right-angles to it. Immediately behind our side of the bank were two 24th Lancer tanks who were joining in the noise, firing their Besas to the front. In front of them and slightly

Cpl G. Cowie.

to the right were a few khaki figures clustered behind the bank. Good old 'D' Company. The men I had spotted and was able to recognize were Company HQ men, including our CSM 'Paddy' Shanks to whom I reported with my twenty odd men. Paddy was a good soldier, a regular. In UK on parade he was perfect, off parade he was OK. He certainly proved his fighting qualities at Rauray and a month or so afterwards he received a Military Medal. To us, he was the perfect Company Sergeant-Major. He was very pleased to see me and all the men I had brought up with me. His orders were as crisp as always. He told me to group my men behind the hedge, in twos or threes, and to keep manning it. He had about six spare Bren guns available and plenty of filled magazines. He had obviously been collecting these weapons from casualties. After all, it is the Company Sergeant-Major's job in action to ensure that its men have all the arms and ammunition they require. There were no further orders really. The unspoken one's were 'we stay here, no one gets past us'.

We were now in front of the two tanks of the 24th Lancers, actually almost under their muzzles. They were firing hard and the noise was terrific. It took me a moment to realize it was not enemy fire. I had just positioned my men in groups of three, almost each party with a Bren gun, and was on the extreme left of the hedge. Crouching low, I retraced my steps back along the hedge to ensure that all were OK. One of the reinforcements in the centre group whom I had just positioned was already dead. He was slumped against the hedge with half of his head blown off. God knows what had happened, but I could only assume that it had been a mortar bomb. I helped his partner to lay him on the ground and covered him up with a gas cape. The latter was in a bit of a state. I told him to take over the Bren and to keep his head down for a while, as he could not possibly be seen, let alone hit from the front. The dead soldier was one of the new draft, he was probably eighteen or nineteen. Hearing voices on the other side of the hedgerow when there was a slight lull in the firing, I was told that it was my own platoon dug in in a very conspicuous position. At some stage a soldier came tumbling down through our protecting hedgerow. He was wounded in the hand. I wrapped his field dressing over his wound and packed him off to the rear, by himself. He appeared shocked and very frightened, at least he had a good 'Blighty'.

1725 hrs • 'D' Company reports four enemy tanks at the end of its field.

1730 hrs • 'B' Company has seen enemy tanks withdrawing on its right, back along the track in front of 'C' Company's original position.

Cpl G. Cowie, Section Commander, 18 Platoon, 'D' Company, 1st TS:
With all hell still being let loose, Sgt E. Parker came up and told me that shortly we were to counter-attack up the field on our right, and that because I was 'fresh', I would lead the remaining members of 'D' Company with my section. I thought it was very kind of him to give me such a star role! The object was of course to relieve 'B' Company,

which was still more or less surrounded, and take over 'A' Company's positions which had been overrun and were now occupied by the enemy.

Pte P. Birkett, Intelligence Section, Battalion HQ, 1st TS:

The CO mustered all cooks and orderly room staff etc. to take up defensive positions facing the Germans. He need not have bothered, they had nearly all done so quite some time before.

The Intelligence Section had originally been dug in some 150 yards behind the Command Post, scattered in the centre of a flat field. Having been rounded up like everyone else, they were now in a hedgerow somewhere, as part of the rearguard.

Pte J. Munro, Intelligence Section, Battalion HQ, 1st TS:

Some time earlier in the day, Sgt Glenday had ordered us (Cpl Lister and Ptes Holt, Birkett, Munro and Baverstock) to move forward and join the rifle companies as they were in danger of being overrun. As we ran over the field, some three or four walking wounded passed through – one was Cpl Beattie of the Signal Platoon. We looked directly eye to eye. He was hit in two or three places. We took our place in the line in any position available.

Pte (A/Cpl) J. W. Barnes, Section Commander, 18 Platoon, 'D' Company, 1st TS:

Captain Alexander came up and took command of 'A' Company. He gave instructions for every man to have a serviceable weapon (my rifle for example had no butt) and that all bandoliers and grenades were to be collected and shared out. During these preparations he noted that my battledress had something stuffed inside and asked me what I had there. I explained that I had several grenades, my pouches being full. He smiled and said that in that case he would stand a bit further away from me! We had previously been reinforced with twenty-four men led by Cpl G. Cowie. Most of these men had been given Bren guns, so the proportion of automatic weapons was very high at that crucial moment. Also, I knew Cpl Cowie to be a very disciplined and businesslike NCO and consequently, given the serious situation which then prevailed, he was an additional stabilizing factor.

Capt H.R. Alexander.

Cpl G. Cowie, Section Commander, 18 Platoon, 'D' Company, 1st TS:

I did not expect to use my Sten to any effect at this stage, so slung it across my chest and acquired a rifle and bandolier of fifty rounds. Just afterwards, we were all issued with a mug of tea brought up by Colour Sergeant 'Pipey' McKay and one of the Company HQ men. I had my tea laced with rum, but gained the impression that 'Pipey' had rum laced with tea! I was not really a 'drinker' then, but on reflection wished I had been, as one could get almost as much rum as one wished. This was the real stuff, brought up in large stone jars. There was always a rum ration issue prior to any engagement of this sort. 'Pipey' told me that Company HQ would be giving us covering fire all the way up, with surplus Brens. They did just that.

Sgt E.A. Porterfield, Platoon Sergeant, Carrier Platoon, 'S' Company, 1st TS:

The Bren guns from all the carriers, with their two-man crews, were sent to join with the a troop of tanks to give the rifle companies covering fire while they cleared up the last few pockets of enemy penetration. At the same time the vehicles and their drivers were used to evacuate the wounded.

Lt I.W. Murray, Platoon Commander, 17 Platoon, 'D' Company, 1st TS:

It was left to the rest of my own company, a company of DLI and a troop of tanks to clear the ground behind and relieve those of us on the ring contour.

1 • 1810 hrs • COUNTER-ATTACK • Behind the cover of smoke and artillery fire, a swift counter-attack goes in to relieve 'B' Company on the edge of ring contour 110 and retake 'A' Company's position. 'D' Company (1st TS) on the right, bravely supported by 141 RAC Crocodiles and a tank troop of the 24th Lancers, heads straight for 'B' Company, while 'C' Company (11th DLI) attacks on the left towards the five-sided field where 'A' Company was overrun.

Cpl G. Cowie, Section Commander, 18 Platoon, 'D' Company, 1st TS:

At 'H' hour, we formed up with myself leading and emerged into the field, and at a semi-crouch, advanced up the left side of it towards 'B' Company's position. About thirty or forty men were following me, in single file tactical formation. A few yards behind me was my own Bren gunner, Taffy Jones, with the gun strapped across his chest so that he could fire it from the hip, behind him the No. 2, then the new Company Commander, Capt J. R. Alexander, with the remainder of 'D' Company. On looking round later, I found that our attacking force seemed to stretch back for some considerable distance. Providing I kept my head down, there was cover on the left, i.e. a small bank and hedge. There were several yards to go before reaching the end of the field which seemed to slope up – our objective being 'B' Company's slit trenches just beyond it. There was no cover on the right, just an open field with an amazing number of 'brewed up' tanks. I felt somewhat exposed. Everyone, including the Company Commander, looked white and tense. I felt OK, although I do not know how I looked. Being an NCO in any case, one had to set an example. I think I did this day.

2 • 1810 hrs • Taking advantage of the counter-attack on the left flank, 'B' Company, 11th DLI, and Major Angus with those left from 'C' Company, 1st TS, move forward to flush the enemy from 'C' Company's original position.

Cpl G. Cowie, Section Commander, 18 Platoon, 'D' Company, 1st TS:

Local support was much in evidence. I could hear behind me, as promised, 'Pipey' McKay's Bren guns, and the tanks of the 24th Lancers firing their Besa machine guns. The 'big stuff' from the enemy was still flying about and it was anything but quiet, one could not hear what one said even if it was bawled out. About a third of the way up the field, bullets started slashing through the grass at my feet. I could have been hit either standing up or lying down, so I just carried on at the same pace, except I was now crossing my fingers and muttering a silent prayer that I would not be hit. The only time we would have had to pause and hit the deck would have been if we had been 'stonked' by mortars on the way up. We weren't. The small-arms fire continued, bullets pinging and whining all around me. I had no idea where it was coming from. It may have been from the front, or it could have been from the hedge on the other side of the field. The following day, we found a dead SS soldier with a Spandau in this hedge, almost at the point opposite where I was when the small-arms fire commenced. However, I believe it was Colour Sergeant McKay who had kept his word, and was ensuring that his Brens were chopping down every blade of grass in front of me in case Jerry was occupying a position en route to our objective.

3 • During the counter-attack, two 24th Lancer Shermans are destroyed by a tank dug in at the north-east corner of Brettevillette village, and to the left of 'D' Company's advance, 'C' Company (11th DLI) edge its way towards the five-sided field, led by Capt W. McMichael. In one company locality, 11th DLI troops find a man with a telephone manning a mortar observation post.

1830 hrs • On the 6th KOSB front, the 6th Royal Scots Fusiliers, supported by tanks and artillery, have moved forward and are now putting in a counter-attack to straighten the line on the far left flank.

Cpl G. Cowie, Section Commander, 18 Platoon, 'D' Company, 1st TS:

With a few yards to go to the end of the field, I ran up the small slope until my head was level with the ground of the field beyond. About a couple of yards ahead of me were several slit trenches, and a group of Jerry infantry were scrambling out of these towards a screen of trees about four hundred yards to the rear. They had probably seen us when we had been advancing and had realised that we were intent on taking over the position again. Taffy Jones joined me at the top of the slope and I grabbed his Bren and fired several bursts after the fleeing Germans, they were zigzagging towards the trees and running fast. I was a first class shot with the Bren, but did not seem to hit any, although I certainly helped them on their way (the only trees visible from the slope would have been those among the large hedgerow which formed the western boundary of 'A' Company's five-sided field, soon to be retaken by 'C' Company, 11th DLI).

2000 hrs • 'D' Company reaches 'B' Company's area. They find twelve exhausted survivors: the remnant of 'B' Company led by Capt Calderwood, and the party from 'D' Company who had joined them at 1240 hrs, still holding on in their besieged slit trenches. The newcomers swiftly leap into the other slits recently vacated by the retreating Panzer-Grenadiers and prepare to consolidate the position. It would appear that both sides, British and German, have been lying low in these trenches since the last enemy attack at 1605 hrs, in the hope of being reinforced. Mortar and machine gun fire continues to come in from the south, but the situation is now firm.

The track in front of 'B' Company's position as it appeared in April 2002, the 1944 hedgerow having completely disappeared.

Cpl G. Cowie, Section Commander, 18 Platoon, 'D' Company, 1st TS:
By now, Capt Alexander had come up alongside us. He bawled out to all to get into the slit trenches in double-quick time. I am not certain how many slits there were, but we ended up with two or three men per trench. A quick assessment revealed that there was a Bren gun in almost every other trench. Plenty of firepower, but we appeared not to have any PIATs or 2-inch mortars. I think we could have dealt with any enemy infantry, but not another tank attack.

As 'D' Company settles into its new position, 'C' Company, 11th DLI, are closes in on its objective, the five-sided field. A platoon led by Lt K. Pallister is about to engage some Spandaus and a heavy machine gun positioned in the field. As they do so, Capt McMichael takes the rest of 'C' Company down the right flank. Between the two groups, the Shermans bring down covering fire.

Cpl G. Cowie, Section Commander, 18 Platoon, 'D' Company, 1st TS:
There was still plenty of firing going on, but not at us, and we had not been in position for long when a section of Durhams walked slowly past our front about a hundred yards away on our left flank (Capt McMichael's group). They were being fired on but seemed to ignore it and kept going. However, the last man was suddenly hit whilst climbing over a single wire fence. He appeared to be shouting to the others in front of him, but he was unable to move and remained hanging on the wire. I shouted over to the chaps on our left, but they must have seen what had happened as Pte J. Barnes and another chap ran out and helped the wounded Durham back to their slit trench.

Lt Pallister and his men get held up as they try to advance across the five-sided field, but Capt McMichael and Corporal Rowe each throw a '77' grenade and rapidly expel the Germans from their positions and they flee in all directions.

2100 hrs • Battalion HQ hands over to the 11th DLI and the position comes under the command of Lt Col J.M. Hanmer. His Tyneside Scottish counterpart, Lt Col de Winton, is ordered to go back to 'B' Echelon and rest.

2210 hrs • 'C' Company (11th DLI) finally reaches its objective. Nearly fourteen hours after the first enemy attack, all the 1st Tyneside Scottish positions are now fully restored. However, some of the men wounded earlier in the day are by now in a very bad state.

Cpl J. Drysdale, No. 2 Detachment Commander, Anti-tank platoon, 'S' Company, 1st TS:

I lay and waited until we made a counter-attack. On hearing voices, I shouted for help but my slit trench was covered with branches and my rescuers thought it might be a trick and trained their guns on me until they saw who I was. An officer produced a flask and gave me a swig. He had been told that there were wounded around, and had immediately sent for an ambulance. I was then taken to the field hospital where they took my forearm off, gangrene having travelled nine inches up my arm. Later, I was transported to a large château before being taken to a hospital ship lying offshore which took me home.

Lt J.T. Griffiths, Platoon Commander, 9 Platoon, 'C' Company, 2nd Kensingtons:

After all the attacks were beaten off, we returned to our forward area and pressed on, passing several destroyed German tanks. Near one of them, lay what looked like part of a marble sculpture – the head and a shoulder of one of the tank crew. He had been a young blue-eyed boy who had been blown apart. I shall always remember the placid almost smiling look on his face and I do wish I had stopped to close his eyes.

Although they had left the immediate area the Germans kept firing solid shot from one of their guns on a low trajectory for some time. This was a particularly nerve-wracking experience for the speed of the shell was such that you heard the shell whip past you before the sound of the gun firing, and since we imagined the shell travelled more or less parallel to the ground and only a few feet above it, one felt the chances of being demolished by one was too high for comfort.

Cpl G. Cowie, Section Commander, 18 Platoon, 'D' Company, 1st TS:

I was now able to take stock of my position. I had a Bren, a Sten gun and plenty of magazines for each. My two companions in the trench had rifles and a couple of 50-round bandoliers apiece. We stayed in these positions overnight.

After dark, the guns now silent, the surviving members of 'B' Company and Lt Murray's platoon from 'D' Company withdraw from 'B' Company's area for a well-earned rest.

Lt I.W. Murray, Platoon Commander, 17 Platoon, 'D' Company, 1st TS:

While they held on throughout the night, those of us who had been relieved lay down and slept on the road.

Sgt A.R. Esplin, Section Commander, Mortar Platoon, 'S' Company, 1st TS:

We were all very relieved to hear 'Cease Fire!' from our Platoon Commander. We spent half an hour digging out our worst affected mortars, some were buried altogether in the clay at Rauray.

The Mortar Platoon has fired a staggering total of 3000 bombs during the fourteen-hour battle – an average of just over 200 bombs per hour.

L/Cpl A. Richardson, Regimental Police Officer, Police Section, Battalion HQ, 1st TS:

One felt the easing off of tension, everything seemed quieter, then as we learned later, although the lads had won the day it was not without heavy casualties. Later that night after making a brew, I sat down behind a felled tree trunk and said a prayer in silence. I'm not ashamed to admit it and I bet I was not alone in doing so.

Pte J.L.R. Samson, Bren-gunner, No. 4 Detachment, Anti-tank Platoon, 'S' Company, 1st TS:

We were told to clean our weapons and rest, so I operated the bolt of my rifle, ejected the round in the chamber, re-cocked the weapon and squeezed the trigger forgetting that I had left the full magazine attached, thus I had drawn another round into the chamber and fired it. My immediate reaction was that of panic, and even though I had realized that I had fired the shot myself, I jumped straight into the nearest slit trench followed by five others close to me. This in the event was ridiculous as the trench had been made for two people only. It then came back to me, all what had taken place that day, and for the first time I began to feel really terrified, especially because there was now less noise. I also found that I was dead tired. Nothing else happened to me that day, except that when all the survivors of the anti-tank platoon were gathered together, I found that there were only twelve of us (about 20 per cent of the platoon).

Lt J.T. Griffiths, Platoon Commander, 9 Platoon, 'C' Company, 2nd Kensingtons:

After dark, we were relieved and pulled back to reserve where once more our losses were made up. I found that several pieces of shrapnel had hit my clothing and helmet but without damage to me. I was beginning to feel a bit nervous and wondered how long my lucky streak would last. I was soon asking that question again. Driving the carrier some days later near Caen while following several tanks down a lane, the carrier was blown over on to its side by a landmine. Fortunately, as a precaution against exactly this eventuality, the floor of the carrier was covered with sand bags which absorbed the shock and retained any bits and pieces which might otherwise have been blown about. The crew were badly knocked about and all taken to hospital where they eventually recovered and rejoined us. My only damage was to be hit on the side of the head by our Pye radio '18' set, which gave me a headache and some amnesia. Nonetheless, according to the rest of the platoon, I behaved rationally and was in control of the removal of the injured and the salvaging of equipment from the carrier, including that blasted Pye set which should have been fastened down. The whole episode was a 'lost day' for me. It created a long term problem of headaches and eventual hospital treatment. The carrier was damaged beyond repair and was therefore bulldozed out of the way and 'lost'. For years afterwards some idiot in the War Office kept writing to demand to know what I had done with it.

During the evening, the day's action is mentioned in a radio broadcast made by 'Lord Haw Haw' of the German Forces Network. The 49th Division troops soon realize that he has a personal

Seated on the remains of a German vehicle, a 1st Tyneside Scottish soldier files a report into his log.

message for them when he declares in his familiar tones 'You Polar Bear Butchers!' He goes on to state that if any man wearing a Polar Bear (49th Division) flash on his shoulder is captured, he will be shot right away without any trial whatsoever, as British soldiers with such a flash, he claims, had massacred surrendering SS-Panzer crews without mercy (one week later, a Tyneside Scottish officer and two other ranks were captured during a reconnaissance patrol. Their bodies were found on 19 July in the cellars of Château Juvigny; they had all been shot. (see page 168). On the edge of ring contour 110, the relief party prepares for a night of tension.

Cpl G. Cowie, Section Commander, 18 Platoon, 'D' Company, 1st TS:
Everyone was just sitting tight. A complete 100 per cent stand to amongst all the forward positions was the norm in a situation like this. Tank engines could be heard revving up to our front and there was sporadic shelling all night with the odd flare illuminating the battlefield now and again. There were no casualties during the rest of the night, but there was one awful moment when footsteps were heard just in front of our position. It could only be an enemy patrol as we had received no information that any of ours were operating. My Bren was loaded and adjusted to 'automatic'. I was really ready to fire it, when a subdued voice from in front said, 'Are you the Tyneside Scots?' It sounded like a south country accent. We had no password, and one normally just got shot if unable to give the correct

one when challenged. We did not reply, then the voice continued, 'we are the Royal Engineers just putting some anti-tank mines down in front'. The Royal Engineers had laid their lives on the line. We had nearly opened up on them.

Sapper W. Hudson, 757 Field Company, Royal Engineers:
In the early hours following the battle, we were in front laying anti-tank mines in case the Germans made another attack. Coming back through the Tyneside Scottish lines, we nearly got shot up by them as they did not know that we were in front of them. That was the only time that they were pleased to see us, normally our presence made them expect trouble from mines or booby-traps.

Cpl G. Cowie, Section Commander, 18 Platoon, 'D' Company, 1st TS:
At first light, I dragged the Bren down into the trench to clean it. I was surprised to see the flash eliminator was squashed flat by shrapnel. A hair would not have passed through, never mind a bullet. It was a good job that I had not had to fire it during the night, as the bullet would have exploded in the barrel. One shell had actually burst nearby, so I should imagine that was what had caused the damage. During the morning, a company of Durhams relieved us, and we dug slit trenches in the field behind. We dug in near to a knocked-out tank and were not happy to see just a head lying on the ground nearby. Bodies were now two-a-penny, but a head by itself was a little bit different and we made a point of skirting round it. We discovered the body of the SS soldier with the Spandau in the hedge opposite where we had advanced the day before. He had a small, neat red hole in the side of the head, just under the rim of his helmet. He was bent stiff and could not be moved, so we left him with his Spandau. Later in the day, 'D' Company was withdrawn and we marched down the road by the side of the field. There were several wrecked German soft-skinned vehicles and motor cycles here. A few miles to the rear, we came across one of our divisional MPs directing traffic at a crossroads. He shouted out, congratulating the Tyneside Scottish, then came over and said we were the talk of the bridgehead. I thought that was nice. I believe we ended up at le Haut d'Audrieu. We were supposed to dig in, but another corporal and I and three others dug down about a foot, making an area about the size of a large double bed, and went straight to sleep. We were shattered.

The 1st Tyneside Scottish plaque on the memorial to the 49th (West Riding) Division, south-east of Fonteney-le-Pesnel.

CF C.W. Chesworth, Battalion Chaplain, Battalion HQ, 1st TS:
I was left behind to deal with burial of the dead as best I could, which was the most colossal job. All I could do in the end was gather together the various limbs and bodies and give them a communal grave, which created problems in relation to trying to label them for the War Graves Commission who would later re-bury them properly. Rauray was just one very long nightmare.

Pte (A/Cpl) J.W. Barnes, Section Commander, 18 Platoon, 'D' Company, 1st TS:

Of all the actions I fought in – and I served as a rifleman, section corporal and platoon sergeant, throughout the western front from Normandy to the last day but one of the campaign when I was wounded – Rauray was by far the worst battle. The company areas were a mass of debris, bodies and burning tanks. At the risk of sounding melodramatic, it was a kind of Armageddon.

Pte J. Munro, Intelligence Section, Battalion HQ, 1st TS:

We in 'HQ' assembled for a religious parade in a field and Pipe Major Tom Imrie played 'The Flowers of the Forest'.

Cpl G. Cowie, Section Commander, 18 Platoon, 'D' Company, 1st TS:

The next day, the survivors paraded. The RSM called the battalion roll (an unusual thing). Perhaps the same number answered their names as those that did not.

INTELLIGENCE DIARY 0005–0835 HRS

TIME	FROM	ITEM	ACTION TAKEN
0005	'C'	Tank noises in Brettevillette, also apparent tank shooting from right-hand edge of Brettevillette.	Artillery informed.
0011–0012	–	Mortar bombs land area 889658.	–
0450	'B'	Patrol under Lt. Allan returns reporting that there are no British wounded or dead in farm.	Brigade informed.
0530	'C'	Report hotting up by MG and Mortar Post at Queudeville.	Artillery informed.
0640	'C'	Being attacked by infantry and tanks moving across towards 'B' Company.	Own tanks (24th Lancers) and Artillery informed.
0645	'B'	Report enemy in their positions.	Coy told to hold. MG Pln informed. 'D' Coy warned.
0645	–	Mortar fire on Battalion HQ area.	–
0655	'B'	4 – 5 tanks and company of infantry attacking.	Carriers warned to stand by.
0710	A/tk '3' Section.	3 tanks knocked out before gun damaged.	Brigade informed.
0711	'B' & 'C'	Ask for ammunition.	Section of carriers sent forward with ammunition.
0718	–	One more tank knocked-out.	Brigade informed.
0725	'C'	Short of men.	DLI to assist by counter-attack.
0725	'B'	Doing well.	–
0730	'A'	Report one tank in their area, request a/tk gun.	Tanks contacted for support.
0735	Tk Liaison Officer.	Two troops lying behind 'A' Company and giving support	–
0745	Brigade	Asking about position on left.	Report situation under control.
0750	'S' Coy Comdr.	Tank firing in area Rauray. Ammunition unable to get through	Use of tanks suggested.
0750	Forward Obvn Off.	One platoon of 'B' Company seem to be at a loss what to do.	'D' Company to send forward an officer.
0755	–	Tanks at 889655, troops at 887654.	–
0800	–	Four prisoners of war brought in I Bataillon, Der Führer Regt, 2 SS-Pz Div.	Sent to Brigade. One is an Alsatian.
0812	'C'	First enemy to attack were in British uniform.	This has not been confirmed.
0822	'C'	2 plns overrun. One pln and Coy HQ still holding Enemy infiltrating rnd right and pressing from left.	11 DLI to deal with right. 'C' form base on 11 DLI.
0832	'C'	Fallen back on DLI.	–
0834	'B'	Situation in hand.	'Well done' passed to 'B' Company.
0835	Brigade	'A' Company to get in touch with KOSB on left and watch flank	Passed to 'A' Company.

INTELLIGENCE DIARY 0848–1147 HRS

TIME	FROM	ITEM	ACTION TAKEN
0848	DLI	Slight infiltration of 'C' Coy being dealt with. Tanks supporting two Coys of 11 DLI on our right.	–
0855	'D'	Smoke being put down in front of Company area.	–
0903	'A'	Tank at 891649.	–
0904	Brigade	11 DLI have beaten back opposition and are standing firm.	–
0915	'B'	Enemy machine gun fire from left.	–
0930	'B'	Pinned down by machine gun fire.	–
0940	To Brigade	SITREP (Situation Report). Help for evacuating casualties asked for.	Suggestion that tanks be contacted.
0942	'C'	Collected two officers and 25 other ranks and are with 11 DLI.	–
0947	DLI	Spandau in knocked-out tank at 890649.	–
0949	A/tk Officer.	15 tanks knocked-out. 10 by own unit. 5 by 217th Battery.	–
1003	'A'	Tank may be dug-in on left near Company area.	Tanks informed.
1005	'B'	Being encircled on right.	Ord to hold their ground. 'D' to reinforce. DF spt.
1040	'B'	Ask for tank support to re-establish themselves.	–
1044	–	'D' Coy platoon meeting resistance on the road as they move fwd, but are being supported by tks.	–
1055	'A'	Two tanks moving on left on KOSB front.	–
1109	Brigade	Situation improving on right.	–
1115	'B'	7 tanks 300 yards north-east of Company position.	Tanks have matter in hand.
1122	'B'	'D' Company platoon not yet contacted us.	–
1126	–	Battalion HQ area mortared.	Several casualties to rear HQ.
1130	–	Gunner asked to push forward Observation Post.	–
1131	'A'	Enemy have gone through KOSB. Tank at 894648.	–
1137	'D'	Tanks shooting at them but being engaged by our tanks. LMG at 891650.	–
1143	'B'	Ask for DF (defensive fire).	Artillery informed. Mortars also laid on.
1145	'B'	Enemy tanks in Company area.	–
1147	'C'	11 DLI being attacked by infantry.	–

INTELLIGENCE DIARY 1148–1400 HRS

TIME	FROM	ITEM	ACTION TAKEN
1148	–	Two German tanks knocked-out by our tanks.	–
1155	'C'	Enemy infiltrating round flank.	–
1157	–	Two Panthers knocked-out at 892649.	–
1204	'B'	Three tanks knocked-out and Coy sitting tight.	–
1215	To Brigade	SITREP (Situation Report) sent.	–
1217	'B'	Report six tanks burning in their area.	–
1223	–	Artillery asked for stonk in front of 'B' Company area.	–
1230	'A'	Company cut off from KOSB by tanks then fired on from flank thus splitting Company up.	–
1240	'B'	'D' Company platoon arrives. 'B' Coy can hold on providing there is tank support to meet enemy tnks.	–
1247	'C'	SP gun on left knocked-out. Smoke being laid 894653.	–
1254	'B'	Attacked by infantry and tanks from the left.	Artillery asked to shift fire over to left.
1300	–	Carrier gets ammunition through to 'B' Company.	–
1303	Brigade	Squadrons of 15th Recce Regt at 901660 & 898655.	–
1306	'B'	Call for continuation of stonk.	–
1310	'B'	Report shortage of two Brens.	Bde informed. Arrgmts to collect from A2 & B Ech.
1320	Brigade	Ask if machine guns required.	Yes.
1320	Artillery	Five tanks at 894638.	Artillery to engage.
1329	'B'	Can tanks clear machine guns on left.	Tanks to assist.
1337	Brigade	13 men of 'A' Company picked up by KOSB and are being returned.	–
1338	'D'	Company mortared.	–
1343	'B'	Enemy passed right of Company moving right.	–
1345	Brigade	Report that situation on right is back to previous.	–
1350	Forward Obvn Off.	12 tanks reported to be forming up in wood 888648.	–
1355	'D'	12 tanks at 892638.	–
1400	–	Capt. Mirrielees takes over command of 'D' Coy.	–

INTELLIGENCE DIARY 1400-2210 HRS

TIME	FROM	ITEM	ACTION TAKEN
1408	'B'	Being attacked again from SE and SW. Reinforcements required.	–
1405	–	Extra machine gun platoon arrives.	–
1410	–	SITREP (Situation Report) to Brigade.	–
1415	–	DF (defensive fire) brought down by Artillery.	–
1416	'B'	Troubled by machine gun in left hedge.	–
1420	'C'	Have remnants of two platoons.	–
1422	–	Friends on left have reached 898645.	–
1430	'B'	Tanks milling around in front of 'C' Company area.	–
1440	Brigade	Report from friends that part of 'A' Company are still in position supported by armour.	On investigation, this was found to be incorrect.
1445	Tanks	No enemy tanks now in view.	–
1510	–	Two 11 DLI Coy COs visited Bn HQ regarding relief of two Companies.	–
1550	'B'	Ask for DF (defensive fire).	Artillery informed
1600	'D'	Four tanks at 892648.	–
1605	'B'	Tanks and men debussing south of 'B' Company.	Artillery and mortar fire brought down.
1625	'B'	Enemy armour moving up on right.	–
1640	–	Three flame-throwing Churchills attached to Bn.	–
1650	'B'	Report that they have seen 'C' Coy 11 DLI moving up behind them and that this heartens them.	–
1651	'D'	Machine gun fire from left.	–
1655	To DLI	Commander of second company required here.	–
1725	'D'	Four tanks at end of field.	–
1730	'B'	Enemy tanks moving across right of 'B' Coy and withdrawing to wood in front of 'C' Coy.	–
1810	–	Attk to re-establish line put in. Right 'D' Coy, left 'C' 11 DLI, supp by 3 flame-throwing Churchills.	'D' to relieve 'B', 'C' 11 DLI to retake 'A' psn.
2000	'D'	Objective reached.	–
2210	'C' 11 DLI	Objective reached.	–
–	–	Lt.-Col. Hamner, 11 DLI, then took over command of Bn HQ, Carriers and Anti-tank guns.	After dark, 'B' Coy moved back.

POSTLUDE TO
THE BATTLE

In his Immediate Report No. 25 – Repulse by 49th Division – Rauray 1.7.44 (CAB106/963), Lt Col A.E. Warhurst concludes that during a day of bitter fighting, the Waffen-SS suffered a severe defeat at Rauray. In Warhurst's estimation, the enemy threw around fifty AFVs into the attack, including Mk V Panthers, Mk IVs and Sturmgeshütz III assault guns, during which his losses in both men and armour was considerable.

Of the enemy AFVs officially reported as definitely having been knocked out:

> 1st Tyneside Scottish Anti-tank Platoon claimed 10
> Det. No. 2, Sgt S. Swaddle – 2 tanks
> Det. No. 3, Sgt D. Watson – 5 tanks (Immediate Report No. 26, CAB106/963 claimed 9 tanks)
> Det. No. 5, Sgt S. Day – 2 tanks
> Sgt T. O'Brien – 1 tank
> 24th Lancers claimed 9 tanks and 2 StuGs
> 217th Battery, 55th Anti-tank Regiment claimed 6
> Artillery: Medium guns claimed 5 in one situation alone. Estimated totals range from 10 to 20.

Warhurst believed the total number of German AFVs put out of operation by British forces on the Rauray front must have been substantial, but conservative estimates put the figure at around 35.

Niklas Zetterling's carefully researched book *Normandy 1944* provides German figures for Hohenstaufen AFV losses for June/July gleaned from a variety of sources, including H. Fürbringer's book about the 9th SS-Panzer Division and the archival documents of OB West and Panzergruppe West. Unfortunately, no single source offers figures for 1 July only, but for the 'Epsom' period including 1 July, equipment losses are judged to have included 6 Mk V Panthers, 16 Mk IVs, 10 StuGs, 11 anti-tank guns, 1 heavy infantry gun, 6 light infantry guns, 13 mortars and 19 machine guns. It is not clear whether tanks of the 3rd Panzer Regiment, 2nd Panzer Division, were supporting the 9th SS-Panzer Division attack (although this was suggested as a possibility in the 49th Division's Intelligence Summary No. 18 of 2 July – WO 171/500). The 2nd Panzer Division had 21 Mk V Panthers and 85 Mk IVs operational on 1 July and had been in the area for some days.

In regard to British tank losses, the 24th Lancers lost 3 Shermans and the Sherwood Rangers Yeomanry lost 2. The successful defence of Rauray was therefore due in no small part to the 8th Armoured Brigade, and in particular, the gallant support of the 24th Lancers whose performance, given the fact that their armour was inferior to that of the enemy, was truly outstanding.

Lt Craig Mitchell, the Battalion's Intelligence Officer, writing in the 1st Tyneside Scottish War Diary (WO171/1382), confesses that he found it difficult to get any cohesion into his account of the day's action owing to the speed and confusion of the battle. He describes each little party caught up in the fighting as having their own story to tell, particularly the anti-tank and mortar platoons. Each mortar, with its barrel searing to the touch from continuous firing, fired 600 bombs out of a devastating total of 3,000 launched at the enemy. If one adds to this staggering statistic the total number of shells fired by a whole range of artillery from 'Big Boys' to naval guns, then one begins to see why the Panzers stood little chance of success and why their commanders were sending reports with quotations from Dante (see Stage Eight • 1200 hrs). In their own special way, the flame-throwing Crocodiles would have added to this hellish vision with their fire-breathing sorties. Lt Mitchell also points to first-class signal communication as being fundamental to the successful defence of Rauray, and claims that much of the task could not have been carried out without it. He of course commends the magnificent efforts of the Battalion's 6 anti-tank guns (he records them having knocked out a total of 12 tanks), but his greatest praise goes to the small band of men who remained all day on the edge of ring contour 110, and in particular to Captain K.P. Calderwood for maintaining wireless contact throughout.

The history of the 1st Tyneside Scottish, *Harder than Hammers*, mentions that the carrier platoon had to fight its way forward in order to get supplies of ammunition through to the hard pressed men of 'B' Company, one driver having to make the trip six times. Understandably, in any account of the Rauray battle, one needs to emphasize the firepower of the British artillery. According to one commentator in *Harder than Hammers* '. . . the air shrieked with the continuous whine and fizz of shells passing overhead.' However, the enemy's shell and mortar fire on ring contour 110 was also described as murderous, reminding us that the Germans themselves had a great deal of firepower at their disposal. The start of each enemy attack was heralded by a massive barrage of artillery and Nebelwerfer rocket bombs, and these aerial assaults must have greatly contributed to the high number of Tyneside Scottish casualties.

During the period from 26 to 30 June, the Battalion had lost 180 trained men. In his immediate post-battle summary, Lt Mitchell offers a preliminary estimate of the Battalion's losses on 1 July by listing 132 casualties. *Harder than Hammers* claims that the Battalion needed to replace some 400 men – nearly half its normal force. Major Samson, in his book *Geordie and Jock*, believed severe losses were sustained and that little over 200 were left at the end the day, a mere shadow of the unit that had arrived in Normandy just a few weeks previously. The Battalion certainly received 350 replacements a few days later at le Haut d'Audrieu (see page 162). Although considerably less in number, casualty figures for

Inspecting a knocked out SS-Pz Regt 12 'Panther' near Rauray, 27 June 1944.

other units who fought at Rauray appear to be in proportion, the 11th DLI needing 200 and the 10th Battalion 150 replacements. German losses were also very high: up to 1 July (inclusive), Kampfgruppe Weidinger had lost 108 killed, 408 wounded and 126 missing, and the 9th SS-Panzer Division's casualties had amounted to 1,145.

The attack on the Rauray gap had been the German's best and last chance to penetrate and drive a wedge into the Allied front while they still had Panzer divisions fresh enough to attempt it. At the end of the war, Dempsey told Montgomery that he looked on the Rauray battle as the turning point in the Normandy campaign; it was the start of the German collapse there.

SUMMING UP

While it is perhaps best to leave readers to form their own views about the Rauray battle from the evidence put forward is this book, it might be prudent to offer one or two observations, given the fact that a number of questions have been asked over the years about the 1st Tyneside Scottish and its performance during the day-long action.

Following the publication in the 1980s of a celebrated book about Normandy which contained a fairly damning passage about the 1st Tyneside Scottish on 1 July, alleging that its men were seen streaming back from their forward positions in disarray, a controversial review of the book, printed in a national newspaper, suggested that the Battalion in fact ran away and was subsequently deemed unfit for vital operations. For those who were aware of the battle honour, Military Cross and three Military Medals won by the Tyneside Scottish at Rauray, the reaction to this review was one of total outrage. Angry complaints were immediately lodged by several prominent, high-ranking Normandy veterans, which resulted in formal apologies being issued and the passage being removed from the book in later editions. However, the damage had already been done, and in response to the whole affair, Major John Samson began his quest for 1st Tyneside Scottish veterans' accounts of the Rauray battle in an attempt to restore the Battalion's reputation.

Having now drawn all the available evidence together, one can contemplate to what extent the Battalion was actually overrun. Clearly, the situation regarding the three forward companies was very confused for much of the day, with even those in the thick of the action unsure as to how many of their number had withstood the first attack. However, it can be stated that some sections were forced back by the ferocity of the enemy's determined onslaught. Some observers reported seeing men of 'B' Company retiring from ring contour 110 soon after the enemy had entered the position, and it would appear that some sections of 'A' Company were given the order to withdraw fairly early on and ended up being scattered over a wide area. Pte T.J. Renouf, rifleman, 7 Platoon, 'A' Company, suggests in his account of the battle that the decision to pull out was premature, although he confesses that he was only seeing the limited area around him. In his words:

I would emphasize that the confusion which followed the 'A' Company withdrawal was not due to panic, on the contrary there was evidence of much bravery. As I remember, I would say it was more likely due to the fact that by then there were no officers or NCOs around to rally the troops.

It is this comment which perhaps holds the key. When the Battalion left the UK, it had spent four years building both its physical and mental fitness for the trials which lay ahead. An important figure in this training programme, and the sort of man to whom the Battalion would look when under duress in action, was Major W.L. McGregor, the officer commanding 'A' Company. A Black Watch sergeant before the war, McGregor had shown sound leadership qualities during the battles of 1940 and was destined to become a MBE. When temporarily in charge of the Battalion in February 1943, he had on one occasion route marched the Battalion 50 miles inside 24 hours over the hilly roads of South Wales. His stock phrase appears to have been 'Your noo verra guid!', an indication of his ebullient style of training. If the Battalion was to live up to its motto, *Harder than Hammers*, then it was he who would cast their mettle. Having arrived in Normandy, Major McGregor was wounded leading his men from the front on 26 June during the first hour of the first action the Battalion took part in at Tessel Wood. Although his replacement, Capt D.C. Mirrielees MC, was a fine officer, such losses were extremely difficult for the Battalion to absorb. Another eight officers besides Major McGregor were lost before Rauray, including 'B' Company Commander, Major J.K. Dunn (MC), and 'D' Company Commander, Major H.B. Boyne. It also has to be remembered that the 40 replacements the Battalion received on 29 June for the 180 men lost during the week before the battle, were all placed in 'A' Company and were unfamiliar with those around them.

Nonetheless, despite the detrimental effect of these catastrophic losses and the withdrawal of 'A' Company, the Battalion still gave a fine account of itself (see the comments of Major-General E.H. Barker, Commander of 49th Division on page 178) with the Anti-tank Platoon setting a particularly brave example. Although the far left platoon of 'A' Company pulled back during the first attack, its position was not altogether lost until midday. Pte (A/Cpl) J.W. Barnes, Section Commander, 18 Platoon, 'D' Company, states that he found some elements of 'A' Company still digging in during late morning (see page 113), and it is important to firmly bear in mind that its men had spent several hours facing a 'last ditch' effort by elite SS-Panzers to break through the shoulder of the 'Epsom' salient before finally being cut up by tanks firing at close range into their lines. In regard to 'C' Company's efforts, Major W.K. Angus mentions in his account of the battle that his forward platoons fought with determination until their commanders were either killed or wounded (see page 84).

However, regardless of how much of its force the Battalion managed to keep at the front throughout the day, its primary objective was to maintain a presence on the edge of ring contour 110 – which it did. The job of the 1st Tyneside Scottish at Rauray was not so much to provide a 'thin red line' of riflemen against a spearhead of SS-Panzers, but to support 'B' Company in its important forward role with every means possible. Defensive artillery fire was always going to be the factor that would win the day for the British, but without the likes of Captain Calderwood in his outlying slit trench on the high-ground above Rauray, shouting out his coded targets above the noise of battle, and Major Frank Lucas, the artillery observation officer in Rauray who processed Calderwood's messages and directed most of the fire, the concentrated DF barrages needed to crumble the enemy's resources would not have been so effective. We have seen throughout this book the quality of determination employed by the Battalion in providing support for the small band who stayed put on ring contour 110, from the bravery of its anti-tank gunners through to the efforts of 'D' Company. Of course, other units, such as the gallant 24th Lancers, provided support at Rauray in equal measure, but none made more sacrifices.

The author has made every attempt to record the events as faithfully as possible given the sources available, but a totally accurate reconstruction of the battle would be virtually impossible to create given the rapidity of the action at Rauray and the resulting confusion, especially after a gap of nearly sixty years. British and German statistical records vary in relation to the type and number of AFVs destroyed on the day, and no doubt other written accounts would interpret the evidence which remains in the archives differently. However, despite these difficulties, the main aims of this book remain undaunted – to resurrect Major John Samson's dossier, preserve information about the Rauray battle which would otherwise have been lost and forgotten, and finally, to restore the Battalion's reputation by fully acknowledging its achievements on 1 July 1944, as a mark of respect for those who accepted sacrifice as a necessary duty.

OBSERVATIONS ON THE DEFENCE OF RAURAY BY CAPT (RETD) BRIAN STEWART CMG, 2ND I/C, 1ST TS ANTI-TANK PLATOON, 1942–4.

Since the Commanding Officer of the day, Lt Col R.W.M. de Winton, died long before the Samson initiative started, we have no one to describe the Rauray battle from the Battalion level. Corporal Cowie's description of the 2nd i/c, Major Nicol, rounding up the sick and the lame to reinforce the beleaguered Rifle Companies, reminds us too that the Major is no longer with us to give his point of view of the battle. The Intelligence Officer's graphic account is not that of a commander and he understandably found the battle confusing. His account is reminiscent of General Clausewitz's 'Fog of War'.

Clearly, I was much less concerned with the Rifle Companies' dispositions than I was with our anti-tank guns, but at least I can say with absolute certainty that as I visited our guns I saw three Rifle Companies doing their duty. We were all ready, willing and able to repel the enemy; the atmosphere was calm and determined, morale seemed high. Since, like Capt MacLagan, I was wounded and removed from the battlefield during the morning, I can add nothing to the accounts of those who survived until the end of the day, but what I saw as I toured all three forward companies while the battle was raging suggested that our Battalion was conducting itself in the best traditions of the Black Watch and of the earlier Tyneside Scottish battalions.

When trying to put Rauray into context, I have consulted many books on military history and philosophy to discover what academics and soldiers have had to say of men in battle. What is to be made of words like cowardice, courage, morale, fear, leadership; the conflict between a natural instinct for self-preservation and the determination not to be seen as a coward, or to let down one's pals? What is the part played by such indefinable morale boosters as regimental spirit and comradeship, in supporting men in the stress of battle and in helping them to overcome fear in the face of the unknown?

These were not subjects discussed at OCTU or amongst the officers of the Tyneside Scottish. The older contingent of lawyers, bankers and businessmen, and the youngsters fresh out of university did not contain

The Black Watch Association Reunion 2001, Regimental HQ, Balhousie Castle, Perth, Scotland.

any Rupert Brookes, nor, with our knowledge of the First World War, was it likely that any poet amongst us would have written as Brooke did: *Now God be thanked who has matched us with this hour, and caught our youth and wakened us from sleeping.* If there were officers or men in the Tyneside Scottish who thought of war in such romantic terms, they probably kept their thoughts to themselves. But although I doubt whether any of us had a romantic vision of war, there is little room for doubt about the depths and strength of the friendships that were forged during our years of male bonding, sharing common experiences and sometimes hardship. We may not have indulged in philosophical discourse about battle, but I think we all knew where our duty lay, and were proud of our Battalion and determined to do our best.

We had one very great advantage over many of our predecessors. We were not going into battle untrained, nor had we to endure years of misery in trench warfare. We had over two years to get to know each other and we were not survivors of a horrendous war of attrition. But even in the Second World War, without the long-lasting horrors of the First World War, some soldiers and officers found the fear of the unknown, death, wounds, capture, whatever it might be, too much to overcome. I have read many memoirs recording this problem, including those of Field Marshal Templer, who recounted having to threaten his men with his revolver in Italy. But clearly, good discipline, training and leadership all played their part in producing an almost perfect performance.

General Marchal, a distinguished American military historian, who called the battlefield *A field of terror*, estimated that three-quarters of fighting soldiers in a modern army would find it difficult to use their weapons to kill an individual enemy soldier, because modern society conditions civilized man not to kill. This may well be true, but in my view the General missed the point. We were not bloodthirsty and I doubt if many of us took pleasure in the idea of killing another human being. But that was by the way; the point was to inflict as much damage on the enemy as possible while minimising our own casualties.

Field Marshal Lord Carver, a fighting soldier as well as a thinking one, in his memoirs *Out of Step*, records a conversation between himself and General Horrocks. The General, having enquired how many tank casualties Carver's Brigade had suffered since crossing the Rhine said, 'That's not much, you can't be trying', to which Carver replied, 'I reckon my success by the casualties we inflict on the enemy, not by the casualties he inflicts on us.' Carver's reply encapsulated the principle most of us were working on by instinct. Our job was to hurt the enemy. Perhaps if we had been in a philosophical mood we might have propounded a useful fighting rote: 'Do unto the enemy before he does unto you.' Our satisfaction was in the effective destruction of the target, not in the destruction of human beings as such.

Whatever the mix of ingredients underlying our soldiers' performance, they fought well and did their duty, morale was high and they overcame what fears they had. The performance of Capt Calderwood sitting at the forefront of the British defences, calling down artillery fire throughout the battle, epitomizes the courage displayed by the fighting troops of the 1st Tyneside Scottish at Rauray, as does the tenacity and selflessness of our anti-tank gunners, Sgts Watson and Swaddle. As I attend the annual Regimental Reunions in Perth and meet the dwindling band of survivors from Rauray, it is a heart-warming and highly satisfying experience to be reminded of the great pride which they all share and the amazingly deep bonds of friendship formed during their time in the Army.

JUVIGNY TO MÉZIDON AND THE DISBANDMENT OF THE 70TH INFANTRY BRIGADE

2 JULY

During the morning of 2 July, several war correspondents visited the 1st Tyneside Scottish and made their way up to the high-ground south of Rauray village to see for themselves the scenes of destruction around the company locations remaining from the previous day's action. Preparations for withdrawing the weary Battalion to the area of le Haut d'Audrieu began around midday, and the move took place at 1400 hrs. Those Tyneside Scots who remained were collected together to form new 'B' and 'C' Companies, while new 'A' and 'D' Companies were made up from the influx of 200 South Wales Borderers, and 100 Herefordshires who came to replace all the missing Geordies and Jocks. This distribution was arranged so that comrades who had fought together could remain in the same company. Following one or two promotions, the new company commanders were: 'A' – Major Mirrielees, 'B' – Major Calderwood, 'C' – Major Angus, and 'D' – Major Alexander. A certain number of the replacements were specialists and these went to Support and HQ Companies.

3 JULY

At 1200 hrs on 3 July, the 70th Infantry Brigade was taken out of the line altogether and the 1st Tyneside Scottish returned to the pleasant atmosphere of Ducy-Ste-Marguerite. In much need of rest and reorganization after its shocking ordeal at Rauray, the Battalion spent the next few days trying to adjust to the massive depletion of its ranks. There was a lot to reorganize and the Battalion's Quartermaster was faced with the enormous task of replacing shattered weaponry and equipment, but despite these difficulties conditions at Ducy were good, with wigwam tents providing the troops with sufficient shelter from the poor weather conditions which were now affecting the area.

A further draft of fifty men from the Gloucestershire Regiment arrived the next day to further help the Battalion reorganize, and at Battalion HQ in the mill at Ducy, a small party, attended by Major-General E.H. Barker, Commander of 49th Division, was held at 2000 hrs to 'celebrate the victory'.

However, this respite from the trials of war was fairly brief: at 1430 hrs on 6 July the Battalion left Ducy-Ste-Marguerite to take up new defensive positions east of Montilly, just north of le Pont de Juvigny, and by 2100 hrs the following day a tactical HQ had reached the area and firmly dug themselves in. Six hours later in the dead of night, the whole Battalion had arrived and taken over from the 11th Royal Scots Fusiliers; with 'B' and 'A' Companies just north of the main Hottot–Fontenay road (GC 9), and 'C' and 'D' Companies behind them on the other side of le Bordel Rau stream.

Pte T.J. Renouf, rifleman, 'B' Company after Rauray, 1st TS:

Our Platoon Commander was Lt I. Murray, who was known to have shown great courage and leadership at Rauray. He had a good way with his men and was greatly respected and liked throughout the Battalion. Our Section Leader was Cpl S. Clarke. I shared a dug-out with him and found that he came from Elphinstone, a few miles away from my home in Musselburgh. 'B' Company faced the deserted village of Juvigny and our section was forward, dug in on a pathway leading into the village and some thirty yards from it. Being the forward section, we were confined to our slit trenches during the day, got our daily meal at sundown and spent the night standing-to on guard. It was an exposed and eerie position, every break in the silence, every moving shadow set alarm bells ringing. Château Juvigny was some 500 yards ahead to our left, on the upward sloping ground and surrounded by woods. It was taken to be a German HQ and it was shelled regularly by our 25-pounders. There were several direct hits during each stonk, and these were demolishing the château bit by bit.

At dawn, the Battalion adjusted its positions, made preparations for new wiring and mining, and during the morning the Mortar Platoon made three assaults on the enemy's positions around Château Juvigny in advance of a series of three-man recce patrols which parties of 'A' and 'C' Companies were set to make just before midnight. 'A' Company patrols had orders to follow a track and hedgerows towards a wood just north of the grounds of the Château and to listen in, pinpointing enemy positions and strengths. Two 'C' Company patrols were to attempt to locate the enemy on the right flank; one would go westwards to Hottot-les-Bagues, and the other south-east by making a circuit through 'B' Company's position and following the line of the Seulles river from the bridge to a church and back, via some buildings south of the main road (GC9) in front of 'B' Company. The 'A' patrols came across movement and sniping during their reconnaissance of the wood north of Château Juvigny, and reported the area full of Spandaus, with six teams in three locations. The 'C' patrol heading for Hottot set out just after midnight.

Pte P. Lawton, rifleman, 'C' Company after Rauray, 1st TS:

The road between Juvigny and Hottot was strewn with debris. There were several sorts of vehicles and guns and also the bodies of dead cattle and horses. We would crawl for ten yards then lie still and listen. From time to time, one of us would disturb a piece of metal, the noise sounded much louder to us than it actually was and we would freeze for a while, waiting for the challenge. Eventually we reached the edge of Hottot and lay for some time on the edge of the road, listening for the slightest sound of any movement in, or around, the buildings. Hearing nothing, we decided that they were not occupied and started to withdraw.

The other 'C' Company patrol, led by Lt A.J. Green, followed the Seulles river. It was not so fortunate and its recce ended in tragedy. Two men were lost during the exploration of the buildings south of the main road and a party of two snipers was sent to find them. One of the missing men was then found, only to be lost again along with one of the snipers.

9 JULY

Early in the morning of 9 July, 'C' and 'D' Companies were hit as the enemy responded to the previous day's mortar fire with their own. They also moved some of their Spandau teams from the wood during the night to occupy positions just south of the main road (GC9). Hidden in the hedgerow on the opposite side of the road, these teams sprayed Spandau fire in a wide arc towards one of the Battalion's forward company localities, causing them considerable discomfort. A defensive line of mines was then laid in front of the Battalion by its Pioneer Platoon, and a standing patrol was sent out at 0930 hrs to one of the buildings south of the road. The Battalion held its position throughout the day, and by 2000 hrs 'C' Company had installed the Intelligence Section at the junction near the bridge over the Seulles river, between the main road (GC9) and the road from Tilly-sur-Seulles (GC6).

Pte J. Munro, Intelligence Section, Battalion HQ, 1st TS:

Here I made a personal mistake. I was detailed to go forward to one of our trenches overlooking the Seulles valley and plot positions on a map. While I was talking to a private in the trench, I leaned forward and the sun caught the cover over the map – magnificent reflection. Jerry got top marks here – he lobbed a mortar very close to me and I was blown on top of the man I had been speaking to. I thought I had lost my left arm and I was scared to look. I felt slowly with my right hand until I was sure it was all there. I then walked back to the Field Dressing Station where they pulled a sliver of shrapnel out of my left elbow where I guess it had hit a nerve. They poured Sulphur crystals into the wound and my arm was dead for the rest of the day. I still do not understand how I escaped with such a light wound.

10 JULY

Some time later in the early hours of 10 July, the ripping sound of the enemy's Spandaus began to open up on the Battalion's front again, but 'A' Company successfully quietened them with its 2-inch mortars. However, peace was not an option for those dug in around Juvigny. Two days later, the 2nd Kensingtons carried out a massive machine gun shoot in the Hottot area, firing 465,000 rounds in a single day, resulting in an ammunition shortage which apparently caused the War Office some concern. The 1st Tyneside Scottish IO, Lt C. Mitchell, wrote in the Battalion War Diary:

. . . from 0730 hrs onwards we remained in our slit trenches waiting for enemy reprisals and being deafened by the noise of Vickers machine guns which fired over our heads all day.

This scene then continued for the next few days, with day and night recce patrols to explore buildings, take prisoners and pinpoint Spandau activity, and the daily trading of mortar and artillery fire. On occasions, smoke could be seen rising from Château Juvigny as the British shells found their targets. Two hungry and unhappy deserters came into the 'C' Company standing patrol around this time, both Poles from the 6th Company/II/986 GR, 276 Infanterie-Division. These men, a *Sturmman* (lance-corporal) and a *Schütze* (private), volunteered the information that Château Juvigny was acting as the company HQ and that the 6th Company was depleted to a strength of about sixty to eighty men. The two were clearly very run down and said that British barrages had been a constant trial to the German troops. A more detailed operation, code-named 'Mango', was then arranged to penetrate the area south of le Pont de Juvigny and the area beyond the Château as far as le Val Fleury to the west of Vendes. 'O' Groups were held, and details about 'Mango' were explained to everyone down to section command level with the help of a special model constructed by the Intelligence Section. However, a fairly major event befell the Battalion before 'Mango' could be launched.

On the night of the 16 July, a considerable amount of activity began to take place around the edge of the Battalion's vicinity. The Battalion's history *Harder than Hammers* takes up the story:

. . . Nothing unusual had been notified as about to come off, and everyone wondered what was happening. The answer came in the morning. With the light, at first glance it looked as if a whole armoured division was parked in the region, with tanks, carriers, lorries, etc., scattered all over the place. Closer inspection revealed these as clever rubber dummies. Jerry aircraft passed over during the day, and must have taken note. Anyway, in the evening at about 2300 hrs, the whole area was subjected to heavy aerial bombardment by German 'planes. One bomb landed right on the Battalion Signal Office, and the Commanding Officer was wounded and evacuated.

Pte P. Birkett, Intelligence Section, Battalion HQ, 1st TS:
I had to go on duty at midnight in the CO's dug-out. As I was fumbling my way to his HQ, over came a bomber and dropped a huge bomb. Not being very brave against bombs, I dived for cover between a jeep and a fallen tree. The bomb, which some said later was a land mine, landed about thirty yards away with a terrific bang. It wasn't until dawn that we saw the hole it made. A direct hit on the Signals . . .

Four signallers were killed and fourteen other Tyneside Scots injured during the bombing. The CO, Lt Col R.W.M. de Winton, was wounded in the leg and the 2nd i/c, Major D.N. Nicol, assumed command. Afterwards, some members of the Intelligence Section had the unpleasant task of searching for human remains in the huge crater left by the bomb which had devastated the Signal Platoon:

16 JULY

Pte E. Holt and I went round with a pail each, picking up bits of this and that, not that there was much left.

The author's father, Pte L. Baverstock, who had been with the Signallers immediately prior to the raid, had narrowly missed being wiped out in the explosion, having, in his words, 'just left them for a moment' – a decision which was to determine the future existence of this book and its author.

The reason behind the deployment of the dummy armoured division at Juvigny on 16 July is uncertain, but a likely explanation is that a diversion may have been ordered prior to Operation 'Goodwood', the major British armoured attack south-east of Caen, which was launched soon after on 18 July. Whatever the reason, the bait was certainly taken – sadly, to the cost of the Battalion.

17 JULY

On 17 July, 'Mango' was cancelled and a fighting patrol of platoon strength was ordered to go forward to the vicinity of Château Juvigny to recce the German HQ of the 6/II/986 GR.

Pte T.J. Renouf, rifleman, 'B' Company after Rauray, 1st TS:

Lt Murray and our Platoon were chosen for this task. We set off late into the night so that we would arrive at Château Juvigny just as dawn was breaking (at 0230 hrs, the very heavy artillery barrage that had been planned as part of 'Mango' went down for 45 minutes). The advance was uneventful, save for the problem of keeping in touch and maintaining fighting formation. As we neared the Château we found the bodies of several of our own troops, of the Hallamshire Regiment as I remember, who had been killed in a previous attack and had been lying there for many days.

(The Hallams had made a brave but costly set of attacks on Vendes on 14 July as part of Operation 'Cormorant'. By the end of it, their casualty figures had become as serious as those of the 1st Tyneside Scottish in June and early July. It would appear that the need to avoid future losses such as these was the reason behind the initial reluctance the 49th Divisional Command had for going ahead with 'Mango').

On reaching the Château it appeared to be deserted and Lt Murray signalled back to the CO who ordered the Battalion to advance. The advance took place on a two company front, since the Battalion would normally be deployed in a two line defence formation at this stage of the campaign.

18 JULY

Another nine deserters came in at 0900 hrs on 18 July, who confirmed that the enemy had indeed withdrawn. 'Mango' was suddenly on again, but without the immediate fire support. However, arrangements were made for artillery to be brought down if and when required. At 1000 hrs, the newly formed 'D' Company, 1st TS, led the advance, with 'C' Company behind them. As the Tyneside Scots made their way towards Château Juvigny, 'A' and 'B' Companies of the 1/4th King's Own Yorkshire Light Infantry headed for la Ferme Barbée on their left flank, an enemy strongpoint situated on a narrow spur of land, which the Yorkshiremen had attacked while the Hallams were making their hazardous bid for Vendes on 14 July. The 11th Durham Light Infantry moved up on the Battalion's right to complete the line of the divisional advance.

Cpl G. Cowie, Section Commander, 'C' Company after Rauray, 1st TS:

We crossed the road and headed for the Château which had been a good enemy OP. The enemy had pulled back and the Royal Engineers were already on the job, clearing grass verges with their Polish mine-detectors.

The Sappers and Battalion Pioneers picked up over 100 Teller mines, thirty-seven on the road leading up to the château alone. As the men advanced through the grounds of Château Juvigny they came across several dismembered Germans, mutilated by the tremendous artillery barrages that had continued throughout the previous week, and on

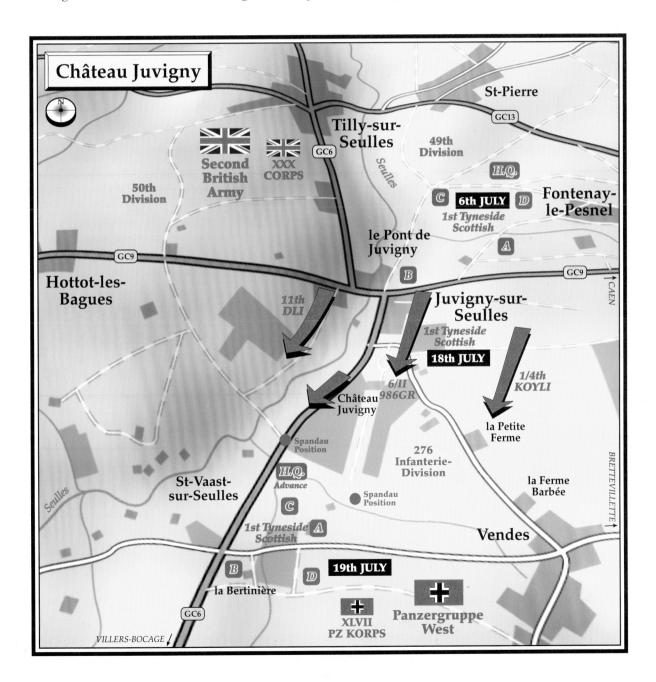

reaching the Château, the Battalion discovered more dead bodies lying around on tables in the rooms and the floors of the reinforced cellars. The leading sections carefully proceeded to carry out a full inspection of the abandoned building, making sure that the enemy had completely gone. The 986 GR had left behind a considerable amount of equipment and great care had to be taken as such items were frequently booby-trapped. Souvenir hunting claimed a number of lives in Normandy.

> *Pte R.D. Hilton, rifleman, 'D' Company, 1st TS:*
> *We went through the Château room by room, all of us knew well not to touch or pick up anything. There was not a sign of any Germans. I don't think our Company had any casualties.*

> *Pte J. Munro, Intelligence Section, Battalion HQ, 1st TS:*
> *I climbed up the four floors of the building and on the top floor I found three cartons of morphine vials, obviously intended for wounded Jerries. I took them to the MO.*

19 JULY

When I first read the 1st Tyneside Scottish War Diary for Normandy (Public Record Office WO171/1382), I noted with much interest that the entry for 19 July 1944 included a passage which mentioned a private in the Intelligence Section finding the bodies of an officer and two other men who had been missing since 9 July. They had been shot. Back in the late 1970s when my father was still alive, I had once quizzed him about his experiences in Normandy and during one recollection he had described to me a deserted château, explaining how he had gone off on his own to explore the cellars and found a group of men who had all been shot. The Battalion War Diary had therefore verified his story for me.

'B' Company later passed through the forward companies and launched an attack up the road leading south from le Pont de Juvigny (GC6) at 0930 hrs on 19 July, and by 1015 hrs was in a new position digging in.

> *Pte T.J. Renouf, rifleman, 'B' Company after Rauray, 1st TS:*
> *The advance continued beyond the Château. The line of attack of our section was up the Villers-Bocage road located some 50 yards to the right. This was a straight open road rising steadily towards the high ground a few hundred yards ahead. Led by Cpl S. Clarke, we had advanced, cautiously, about 100 yards when the order was given to take up positions in the roadside ditch. As we moved into the ditch a very short burst of Spandau fire struck the section. We all dived into the ditch which gave us good cover, but since we were in the sights of the enemy we were virtually pinned down. The only casualty was Corporal Sammy Clarke who was badly hit in the lower groin. He was in great pain and shouting for help. The Section was well spread out but those nearest to Sammy were bravely giving him help and calling for stretcher bearers. The Spandau crew were obviously positioned on the high ground by the roadside some 200 yards ahead and were covering everything on the road. One of the other sections moved forward on the right flank under the cover of the trees, to deal*

with the Spandau and so allow our section to move. After some 15 minutes, the stretcher bearers, again showing great courage, arrived to attend to Sammy and took him away.

The order then came for our section to withdraw back to the Château. We moved quickly across the road and into the woods, fortunate not to be fired on. It was there that we learned that Sammy had died almost before he had reached the RAP. Seemingly the bullet or bullets that hit him had punctured an artery, and despite all the efforts the bleeding could not be stopped. This was a cruel blow that affected everyone in the platoon because he was highly regarded as a section leader and very popular. Because of my connection with him back home, it was particularly distressing to me. Reluctantly I wrote and told my mother in a guarded way what had happened and she went to visit Sammy's widow. The girl was prostrate with grief and all the more distressed for the sake of their year-old daughter.

Back at the Château, I discovered that the pick that I carried down my back, wedged there under my backpack, had a lump taken out of the shaft by one of the Spandau bullets. Later, I found a Spandau bullet in my pack which had been stopped by the thick wad of writing paper that I had recently received from home. Then I remembered that a bullet had hit the concrete telegraph post about two feet in front of me when we were fired on. Three bullets had whizzed past me missing my body by inches and made me realize that in the lottery of battle much depended on Lady Luck. What I took to be a short burst of Spandau fire, was in effect a lethal dose. In half a second this deadly weapon had delivered over 10 rounds.

The German MG42 'Spandau' was a very flexible machine gun which could fire roughly 1,200 sustained rounds a minute using connectable 100-round belts, but in combat it was generally used as a light machine gun, firing short economic bursts.

20 JULY

Battalion HQ having been established in the cellars of Château Juvigny, the 1st Tyneside Scottish rifle companies moved southwards the following day to take positions around le Bertinière, half a mile east of St-Vaast-sur-Seulles, where they were subjected to some sporadic shelling during the night. In the American sector, the US XIX Corps had finally expelled the enemy from St-Lô.

21 JULY

Returning from a night recce of the area south of the position, a patrol brought back news the next morning that the enemy was digging in less than a mile south of Etregy, just north of the Ruisseau du Coisel (a stream). However, before any further actions could be launched, the position was handed over at 1400 hrs to the 1/7th Warwickshire Regiment of the 59th (Staffordshire) Division, and by 1800 hrs the whole of the 70th Brigade had been moved back to an assembly area at Folliot, three and a half miles north-west of Tilly-sur-Seulles. The reason for this sudden withdrawal from the line soon became apparent when orders were received that the 49th Division was to leave XXX Corps and be transferred to I Corps on the Caen sector. Reconnaissance parties were quickly organized and despatched from Folliot to prepare the ground for the arrival of the bulk of the Battalion in an area just east of Caen. The narrow roads were rutted with mud, churned

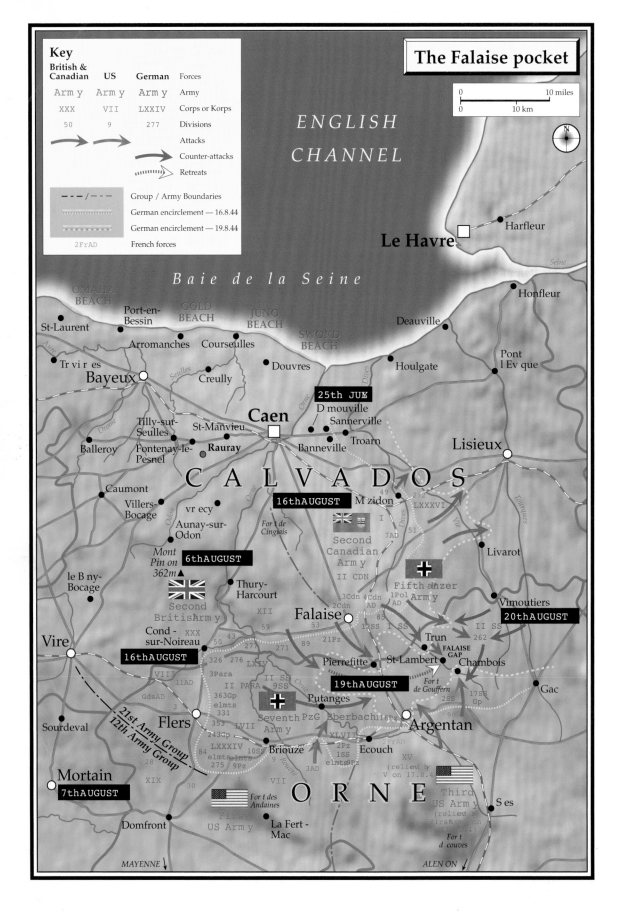

The Falaise pocket

Key

British & Canadian	US	German	Forces
Army	Army	Army	Army
XXX	VII	LXXIV	Corps or Korps
50	9	277	Divisions
→	→	→	Attacks
			Counter-attacks
			Retreats
— · · — / — · —			Group / Army Boundaries
			German encirclement — 16.8.44
			German encirclement — 19.8.44
2FrAD			French forces

0 — 10 miles
0 — 10 km

N

ENGLISH CHANNEL

Le Havre

Harfleur

Honfleur

Seine

Baie de la Seine

OMAHA BEACH

GOLD BEACH

JUNO BEACH

SWORD BEACH

Deauville

St-Laurent

Port-en-Bessin

Arromanches

Courseulles

Douvres

Houlgate

Pont l Ev que

Tr vi r es

Bayeux

Creully

Seulles

Aure

Drome

Tilly-sur-Seulles

St-Manvieu

Caen

25th JUN
D mouville
Sannerville

Lisieux

Banneville

Troarn

Orne

Balleroy

Fontenay-le-Pesnel

Rauray

Dives

CALVADOS

M zidon

49

LXXXVI

51

Caumont

Villers-Bocage

vr ecy

Aunay-sur-Odon

Fort de Cinghais

16thAUGUST

272

Livarot

Vire

Touques

I

7AD

Second Canadian Army

II CDN

Fifth Panzer Army

Vimoutiers

Mont Pin on 362m▲

6thAUGUST

Thury-Harcourt

Odon

Second British Army

XII

3Cdn 4Cdn AD

2Cdn

1Pol AD

85

1SS

I SS

II SS

262

le B ny-Bocage

Cond -sur-Noireau

XXX

50

43

59

Falaise

53

89

21Pz

271

Trun

FALAISE GAP

St-Lambert

Chambois

16thAUGUST

VIII

326 276

277

3Para

LXIV

II SS

Pierrefitte

Fort de Gouffern

17SS Gp

2SS

Gac

11AD

GdsAD

363Gp
elmts
331

II PARA

9SS

19thAUGUST

Putanges

Flers

353
243Gp

LVII

Seventh PzG Army

Eberbach

16Pz

Argentan

90

Sourdeval

21st Army Group
12th Army Group

28

LXXXIV
84 elmts
275 9Pz

10SS
elmts
9

Briouze

Rouvre

3AD

XLVII

2Pz
1SS
elmts 9Pz

Ecouch

2FrAD

XV
(relied by V on 17.8.4

Mortain

7thAUGUST

XIX

30

VII

Fort des Andaines

First US Army

O R N E

La Fert -Mac

Third US Army
(relied b
First Army on

S es

Domfront

Fort d couves

MAYENNE↓

ALEN ON↓

up by the vehicles of the 11th Armoured Division. They were trying to leave the area just as the first Polar Bear groups were arriving and the inadequate width of the low grade Normandy roads caused huge traffic jams.

Cpl G. Cowie, Section Commander, 'C' Company after Rauray, 1st TS:

I was in the advance recce party. There were about eight of us; representatives of all companies and sub-units, under the command of Capt Brennan. We arrived in the area just east of Caen and dug in near some vehicles with the 'HD' sign of the 51st (Highland) Division in a small embankment. There was a lot of German equipment laying around, greatcoats etc. but no weapons. The rest of the Battalion arrived over the next few days.

The whole Battalion moved in troop-carrying vehicles to a position south-east of Démouville, taking over from units of 3rd Infantry Division on 25 July. On the same day, the Canadian II Corps launched Operation 'Spring', an unsuccessful attempt to strike out along the Caen–Falaise road, and the US VII Corps began Operation 'Cobra', the push that would eventually allow the Allies to break out in the Western sector. Very different to the confined bocage of the Fontenay-le-Pesnel area, the countryside south-east of Caen was an open rolling landscape of cornfields, recently scarred by the massed tank formations of the 7th, 11th and Guards Armoured Divisions when they had attacked through the area the previous week during Operation 'Goodwood'. Not long after arriving, the enemy started to shell the Battalion's position using 10.5 calibre long-range guns, the heaviest pounding that the Tyneside Scots had experienced in Normandy, then during the following night, Luftwaffe night fighters added to their torment by bombing and strafing the area. An elaborate network of deeply dug trenches, with strong, thick head cover, offered the Battalion reasonable protection from the shelling and mortaring and casualties were kept fairly low, but the intense claustrophobia of trench life under heavy shellfire created an atmosphere much like the Western Front during the First World War. Everyone lived below ground during the day, midday meals consisting of haversack rations and main feeding taking place only at night. Over the next few days, the heat of a baking July sun began to harden the muddy troughs that had been carved in the battered roads by the wheels and tracks of heavy traffic, and vehicles had to maintain a 5 mph speed limit to avoid raising clouds of dust which were conspicuous to the enemy. Slow-moving columns virtually became sitting targets, and to ride along the roads at this speed was a nerve-wracking experience.

Towards the end of the month, the 49th Division artillery arrived and began to dominate the battlefield with their fire, putting over four to six shells to every one the Germans fired, which brought about a considerable reduction in enemy artillery activity. It was around this time that XXX Corps began Operation 'Bluecoat', finally taking the prominence of Mont Pinçon on 6 August, the same day that the US XIX Corps, attacking alongside the British VIII Corps, had taken Vire. On the evening of 6 August, 'Ultra', the Allied code-breaking system, warned that the Germans were about to launch their 'Lüttich' attack on the US VII Corps at Mortain, about 10 miles south of Vire. Knowing that the Germans, under Hitler's orders, would make a

25 JULY

6 AUGUST

final stand at Mortain, Montgomery issued a directive for a large enveloping encirclement to be made around the German Fifth Panzer-Army and Seventh Army. In the east, the First Canadian Army would strike out towards Falaise, then head east towards the River Seine; in the centre the Second British Army would initially drive south-east and then thrust eastwards also; and in the west the Third and Twelfth US Armies would sweep round towards Alençon to form the southern arc of the encirclement.

7 AUGUST

On the night of 7 August, the Canadian II Corps, supported by tanks of the Polish 1st Armoured Division, began Operation 'Totalize', the attack against the German forces around Falaise, which Montgomery hoped would begin the northern phase of the encirclement. However, the attack was held up short of Falaise. Although it was not engaged in the operation, the Battalion had a grandstand view of the supporting air bombardment by the RAF on the Falaise Road positions, and cotton wool was issued to all troops to put in their ears, to counteract the effect of the 4,000 lb bombs. Along with heat came the discomfort of insect bites as swarms of mosquitoes infested the area. *Harder than Hammers* describes them thus:

> *These pests appeared absolutely ravenous, and it was impossible to get away from them. In spite of liberal supplies of anti-mosquito cream being issued and a generous allowance of 'Flit' for the trenches, they made life thoroughly uncomfortable. One company, through an error, discovered that a pressure lamp would burn brighter on 'Flit' than on its normal paraffin.*

> *Pte P. Lawton, rifleman, 'C' Company after Rauray, 1st TS:*
> *We tried anything and everything to discourage the millions of mosquitoes but nothing worked. I remember being in a forward observation trench watching for enemy movement. As this trench was in sight of the enemy, any sudden movement could be fatal, so when a mosquito landed on your hand all you could do was wait for it to go away.*

> *Pte P. Birkett, Intelligence Section, Battalion HQ, 1st TS:*
> *The mosquitoes finally met their 'Waterloo' in the form of anti-gas ointment. I wasn't surprised, the smell nearly killed us as well.*

8 AUGUST

A few hours later during the morning of 8 August, the 1st Tyneside Scottish were moved a few miles east to the bomb-shattered and gutted villages of Sannerville and Banneville, holding defensive positions there for the following week. Strong trenches were once more necessary, as again enemy shelling and mortaring was heavy. Battalion HQ was particularly badly stonked, and at one point the Intelligence Section had to deal with a fire carrier that had been set ablaze. Around this time, RSM Sands, 1st TS, was accidentally killed through a mishap with a Sten gun.

> *Pte J. Munro, Intelligence Section, Battalion HQ, 1st TS:*
> *RSM Sands was waking a sleepy soldier for a 'stand to' using the butt of his Sten gun. As so often happened, the heavy bolt action cocked the gun and it fired right into the RSM's chest. I believe he died instantly.*

Patrols were sent out each night, in order to consolidate the ground in front of the position.

> *Cpl G. Cowie, Section Commander, 'C' Company after Rauray, 1st TS:*
> *We had the task of manning both day and night standing patrols. Our party normally consisted of half a dozen men and a signaller. One day our platoon was tasked to take a fighting patrol to a château on the other side of the road from our position. The object was not to take prisoners but to occupy it if the enemy were not there. We approached the château carefully, it was a lovely day and all was still. As we entered the garden to the château someone stopped me and pointed to the ground There were a dozen or so small prongs sticking up an inch or two above the surface – anti-personnel mines. These would have taken one's leg off if stepped on. We marked a safe route up to the house with bottles we found laying around, and posted the majority of the patrol outside while the members of the Platoon HQ searched inside the premises. It was furnished but there was no sign of the enemy. While we looked around, a message came from outside that some Germans had been seen. A couple of the chaps were in firing positions watching a leafy path at the rear of the building. I thought it was a false alarm, but then a couple of German soldiers walked across the path about 100 yards away. They were obviously in position there and had no idea we were in the château. It was a case of 'live and let live'. We contacted Company HQ, after which we were instructed to withdraw but to leave a strong section behind.*

In the south, General Patton's rapidly advancing US Third Army had raced up from Le Mans through Alençon, finally reaching the outskirts of Argentan on 12 August. Two days later, the First Canadian Army began Operation 'Tractable' – the attack which it was hoped would finally break the enemy's resistance around Falaise. Time was pressing. Despite having successfully trawled von Kluge's battered Army Group B into a catchment area known as the 'Falaise pocket', the gap at its eastern end was still open and some key German units were being allowed to escape (see map on page 170).

12 AUGUST

THE ACTION AT MÉZIDON

By the middle of August, the German front had virtually collapsed and the withdrawal that was later to be known as the 'Flight to the Seine' had begun. On 15 August, Operation 'Dragoon', the Allied landing in the south of France, took place, and the Battalion was moved south-eastwards, first to le Torp where all the 3-ton lorries were emptied of their stores, and then on to le Mesnil, prior to an attack to seize the town of Mézidon and the high ground beyond. By midnight, the whole Battalion had settled down, resting for the operations on the next day. On 16 August at 1430 hrs, the Battalion was carried forward, two rifle companies in the 3-tonners and one rifle Company on Support Company fighting vehicles. 'D' Company proceeded on foot, a distance of about eight to nine miles. Once HQ and 'D' Company had arrived in position at 17.30 hrs, the Battalion was ready to attack.

15 AUGUST

16 AUGUST

'A' Company pushed straight through to the western outskirts of Mézidon, and 'D' Company, embussed in the scout cars and armoured half-tracks of the 49 Division Recce Regiment, followed them through on arrival. The intention was for 'A' and 'D' Companies to clear the town through to the eastern side across the Dives river, and for 'B' and 'C' to take up positions behind on the western side of the town. 'A' and 'D' Companies had of course been formed from the replacement troops after the Rauray battle and were therefore fresher than the original Tyneside Scots of 'B' and 'C' Companies.

Unfortunately, the bridges over the Dives had been blown by the enemy, and resistance in Mézidon slowed the progress of 'A' and 'D' Companies as they fought to break through the town. They were still only half-way to their objective by the time darkness fell. As the town had to be cleared before the Sappers could get on with mending the bridges, 'A' and 'D' were forced to carry on clearing the remaining part of the town in the dark, in the face of strong enemy opposition.

Cpl G. Cowie, Section Commander, 'C' Company after Rauray, 1st TS:

We had been marching in tactical formation on either side of the road, with about five yards between each man and more between the various sub-units, therefore a company extended over quite a distance of roadway. The two leading Companies were already advancing through the town. All was quiet and it was getting near dusk. I stopped a 49th Recce Regiment armoured car coming out of the town and was told 'It's all right, the town's clear' – famous last words! We had only advanced a short way up the main street when the enemy's artillery opened up. Shells began to fall in our (western) part of the town and we immediately deployed off the road. Those of us on the left-hand side went through gardens and between houses, eventually advancing across a field in an easterly direction. We could now hear small arms fire up ahead and some mortar bombs were dropping in our area. We stopped and started to dig-in, but the ground was hard and we could not get very far down. The mortar bombs then began to fall very nearby, and so as our slit trench was no good as yet, the Platoon Officer and I dived under a table situated in the corner of the field as it seemed to have a stone top to it. It seems ridiculous now, but at the time we sought anything for a bit of cover rather than be caught out in the open. The firing ceased and I turned over on my back, still under the table, and listened for more mortar bombs. Being six foot tall, my legs were sticking out from underneath the table. All of a sudden a mortar bomb dropped a yard or so away and I felt a dig in my left knee. The wound did not hurt and was not bleeding, but when I tried to stand up after the stonk I found that I could not bend my knee. I wanted to stay but the young officer ordered me to go back to the RAP and get the wound dressed. It was completely dark when I eventually arrived at the RAP which was situated near the bridge on the west bank of the river. Here I saw Piper Bruce with a large shell dressing on his stomach. He had been hit by Spandau fire while carrying wounded on his stretcher. He died before he left the RAP. The following day I was taken, via the Advanced Dressing Station, to a tented hospital in Bayeux where I was *operated on to have a piece of shrapnel removed from my knee, and a day or so later I was flown back to the UK. I later returned to serve with the 1st Black Watch alongside others from the Battalion who by then had been transferred to the 51st (Highland) Division.*

Clearing each house and garden in turn, the companies fought on in the dark, much of the time unsure as to their exact positions. However, 'D' Company finally managed to force a way through the town, Cpl C. Williams dealing with two Spandau posts on the way. Behind them, 'B' and 'C' moved up and an advance HQ post was established near the church on the west bank of the Dives. By about 0100 hrs, the eastern outskirts of Mézidon had been cleared, but the men were exhausted. No one had got to bed before midnight the night before, and 'D' Company had marched eight miles in full kit in the sweltering heat of the noon day. However, despite the success in Mézidon itself, stiff opposition was still coming from the high ground that rose steeply from the east of the town, and it was decided to consolidate the ground won so far and dig in for the night.

Harder than Hammers describes the scene:

> *. . . Owing to the broken bridges and enemy artillery, mortar, and small arms fire landing in the streets, it was not possible to bring forward any rations. The companies were in continuous action all through the night against parties of enemy infantry trying to regain possession of the town, and considerable casualties were sustained and inflicted.*

The advance Battalion HQ was situated in the town square, and several losses in personnel were suffered here, including Lt Craig Mitchell, the Intelligence Officer, who was cut down by a mortar bomb while crossing over to the command post. These were French mortars – silent in flight, with no warning other than the explosion of the first bomb, and the enemy was using the church tower just opposite as an aiming mark for them. This dreadful spell of mortaring continued all through the night and the following morning, and the area became known as 'Bomb Alley'. Ten prisoners of war were brought in during the day – from the 7th Company/II/858 GR and the 9th & 10th Companies/III/858 GR of 346 Infanterie-Division.

The first signs that the enemy might be finally withdrawing came during the afternoon of the following day, when the town's civilians suddenly began to appear in the forward area at 1500 hrs. 'A' and 'D' Companies immediately sent out patrols, who witnessed the main body of the enemy pulling back. At 1615 hrs, 'A' and 'D' Companies moved forward and gained possession of the ridge which dominated the eastern outskirts of the town. Here, two deserters from the 2nd Company/I/858 GR were captured, dressed in civilian clothes.

Harder than Hammers again:

> *. . . With the capture of the town completed and the high-ground beyond in our hands, other units of the Division passed through and there was time to rest and bury our dead. The French population of the town displayed incredible enthusiasm at their liberation. Many*

17 AUGUST

did not appear to know whether to laugh or cry as they attended the funerals of our men, at the same time celebrating with the Scots the day of liberation – and forming the inevitable Resistance Movements.

Having passed through the 1st Tyneside Scottish at Mézidon, the 10th Durham Light Infantry crossed the Dives and the Vie beyond it, and tried to fight its way up to the high-ground of Mont de la Vignes. On the crest of the hill was a wood enclosing a château where the enemy commanded a strong defensive position. Fighting uphill, the Durhams were severely ripped into by Spandaus concealed in hedgerows along the way. Storming the château, they set about clearing it of enemy troops, and after much close fighting they made the position as secure as they could with the few men that remained, taking fourteen POWs. However, by now it was totally dark and ammunition and supplies were taking a long time to come up to the high-ground. At 0300 hrs disaster struck a massive mortar strike was immediately followed by a strong enemy counter-attack. The small band of Durhams gallantly fought back, but when at dawn a second German company appeared, the Durhams had to fight their way out in small groups and try to dig in at the foot of the hill. Two hundred men of the 10th DLI were either killed, wounded or taken prisoner in this one costly encounter.

Displeased with way his forces in Normandy were crumbling, Hitler replaced *Generalfeldmarschall* von Kluge as Commander OB West and Army Group B with *Generalfeldmarschall* Model, but it was too late – the gap which formed their only means of escape was tightening. The Falaise pocket had almost been closed.

19 AUGUST

At midday on 19 August, the 1st Tyneside Scottish were moved back to Moult, where they were to receive a stunning blow.

THE DISBANDMENT OF THE 70TH INFANTRY BRIGADE

In order to describe the break-up of the 70th Infantry Brigade, one can do no better than quote one of the officers of the 1st Tyneside Scottish, who wrote in 1947:

At 1500 hrs, the Commanding Officer summoned all officers to Battalion HQ, and in an atmosphere of intense gloom, amounting almost to despair, announced that the whole of 70th Inf Brigade was to be broken up. This sudden and unexpected bombshell was a terrible shock to all, and disappointment was bitter that after the fine record the Battalion had achieved during the hard days, now that the first round of the campaign had been won, it was not to be allowed to share in the fruits of victory.

The Commanding Officer explained that this decision had been forced upon higher authority because of the desperate shortage of reinforcements, which could now be found in no other way. On 20 August, Major-General Barker, GOC, 49 Div, addressed all officers and warrant-officers of the Brigade, expressing his sorrow at losing the brigade and his sympathy with all concerned. 56 Brigade, who had served so far as a fourth brigade in 50 Div, was to replace the 70th, which was now transferred to 59 Div, the whole of which was to be broken down. Before leaving Moult, Major-General Barker arranged for the transfer to the Essex Bn in 56 Brigade of all the Herefords in the TS, and of all the SWBs to the SWB Bns in the same brigade.

On 21, the Battalion moved to Fresnay, where the breaking up was to take place, being housed in comfortable surroundings; the whole Battalion in houses for the first time since landing on the Continent. On the next day all officers of 59 Div (including 70 Brigade) were addressed by the C-in-C, General Montgomery.

The C-in-C began by outlining the progress of the campaign to date, explaining on the broad scale how and to what extent total success had been achieved. He expressed his deep sorrow that he had had to order the breaking down of the formations in this way and explained that the decision to do this had been anticipated to be necessary at this stage, before the invasion was launched. On the whole, casualties had been lighter than had been expected, but in order to press home the initiative we had secured, it was vital that units should be brought up to strength. Rather a slightly smaller army with units complete than a larger army with incomplete units. It was a bitter pill to swallow, but all would have the opportunity of finishing the job, if with other formations.

The breaking down started almost immediately. On 23, Major Alexander, Captain Mackenzie and twelve other ranks were posted to 11 RSF, 49 Div On the 24th, Lt Col Nicol, Major Calderwood, Captain Dempster, Captain Brennan, Lt Wykes, Lt Irwin, Lt Hoare, Lt Armstrong, Lt Lindsay, and 164 other ranks were posted to 7 Argyll and Sutherland Highlanders in 51 Div, with Major Mirrielees, Captain Barr, Lt Crockett, Lt Murray, Lt Salisbury and 101 other ranks going to 5th Black Watch. Also on the 24th, posting orders to 7th Black Watch were received for Major Angus, Captain Gelston, 2/Lt Shanks and 57 other ranks (Other Battalion members were also posted to 1st Black Watch).

It was understood that the Battalion would be placed in 'suspended animation', and that its name would still continue in the Army List, and it has now been decided that the Tyneside Scottish will have its place in the Territorial Army, and that it will continue its proud and happy connection with The Black Watch. We feel sure that all of us would wish to send to this new Tyneside Scottish our greetings and to express our confidence that it will uphold the traditions of the Battalion and of the Regiment and will add new honours to those achieved by the bitter and heroic endeavours of the two Great Wars.

Alas many have fallen, but the proudest tribute to them all is that they did not die in vain, and that if the call should come again the Tyneside Scottish will be there and they in their turn will become 'Harder than Hammers'.

By 25 August – the day the French 2nd Armoured Division entered Paris – the British, Canadian and US Armies had driven the German Army Group B back across the Seine, and the Battle of Normandy had been brought to a close.

APPENDICES

APPENDIX 1: TRIBUTES FROM COMMANDERS

Major-General E.H. Barker, Commander of 49th Division, wrote in his diary on 2 July 1944 that the division was feeling pretty pleased with itself, having given the enemy a real 'bloody nose', and that the 1st Tyneside Scottish had particularly distinguished themselves.

Soon after, the 1st Tyneside Scottish received this message from Major-General Barker:

Will you please pass on to your troops my congratulations on the magnificent stand made by you today. You have today made a great name for yourselves not only in the Division but in the Army as a whole. I deplore the casualties you have sustained, but it is most gratifying to know that the gallant band who remained on point 110 were successfully relieved. I hope in the near future that we shall be able to get you all out for a rest, but meanwhile I must ask you to remain with your fellow-battalion – 11 DLI – on the important feature. Again the congratulations of myself and the whole Division, and our best wishes.

Capt J.S. Highmore, Company Commander, 'D' Company, 1st Tyneside Scottish:
Two or three days after I had been operated on, Maj Gen Barker, the Divisional Commander, visited the field hospital and asked me my unit and where I had been wounded. When I told him, he replied that I would be pleased to hear that he had issued a Divisional Order commending the performance of the 1st TS at Rauray.

At 1300 hrs on 3 July, another message was received by the Battalion, this time from the XXX Corps Commander, Lieutenant-General B.C. Bucknall:

The following message sent by the Corps Comd to the Div Comd is forwarded for infm. At close of their arduous and extremely successful defeat of best German SS tps, please convey my great felt and heartiest congratulations to all ranks and especially 8 Armed Bde and 70 Inf Bde. Their alert and stubborn resistance will make a great contribution to our Comds plan. Jolly good work.

Pte L.J.C. McLaren, Batman-Driver to IO, Intelligence Section:
We had a visit from one of our former Commanding Officers, Brigadier A.J.H. Cassels, who spoke and congratulated the Battalion on its magnificent performance at Rauray.

(Brigadier Cassels was a highly respected commander who had been instrumental in moulding the 1st Tyneside Scottish into a fighting unit during 1943 (see page 12 for details).

In his book *Normandy to the Baltic*, Lord Montgomery wrote:

On 1 July, the SS formations made their last and strongest attempt against the Second Army salient. 1, 2, 9, 10 and 12 SS Divisions formed up with their infantry and tanks and made repeated, though not simultaneous, attacks against our positions. All these attacks were engaged by our massed artillery with devastating effect, and all but one were dispersed before reaching our forward infantry positions. At the time, the strength of these attacks was perhaps under-estimated owing to the efficiency of our defensive fire. Later identifications and captured strength returns showed how many units were involved and how heavy their casualties had been. At one place alone, on the Rauray spur, the enemy got to grips with our defences. An infantry battalion of 2 SS Division and a tank battalion of 9 SS Division closed with a battalion of 49 Division and a regiment of 8 Armoured Brigade. Heavy fighting continued at intervals throughout the day, and at the end of it our positions were intact, while thirty-two enemy tanks had been knocked out.

Later on, the 1st Tyneside Scottish was among those who were awarded a major battle honour for their efforts on 1 July 1944. This honour is retained by the Battalion's parent regiment, The Black Watch (RHR), and is listed as 'Defence of Rauray'. The citation includes the following passage:

This subsidiary action was a turning point in the campaign. Increasing enemy counter-attacks which forced the British on to the defensive, developed into a counter-offensive which was crushingly defeated, a process in which the enemy lost some of his best troops and was not again able to launch a force of equal size and quality.

APPENDIX 2: RAURAY DECORATIONS

Distinguished Service Order

Anderson, W. A. C., Lt.-Col., 24th Lancers
Mackay-Lewis, K. F., Lt.-Col., 185th Field Regiment

Military Cross

Calderwood, K. P., Capt., 1st Tyneside Scottish
Lucas, F. R., Major, 185th Field Regiment
Luddington, W. H. C., Major, 24th Lancers
Vaughan, W. S., Lt., 217th Battery, 55th Anti-tank Regiment

Distinguished Conduct Medal

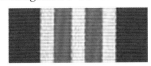

Hall, W., Sgt., 217th Battery, 55th Anti-tank Regiment

Military Medal

McMillan, J., Sgt., 1st Tyneside Scottish
Shanks, O., CSM, 1st Tyneside Scottish
Watson, D., Sgt., 1st Tyneside Scottish
Wilcox, W., L/Sgt., 24th Lancers

Croix De Guerre

Sparrow, L. W., Bdr., 217th Battery, 55th Anti-tank Regiment

'Geordie and Jock' Sam Swaddle (left) from Newcastle and Hugh Allen from Cambuslang, Glasgow, reunited thirty-eight years after Sam had carried the badly injured Hugh away from the Rauray front line to safety.

APPENDIX 3: RAURAY VETERANS

Here is a full list of the Rauray veterans who over the years have responded to requests for recollections about the events of 1 July 1944, and whose accounts have subsequently been recast for this book:

1ST TYNESIDE SCOTTISH (BLACK WATCH)
Battalion HQ

Birkett, P., Pte Intelligence Section; Campbell, A.J., Major; Chesworth, C.W., CF Battalion Chaplain; Leedale, S., Pte Medical Orderly, Medical Platoon; McLaren, L.J.C., Pte Batman-Driver to IO, Int Section; Munro, J., Pte Intelligence Section; Richardson, A., L/Cpl Reg Police Officer, Police Section; Thomson, R.S., Sgt Sniper Section.

HQ Company

Armstrong, T., Lt Motor Transport Officer, Admin Platoon; McGowan, R., Pte MT Driver, 'A' Echelon, Admin Platoon; Taylorson, E., L/Cpl i/c Petrol, 'A' Echelon, Admin Platoon.

Support Company

Allen, H., Pte Gun Nr, Det No. 2, Anti-tank Platoon; Brown, W., Sgt Platoon Sgt, Anti-tank Platoon; Capaldi, J., Pte Gun Nr, Det No. 5, Anti-tank Platoon; Drysdale, J., Cpl Det Cmdr, Det No. 2, Anti-tank Platoon; Esplin, A.R., Sgt Section Cmdr, Mortar Platoon; MacLagan, Capt, A. Platoon Cmdr, Anti-tank Platoon; Porterfield, E.A., Sgt Platoon Sgt, Carrier Platoon; Samson, J.L.R., Pte Gun Nr, Det No. 4, Anti-tank Platoon; Stewart, B.T.W., Lt 2nd i/c, Anti-tank Platoon; Swaddle, S.C., Sgt 'A' Section Cmdr, Anti-tank Platoon; Walker, J.C., Pte Bren gunner, Det No. 3, Anti-tank Platoon; Watson, D., Sgt 'B' Section Cmdr, Anti-tank Platoon; Wright, J.D., Sgt Section Cmdr, Carrier Platoon.

Rifle Companies
'A' Company

Corris, A., Pte rifleman, 7 Platoon; Forrest, R.S., Piper stretcher-bearer; Renouf, T.J., Pte rifleman, 7 Platoon.

'B' Company

Jarvis, D.W., Pte stretcher-bearer; McLaren, J.F., Lt Platoon Commander, 12 Platoon; Quigley, J., Pte rifleman, 12 Platoon.

'C' Company

Angus, Major, W.K. Company Commander; Henderson, A., Pte rifleman, 13 Platoon; Malone, G.J., Pte rifleman, 13 Platoon; Waters, N.E., L/Cpl Section Commander, 14 Platoon; Stephens, A.J. , Pte LMG No. 1, 13 Platoon.

'D' Company

Barnes, J.W. Pte, (A/Cpl) Section Commander, 18 Platoon; Bidwell, K.A., Pte LMG No. 1, 17 Platoon; Cowie, G., Cpl Section Commander, 18 Platoon; Highmore, J.S., Capt Company Commander; Hilton, R.D., Pte rifleman, 18 Platoon; Hodgkyns, J.R., Pte rifleman, 18 Platoon; Huxstep, D., L/Cpl Section Commander, 18 Platoon; Lawton, P., Pte PIAT No. 1, 18 Platoon; Murray, I.W., Lt Platoon Commander, 17 Platoon; Rolle, G.E., Pte rifleman, 18 Platoon; Tipler, J.W.H., Cpl Section Commander, 18 Platoon.

11TH DURHAM LIGHT INFANTRY

Baxter, R.C., Cpl Section Commander, 18 Platoon, 'D' Company

2ND KENSINGTONS (PRINCESS LOUISE'S)

Clark, T.H., Pte Batman driver, Company HQ; Greenland, A., Sgt 11 Platoon, 'C' Company; Griffiths, J.T., Lt Platoon Cmdr, 9 Platoon, 'C' Company; Hebdige, S., Cpl 9 Platoon, 'C' Company.

217TH BATTERY, 55TH ANTI-TANK REGIMENT

Moss P. Gnr. Gun aimer, 'B' Troop.

143RD AND 185TH FIELD REGIMENTS

Cooke H., Sgt Gunner, 185th Field Regiment; Wood, A.J., 507th Battery OP, 143rd Field Regiment; 143RD

757TH FIELD COMPANY, ROYAL ENGINEERS

Hudson, W., Sapper.

Gordon Cowie.

Left to right: Tom Renouf, John Hodgkins, John Tipler and Percy Lawton.

J. Drysdale and Sam Swaddle.

David Watson.

Jim Barnes.

John Munro.

Peter Birkett.

1st Tyneside Scottish, Black Watch Reunion 1989.

1st Tyneside Scottish Senior Officers. From left to right: Major Ken Dunn, Major Jim McLaren, Capt Aldo Campbell, Major Harry Boyne, Capt Tom Armstrong, Lt Col Ambrose Walton.

APPENDIX 4: MAJOR JOHN SAMSON

In 1991, Sir Harry Boyne ('D' Company Commander, 1st Tyneside Scottish, wounded during the attack on Brettevillette, Normandy, 28.6.44) wrote these lines about the work of Major J.L.R. Samson FSA (Scot):

Major John Samson spent much of the last four years of his life in seeking by correspondence, telephone and personal interview, authentic recollections from every survivor he could trace who had taken part in the Rauray encounter. The quest, a labour of love, was pursued without regard to the rank of the potential informant or his particular duties on the day in question. It was inevitably frustrated to some extent by the fact that, forty years after the events under inquiry, various officers and other ranks who might have had pertinent reminiscences to contribute had died or were untraceable. But John, with characteristic thoroughness and persistence, succeeded in amassing a remarkably voluminous dossier. At the time of his death, it amounted to forty-eight of the foolscap-size proforma requests he had sent out. Despite this comparative wealth of material on which to draw, John could not be persuaded by friends that it was enough to provide him with the making of a reliable word picture of the historic day. He was particularly insistent that it would be a mistake to begin his task of drawing it all together without contributions from surviving members of the Battalion's Pioneer and Signal Platoons who, in his opinion, would probably have been best placed to survey the battlefield as a whole. Always a perfectionist in everything he tackled, John unfortunately did not live to succeed in his efforts to track down any pioneers or signallers.

(Given a little more time, John would have realized that the Signal Office had been wiped out during the Juvigny air raid on 17 July 1944, making it practically impossible for him to find enough Rauray signallers to contact forty years later).

In 2000, Gordon Cowie, then Secretary of the Newcastle Branch of the Black Watch Association and fellow Tyneside Scot, paid this tribute to his friend John Samson:

I first met John Samson in 1945 when I was with a holding battalion at Stewarton, near Kilmarnock in Scotland, awaiting a posting to an OCTU. The war had just ended in Europe but was still going on in the Far East. We seemed to be on the same wavelength, both being Black Watch – I was 1st Battalion, John was 7th – and after we discovered that we had both served with the 1st Tyneside Scottish in Normandy the previous year, we became firm friends. However, we were eventually posted to different OCTUs and lost contact, and it was thirty-four years before we were able to renew our acquaintance.

In 1979, I read an article in the Newcastle Journal about a Tyneside Scottish Memorial which was about to be unveiled in Normandy. The man behind this project was a Major John Samson of Leatherhead in Surrey, who was making an appeal for any former 1st TS men to join him at the ceremony. This, I thought, could only be my old friend John and I immediately wrote to the address given in the article. Within a few days, John telephoned me and we shared the delight of speaking to one another again after so many years. Unfortunately, I was not going to be able to join the unveiling party as I had already made plans to go to Normandy a few weeks later, but I agreed to call in on John at his Surrey home on my way back. Although unable to attend the unveiling, I paid my own tribute at our new Tyneside Scottish Memorial at Ducy-Ste-Marguerite during my later visit. It was very moving for me. The monument honours the many officers and men of the 1st Tyneside Scottish who lost their lives in just a few weeks of fighting in Normandy. The Union flag and French Tricolour were still flying and a number of Royal British Legion wreaths remained where they had been laid during John's ceremony. It had been solely his brainchild and he had obviously done an excellent job. I later learned that Brigadier Montieth, Colonel of the Black Watch at the time, had unveiled the monument.

As promised, I visited John on my way back from Normandy and we spent several hours together in his study. He told me that he had left The Army with the rank of Lieutenant, as I had done, then joined the London Scottish (Territorial Army). He later transferred to the CMP (TA), eventually gaining the rank of Major with them. He then asked me how many 1st TS there were left in the

Tyneside area, and when I said that I thought that there must be quite a few, he told me that if I ever thought of reforming my local branch of the Black Watch Association he would give me every possible assistance. The original Northumberland and Durham Branch, of which I had been a member, had sadly petered out a few years after its formation in 1946 and so I readily agreed to John's suggestion. Being Secretary of the London Branch, he was able to pave the way with Regimental HQ in Perth and our plans for a Newcastle Branch were soon under way.

A former officer of field rank was essential for setting up a new branch, and so Lt Col Ambrose Walton, a former 1st TS officer, whom I had known, was was elected Chairman and I became Secretary/Treasurer. Afterwards, John was as good as his word; if I had any problems or needed advice – he was there.

About a year after we had renewed our friendship, John informed me that he intended to write the Rauray story and that he was going to send out questionnaires to see if any former 1st TS men could write down their experiences of the battle. I immediately trawled through my list of members and came up with about fifty names of those whom I knew had served at Rauray. Over the following months – and years – I often asked John how work was proceeding. Latterly, it was always the same answer; he was merely waiting to trace former members of the Signal and Assault pioneer Platoons. I could not help further and had a feeling that he would never manage to locate anyone. In 1988, I was informed almost simultaneously, by both Mrs Greta Samson and RHQ, that John had died. I was devastated. I got in touch with Sam Swaddle, a colleague of John's from the 1st TS Anti-tank Platoon, and we travelled down from Tyneside to the funeral in London. Major General Watson CB, who was Colonel of the Black Watch at the time, also attended. Several months after the funeral, Sir Harry Boyne informed me that Greta Samson had given him her husband's Rauray dossier. Shortly afterwards, Sir Harry suffered a stroke which resulted in him being incapable of carrying on with the Rauray story, and so he sent all the relevant papers to me. I had written the odd article and no doubt could have written a brief account of the Rauray affair, but I think Sir Harry had overestimated my abilities as I did not have the know-how to write a book. I did manage to group all the accounts as per company and make some notes, but that was all. Only Sam Swaddle knew that I possessed the dossier and he often used to ask me about my progress with it. I used to fob him off and eventually he forgot all about the matter. I had not. I knew that Sir Harry Boyne had full confidence in me and that I owed it to John Samson to ensure that his work was completed. I felt I was letting everyone down.

Then suddenly in 1999, right out of the blue, I received a letter from Kevin Baverstock. He had been informed by the military historian Pat Delaforce that I had fought at Rauray (I had earlier contributed to Delaforce's book about the 49th Division). Kevin explained that he had done much research on the Rauray battle, the idea having originated from the fact that his father had served with the 1st TS during the action. I realised that he meant business and that in due course, given access to John Samson's dossier, the kind of Rauray story that John had originally envisaged might now be written up by Kevin. As far as I was concerned, Kevin had saved the situation. I was therefore determined to give him all the assistance he required, and he quickly appreciated that I, along with a few of my friends, could offer some useful information given that we had been at the sharp end on the day. Kevin also made contact with other veterans' associations and sought the advice of several military historians. Nevertheless, I think he would agree that had there not been a Newcastle Branch of the Black Watch Association in existence he would not have been able to amass such a wealth of material. I know he would have written a story about Rauray and would have come up with a very interesting effort, but it would not have been quite the same without John Samson's dossier. With it, I believe this book is a most excellent and convincing story of the heroism of the young men of the 1st Tyneside Scottish who served both their Regiment and their country well.

Finally, I know I can take credit for forming the BWA Newcastle Branch and for making it what it is, but I would like to point out that it was John Samson's suggestion and prompting that encouraged me to do so. John was an officer and indeed a gentleman. An old comrade and a great friend. I owed him a lot, not least to ensure that his dossier was put to good use. By passing it on, I now feel that I have honoured that particular debt as this book successfully completes the project that he began some twenty years ago. To John Samson I would say only one word – quits!.

APPENDIX 5: ROLL OF HONOUR

Listed below, are the names of the 1st Tyneside Scottish (Black Watch) soldiers of all ranks reported killed in action or otherwise, and those who died of wounds, Rauray, 1 July 1944. It is by no means a full register, as many more died later in the United Kingdom, having been brought back from Normandy severely wounded, and as such were never recorded.

3322721	Pte	Anderson, F.B.	St-Manvieu War Cemetery, Cheux
2884647	Sgt	Anderson, W.	St-Manvieu War Cemetery, Cheux
2760087	Pte	Anderson, W.	Bayeux War Cemetery
2883970	Sgt	Asher, A.K.	Bayeux War Cemetery
14268230	Pte	Bailey, J.H.	St-Manvieu War Cemetery, Cheux
2760378	Pte	Black, J.	St-Manvieu War Cemetery, Cheux
2760378	L/Cpl	Black, W.C.L.	St-Manvieu War Cemetery, Cheux
14412967	Pte	Blackburn, D.	St-Manvieu War Cemetery, Cheux
269413	Lt	Bolton, R.C.	The Bayeux Memorial, Normandy
2766580	Pte	Braid, J.M.	St-Manvieu War Cemetery, Cheux
3062121	L/Cpl	Burrel, A.	St-Manvieu War Cemetery, Cheux
2760304	Pte	Caldwell, J.H.	Bayeux War Cemetery, Normandy
2886411	Pte	Davidson, A.	St-Manvieu War Cemetery, Cheux
14514282	Pte	Dorrell, D.H.W.	The Bayeux Memorial, Normandy
14424005	Pte	Drysdale, P.	Tilly-sur-Seulles War Cemetery
14420926	Pte	Hamer, C.	The Bayeux Memorial
14416637	Pte	Holden, H.	The Bayeux Memorial
14428656	Pte	Hughes, D.L.	The Bayeux Memorial
4455918	L/Cpl	Jewett, E.	The Bayeux Memorial
14420198	Pte	Johnston, J.	St-Manvieu War Cemetery, Cheux
14620895	Pte	Johnstone, G.	St-Manvieu War Cemetery, Cheux
2760067	Pte	Knowles, A.	St-Manvieu War Cemetery, Cheux
2766607	Pte	Low, J. McK.	St-Manvieu War Cemetery, Cheux
2760231	Pte	McCormack, C.	St-Manvieu War Cemetery, Cheux
2883706	Pte	McDowell, F.L.G.	St-Manvieu War Cemetery, Cheux
3060964	Pte	McLintock T.H.	The Bayeux Memorial
2760071	Pte	McMillan, J.	St-Manvieu War Cemetery, Cheux
4456745	Pte	McMurchie, D F.	St-Manvieu War Cemetery, Cheux
3060962	C/Sgt	Mackay, A.McB.	Tilly-sur-Seulles War Cemetery
4461048	Pte	Millar, H.	St-Manvieu War Cemetery, Cheux
14413239	Pte	O'Connor, D.S.	The Bayeux Memorial
4461062	Pte	O'Hagen, J.	Fontenay-le-Pesnel War Cemetery, Tessel
4456016	Pte	Richards, T.	St-Manvieu War Cemetery, Cheux
2760181	Pte	Robb, A.	Tilly-sur-Seulles War Cemetery
4456713	Pte	Robison, A.	Tilly-sur-Seulles War Cemetery
2760147	Pte	Shepherd, A.	St-Manvieu War Cemetery, Cheux
407007	Cpl	Simpson, J.G.	Fontenay-le-Pesnel War Cemetery, Tessel
14416901	Pte	Skinner, B.	Bayeux War Cemetery
249822	Lt	Wallace, D.C.	Bayeux War Cemetery
14417076	Pte	Warr, A.L.	St-Manvieu War Cemetery, Cheux
3061144	Pte	Watson, W.B.	St-Manvieu War Cemetery, Cheux
14417302	Pte	Williamson, T.	Bayeux War Cemetery
14424669	Pte	Young, J.T.	St-Manvieu War Cemetery, Cheux

SOURCES, ACKNOWLEDGEMENTS AND CARTOGRAPHIC NOTES

SOURCES

Public Record Office

War Diaries

1st Tyneside Scottish in Iceland WO176/339
1st Tyneside Scottish in the U.K WO166/9000, 12676
1st Tyneside Scottish in Normandy WO171/1382
2nd Kensingtons WO171/1314
4th Lincolns WO171/1335
6th King's Own Scottish Borderers WO171/1322
4/7th Dragoon Guards WO171/838
8th Armoured Brigade WO171/613
10th Durham Light Infantry WO171/1292
11th Durham Light Infantry WO171/1293
15th (Scottish) Division WO171/466
21st Army Group WO171/110-113
24th Lancers WO171/849
XXX Corps WO171/336-338
49th (West Riding) Division WO171/499-500
70th Infantry Brigade WO171/653
141st Royal Armoured Corps WO171/877
185th Field Regiment WO171/1001
217th Battery, 55th Anti-tank Regiment WO171/916

Official Histories and Narratives

Immediate Reports of Actions in Normandy (Nos. 25 & 26) CAB106/963
Normandy CAB44/248, 250
Northern Troops in the Memorable Battle . . . . .Military Observer, M.O.I. No: 6021/A744

Books and Regimental Histories

The 6th (Border) Battalion K.O.S.B., 1939–1945 .Capt J.R.P. Baggalay
Churchill's Secret Weapons . . . . .P. Delaforce
Polar Bears – Monty's Left Flank, The . . . . .P. Delaforce
Black Watch and The King's Enemies, The . . . . .B. Fergusson
9. SS-Panzer-Division Hohenstaufen . . . . .H. Fürbringer
Kriegsgeschichte der 12. SS-Panzerdivision 'Hitlerjugend' .S. Meyer

Kensingtons, The . . . . The Regimental Old Comrades Association
Harder Than Hammers – 1947 history of 1st The Tyneside Scottish . . . . . .Officers of 1st Tyneside Scottish
Steel Inferno . . . . .Maj Gen (Retd) M. Reynolds
DLI at War, The . . . . .D. Rissik
10th and 11th Bn Durham Light Infantry History . . . . .D. Rissik
Geordie and Jock – A Brief Account of The Tyneside Scottish . . . . .J.L.R. Samson
First and the Last, The. The story of the 4/7th Royal Dragoon Guards . . . . .Major J.D.P. Stirling
Comrades to the End – The 4th SS-Panzer-Grenadier Regt 'Der Führer' 1938–45 . . . . .O. Weidinger
None Had Lances – The Story of The 24th Lancers . . . . .L. Willis
Normandy 1944 . . . . .N. Zetterling
Official History of World War Two – Victory in the West, The . . . . .Major L.F. Ellis

ACKNOWLEDGEMENTS

The author would like to thank the following 1st Tyneside Scottish veterans: Peter Birkett, Major (Retd) Aldo Campbell, Gordon Cowie, R. Hilton, Percy Lawton, John Munro, A. Stephens, Capt (Retd) Brian Stewart, Sam Swaddle, John Tipler, Lt Col (Retd) Ambrose Walton and Capt (Retd) Arthur Whitehead.

Additionally, the author is indebted to the following people and organizations for their assistance: Bill Ashby, Brig. (Retd) Garry Barnett, Ralph Baxter, Jon Beck, Peter Caddick-Adams, T. A. Clark, Harry Cooke, Ian Daglish, Patrick Delaforce, Colin and Ian Dewey, Jonathan Falconer, David Fletcher, Tony Greenland, Capt (Retd) James Griffiths, Stephen Hebdige, Prof. Richard Holmes, Bill Hudson, Lt Col (Retd) Stephen Lindsay, Louis Meulstee, Percy Moss, Jack Oakley, James Parker, Maj Gen (Retd) Michael Reynolds, Maj (Retd) John Robson, Lt Col (Retd) David Rose, Thomas Smyth, Kevin Storey, Jim Wood and Niklas Zetterling.

And thanks are also due to 49th (West Riding) Infantry Division Polar Bear Association; the Black Watch Association (Newcastle Branch); the Black Watch Regimental Headquarters and Museum; the Durham Light Infantry Association; the Imperial War Museum Film and Photograph Archives; the Imperial War Museum Reading Room; the Kensington Journal; the Liddell Hart Centre for Military Archives, King's College London; the National Army Museum Reading Room, the Public Record Office and the Tank Museum.

CARTOGRAPHIC NOTES

The author has attempted to avoid any breach of copyright when preparing the maps included in this book, by careful use of a wide range of contemporary sources including aerial photographs. No modern surveys have been used as base compilations. Place names, road alignments and topographical features have been edited to reflect the terrain and countryside of Normandy as it appeared in 1944. Certain geographical locations have been selected in accordance with what was accepted by military intelligence as being accurate at the time, such as 'ring contour 110'. The British Army, which was considerably better prepared than its Wehrmacht counterpart, was using War Office maps of Normandy prepared by the Ordnance Survey, showing contour lines at 10 metre intervals. These contours had been interpolated from spot heights and hachures found on French maps, and as a result some minor errors in height information were unavoidable. Of course, this was of no importance at the time, and somehow an encircling 'ring contour 110' seems to describe the exposed nature of the feature's isolation perfectly. However, errors other than those which derive from the historical material are the sole responsibility of the author who apologises to any reader who discovers faults or inconsistencies. For those who are interested in such matters, all the maps and diagrams were drawn digitally on a Macintosh using a combination of software packages. Linework and lettering were created using Macromedia Freehand ™ and Adobe Illustrator ™. Hillshading and 3D effects, including mosaicking and manipulation of aerial photography, were achieved using Adobe Photoshop ™ and Corel Bryce ™.

INDEX